BEFORE YELLOWSTONE

BEFORE YELLOWSTONE

NATIVE AMERICAN ARCHAEOLOGY
in the NATIONAL PARK

DOUGLAS H. MacDONALD

UNIVERSITY OF WASHINGTON PRESS

Seattle and London

Copyright © 2018 by the University of Washington Press

Printed and bound in the United States of America

Design by Laura Shaw Design

Composed in Miller Text, typeface designed by Matthew Carter, Carter & Cone;
Neutra Text, typeface designed by House Industries; and Toyler, typeface designed
by Chatnarong Jingsuphatada, Typesketchbook

All photos by the author unless otherwise credited

Cover photo: Bison hoofprints. Courtesy Ludovic Bertron/Wikimedia Commons

Frontispiece: Courtesy Kimon Maritz/Unsplash

22   21   5   4   3   2

University of Washington Press

www.washington.edu/uwpress

Library of Congress Cataloging-in-Publication Data

Names: MacDonald, Douglas H., 1968- author.

Title: Before Yellowstone : Native American archaeology in the national park / Douglas H. MacDonald.

Description: Seattle : University of Washington Press, 2018. | Includes bibliographical references and index.

Identifiers: LCCN 2017026640 (print) | LCCN 2017027431 (ebook) | ISBN 9780295742205 (pbk. : alk. paper) |
   ISBN 9780295742212 (ebook)

Subjects: LCSH: Indians of North America—Yellowstone National Park—History. | Indians of North
   America—Yellowstone National Park—Antiquities. | Excavations (Archaeology)—Yellowstone National
   Park. | Yellowstone National Park—Antiquities.

Classification: LCC E78.Y44 M33 2018 (ebook) | LCC E78.Y44 (print) | DDC 978.7/52—dc23

LC record available at https://lccn.loc.gov/2017026640

CONTENTS

A NOTE FROM THE AUTHOR

In this book, I wanted to convey to the reader the important role Native Americans played in the history of Yellowstone National Park. While it is against the law under the Archaeological Resource Protection Act of 1979 to take artifacts from federal lands, looting of archaeological sites is still a problem in many parks, including Yellowstone. So in writing the book, I attempted to keep certain site locations obscure to the public to protect them. I also use photographs and illustrated maps that do not specify site locations. The original inhabitants of Yellowstone safeguarded the region's beauty and natural wonders for over 11,000 years, and it is my sincere hope that we can continue that tradition.

Keep in mind the dangers of Yellowstone during your travels. The wildlife and thermal features are beautiful, but they can also be dangerous. Do not approach large mammals in the park, including bears, bison, elk, pronghorn antelope, deer, and sheep; keep a safe distance. Always stay on marked trails and boardwalks in the park, and do not walk on the ground near thermal features and springs to avoid breaking through. While they may look safe to walk on, thermal landscapes pose a hazard to people and are fragile and prone to impact from human use.

ACKNOWLEDGMENTS

Many archaeologists have contributed to the understanding of Yellowstone National Park's Native American precontact history. Among them, I would like to acknowledge Ann Johnson and Elaine Hale (retired park archaeologists) for all their assistance in my University of Montana projects over the years. In addition, Ken Cannon, Leslie Davis, and Craig Lee, among others conducted outstanding archaeology in the park. Montana State Historic Preservation Officer Mark Baumler and the Crow Tribal Archaeologist Timothy McCleary provided insightful comments and information that offered much to the quality of the book.

Many University of Montana faculty and students contributed field and laboratory efforts that helped produce much of the archaeology in this volume. Among those who directly contributed are Matt Nelson (maps) and Cathy Beecher (ethnobotanical information). Still others, including Steven Sheriff, Pei-Lin Yu, Michael Livers, Jordan McIntyre, Jacob Adams, Samuel White, Justin Pfau, Brandon Bachman, Lester Maas, and Michael Ciani, contributed multiple years of field, lab, and report assistance that resulted in outstanding research forming a basis for this book. Richard Hughes conducted obsidian source analysis for our projects, while Beta Analytic conducted radiocarbon dating. Jannifer Gish and PaleoResearch conducted pollen and ethnobotanical analysis.

Thanks to the University of Washington Press, especially Regan Huff, Margaret Sullivan, and Ellen Wheat, who facilitated the book being published. Artist Eric Carlson created the illustrations in the book; I am grateful for his work on this project.

All photographs in this book were taken by me, unless otherwise noted. The National Park Service permitted use of Yellowstone photos (which are in the public domain), many of which were taken by the remarkable park photographer Jim Peaco. The following individuals and entities graciously allowed the use of other figures/photographs in this book: Staffan Peterson, Carl Davis, Lisa Smith,

Kenneth Cannon, Craig Lee, Christopher Morgan, Scott Carpenter, Molly MacDonald, Richard Collier, Robin Park, Billings Public Library, Aaron Brien, Montana Historical Society Research Center Photograph Archives, and the Wyoming State Historic Preservation Office. Samuel White provided the cast of the Anzick Clovis point for photography, and Lithics Casting Lab provided casts of other Clovis and Hopewell artifacts to be photographed for the book.

I would like to thank the University of Montana Department of Anthropology faculty and College of Humanities and Sciences for providing resources that supported this effort. Thanks also to Yellowstone National Park cultural resource staff members Elizabeth Horton, Staffan Peterson, and Tobin Roop, who encouraged me to write this book and provided comments that enhanced it. The book was peer reviewed, and I am thankful for those comments. Any remaining errors are my own.

My special appreciation goes to my wife, Amy Keil, my children, Molly and Otto, as well as the families of Charles and Tracy Edmundson, Jeffrey Keil, Leigh and Dave Jurman, and Lynn Keil for the wonderful trips we took to Yellowstone, when Molly and I took most of the book's photographs.

BEFORE YELLOWSTONE

CHAPTER ONE

YELLOWSTONE, PAST AND PRESENT

YELLOWSTONE NATIONAL PARK occupies a special place in the hearts of Americans as well as the rest of the world. As the first federally recognized national park, Yellowstone represents the ancient Wild West. With its well-known nickname, "Wonderland," the park is considered a utopian landscape in the minds of many. Yellowstone is a singular place of untouched geothermal wilderness that strongly contrasts with the urban sprawl characterizing much of modern America. As if stepping back in time, travelers can venture along the winding roads and trails of Yellowstone and see exploding thermal geysers, wandering grizzly bears, herds of bison, and dramatic pristine landscapes.

Visitors to the park, especially those who arrive during the off-season, can feel like the first people who set foot there. The place has an eerie, quiet, prehistoric quality, despite the many modern developments since the park's formation in 1872. Many travelers in Yellowstone do not know that humans have lived in the region for at least 11,000 years. Soon after half-mile-high glaciers melted and formed Yellowstone Lake during the Late Pleistocene era, early Native Americans made their way to Yellowstone, leaving behind spear points and bison bones that tell the stories of

◀ FIGURE 1.1 Archaeologists look for Native American archaeological sites across all of Yellowstone National Park, including the northern mountains, to identify site locations so they can be protected and managed by the National Park Service.

FIGURE 1.2 The Grand Canyon of the Yellowstone River is a popular visitor attraction in the park.

their lives there. These people likely arrived from northeast Asia, along the Pacific Coast, and up the Columbia and Snake Rivers, or they may have traveled from Alaska by way of a region between two giant glaciers that encompassed Canada.

In this book, I use archaeological research to paint a picture of the lives of Native Americans in the park for the previous 11,000 years. The book describes the Native American era before European contact, often referred to as the precontact, or prehistoric, period. The book also discusses how various Native American tribes used special places of the region, including mountains, rivers, geysers, and lakes. Starting with the first historic record of Obsidian Cliff in the 1870s by geologist and naturalist William Henry Holmes, scientists have continued to discover abundant material evidence of Native Americans in Yellowstone. Today, nearly 2,000 archaeological sites in the park dating from 11,000 to 100 years ago have been recognized, surveyed, and documented. This Native American precontact history in Yellowstone National Park is not well known to the general public.

MAP 1.1 Yellowstone National Park, within the United States

YELLOWSTONE, AMERICA'S FIRST NATIONAL PARK

Of the US national park system that now contains 59 preserved parks scattered throughout the United States, Yellowstone was the first. Since its founding in 1872, more than 150 million visitors have flocked to Yellowstone to witness its fascinating natural landscape and geothermal features. In 2015 alone, nearly 4.1 million tourists visited the park, most in the summer. Spring and fall are slower seasons with fewer visitors, while winter has even fewer. During any season, a short hike can quickly take you to areas where you will feel as if you are alone in the park. I've done this numerous times—always in groups of three or more, for safety regarding bears—and it always results in wonderful experiences. Almost anywhere in Yellowstone you will find unbroken ancient forests, amazing mountain vistas, and even archaeological sites used by Native Americans thousands of years ago. You just have to know how and where to look.

After California's Death Valley National Park (at 3.4 million acres/1.4 hectares), Yellowstone—at 2.2 million acres (890,000 hectares)—is America's second-largest national park in the Lower 48 states. There are six even bigger national parks by acreage in the continental United States, and they are in Alaska. Approximately

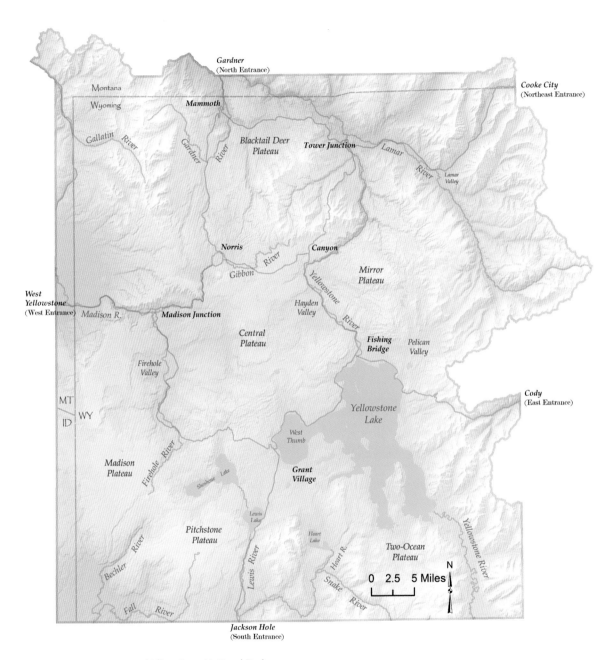

Montana
Wyoming

Gardner
(North Entrance)

Cooke City
(Northeast Entrance)

Gallatin River

Mammoth

Gardner River

Blacktail Deer
Plateau

Tower Junction

Lamar River

Lamar
Valley

Norris

Canyon

Mirror
Plateau

Gibbon River

Yellowstone River

West
Yellowstone
(West Entrance)

Madison R.

Madison Junction

Hayden
Valley

Central
Plateau

Fishing
Bridge

Pelican
Valley

Firehole
Valley

MT
ID

WY

Cody
(East Entrance)

Yellowstone
Lake

West
Thumb

Madison
Plateau

Firehole River

Shoshone Lake

Grant
Village

Lewis
Lake

Pitchstone
Plateau

Bechler River

Lewis River

Heart
Lake

Heart R.

Two-Ocean
Plateau

Yellowstone River

0   2.5   5 Miles

N

Snake River

Fall River

Jackson Hole
(South Entrance)

MAP 1.2 Yellowstone National Park

96 percent of Yellowstone National Park is in Wyoming, while 3 percent is in Montana and 1 percent in Idaho. Most of the center of the park—often referred to as the Yellowstone Plateau—is pushed upward in elevation by a vast geothermal bulge that marks the location of a large volcanic caldera. Because of this volcanism and the surrounding Rocky Mountains, more than 90 percent of the park is above 7,000 ft. (2,100 m) in elevation. The thin air at that altitude can be a shocker for many visitors whose homes are near sea level on the Atlantic or Pacific Coasts.

Yellowstone's geothermal activity is also the cause of the park's many thermal features, such as Old Faithful, which are popular among tourists in the central portion of the park. The lowest elevation in the park—about 5,300 ft. (1,600 m)—is near Gardiner, Montana, along the Yellowstone River, while the park's highest mountains include Eagle Peak (11,372 ft./3,466 m) in the Absaroka Range in the eastern part of the park, as well as Electric Peak (10,969 ft./3,343 m) and the famous Mount Washburn (10,243 ft./3,122 m) in the northern tier of the park.

FIGURE 1.3 Old Faithful is one of Yellowstone's most popular attractions. Even severe winter weather doesn't stop the geothermal features of the park.

The natural setting of Yellowstone varies from those low-elevation areas in the Gardiner Basin of Montana to the high-elevation areas of Yellowstone Lake and the surrounding mountains. The Gardiner Basin in the northern part of the park, as well as the Madison River Valley in the western portion of the park, offer comparatively moderate winters and, therefore, refuge for bison, elk, deer, and pronghorn. These large animals seek the forage of the sagebrush prairies and grasslands in the lower elevations. In summer, they flock to the cooler higher elevations in central Yellowstone that are dominated by pine and spruce forests with scattered grassy meadows. Native Americans in the past followed a similar migration pattern, moving up in elevation in summer and down in elevation in winter. Their annual settlement patterns were oriented around the seasons, based on availability of food sources. With few resources available in the high-elevation, snowy uplands in winter, they sought the security of the valleys that surround Yellowstone National Park, including the Yellowstone, Snake, Madison, and Shoshone Rivers.

VISITING THE PARK

Just as the river corridors were the routes Native Americans traveled to and from the Yellowstone Plateau, they also are the major entry points to the park today. Visitors can enter Yellowstone National Park from five different entrances: the north (Gardiner, Montana, via the Yellowstone River Valley), the northeast (Cooke City, Montana, via the Lamar River Valley), the east (Cody, Wyoming, via the Shoshone River Valley), the south (Jackson, Wyoming, via the Snake and Lewis Rivers), and the west (West Yellowstone, Montana, via the Madison River Valley). Traveling through these river valleys—both in the past and in the recent times—brought people from the sagebrush grasslands up onto the heart of the Yellowstone Plateau, a lush, cool summer haven for Native Americans and modern visitors alike.

While more than 95 percent of Yellowstone is within the state of Wyoming, more than two-thirds of park visitors enter the park through the state of Montana. The West Yellowstone Entrance, in Montana, witnessed the most visitors in 2016—approximately 42 percent—followed by the South Entrance (20 percent), the North Entrance (19 percent), the East Entrance (13 percent), and the Northeast Entrance (6 percent).

The National Park Service operates Yellowstone and the other national parks through funding from the US Department of the Interior. The annual operating budget for Yellowstone is more than $30 million. Most of the park's administrative offices are in the northern portion of the park in Mammoth Hot Springs, Wyoming. If you are visiting the park's northern area, you will enter through the well-known North Entrance Arch in Gardiner, Montana. Gardiner is a small town of about 1,000 people. It has a variety of fine hotels, motels, and campgrounds that house many of Yellowstone's tourists.

While the northern portion of the park around Gardiner is most popular in the summer, it is also one of the only portions of the park open year-round; most of

FIGURE 1.4 My crew from the University of Montana conducted an archaeological survey in the sagebrush grasslands of the northern portion of Yellowstone near Gardiner, Montana (2007).

the roads there are maintained throughout the winter in the park. Because of its comparatively low elevation, the Gardiner Basin is a winter retreat for large game, including bison, elk, and pronghorn antelope. Early Native Americans often spent portions of their winters in this valley around Gardiner as well.

During our University of Montana archaeological expeditions near Gardiner between 2007 and 2009, my team and I identified dozens of important archaeological sites there that were used by Native Americans over the past 11,000 years (figure 1.4). This portion of the park is dry and largely covered by sagebrush grasslands along the winding Yellowstone River. The river offers abundant fishing and rafting opportunities for tourists.

Following the Grand Loop Road, the North Entrance road connects Gardiner, Montana, with Mammoth Hot Springs, Wyoming, some six miles south. The road passes a popular swimming hole—the Boiling River—just south of the Montana-Wyoming state line. A hot spring—with scalding water of above 130°F (54°C)—flows directly into the very cold water of the Gardner River, and the waters

combine to provide a wonderful hot-tub-like experience in a roaring river setting. The Boiling River is closed in the spring because of high water conditions, but it is open the rest of the year. Native Americans lived along the Gardner River, leaving traces of their activities behind at numerous archaeological sites in the vicinity of Boiling River (elevation 5,700 ft./1,730 m). One of the most important Native American trails—the Bannock Trail—passed through this area. Used by the Shoshone, Bannock, Salish, and Nez Perce tribes, among others, this trail connected the Snake River region of Idaho to the west with the popular bison hunting grounds of the Great Plains east of Yellowstone.

Continuing southward, the Grand Loop winds up onto the vast Yellowstone Plateau. Approximately 1 mi. (1.6 km) along the winding highway, you come to Mammoth Hot Springs, Wyoming, at 6,350 ft. (1,930 m). Here, you will find the park's administrative offices, a post office, a small medical clinic, as well as tourist lodging and restaurants. A tourist attraction here is the monumental Mammoth Hot Springs, which towers above the park facilities. There are numerous boardwalks where tourists can walk among the beautiful hot springs and terraces.

From Mammoth Hot Springs in winter, you can drive on the Grand Loop Road for 18 mi. (30 km) eastward to its intersection with the Northeast Entrance road at Tower Junction. On that road, you will pass a significant outcrop of chert—called Crescent Hill chert—which was collected and used by Native Americans. Chert is a highly siliceous rock that was popularly used throughout the world, including Yellowstone, by prehistoric people to make stone tools for survival. Yellowstone is rich with many sources of stone, including chert and obsidian, which provided raw material for tool making.

The Northeast Entrance road subsequently winds for about 30 mi. (48 km) along the Lamar River Valley to the park's Northeast Entrance at Cooke City, Montana. The Lamar Valley is one of the park's most popular areas to look for wolves, which often have dens in the foothills above. In a recent winter trip through this valley, my son and I watched a lone wolf compete for a bison carcass against a large grizzly bear and a pack of coyotes. The open sagebrush flats of the valley provide abundant grasslands for herds of bison, elk, bighorn sheep, and pronghorn, while the foothills are dominated by pine, fir, and spruce woodlands. Pockets of aspen and willow are present in wetlands throughout the valley.

◀ FIGURE 1.5 After passing through the park's North Entrance near Gardiner, Montana, visitors travel south on the Grand Loop Road along the Gardner River toward Mammoth Hot Springs. The Boiling River, where hot springs spill into the Gardner River, is a popular scenic spot.

FIGURE 1.6 Beartooth (top) and Dead Indian (bottom) Passes look out on spectacular mountain landscapes in the park's northeast region.

Lamar Cave lies just to the north of the winding Lamar River. The cave has yielded the remains of 36 species of mammals—including predominantly voles, ground squirrels, rats, mice, and gophers, as well as fish, reptiles, and birds—dating back nearly 2,000 years. The fossil remains from the cave indicate the evolution of the modern sagebrush-grassland ecosystem of the Lamar Valley within the past millennia.

In winter, the road from Mammoth Hot Springs through the Lamar Valley ends at Cooke City and bustles with snowmobilers and snowboarders exploring the snowy mountain terrain. If you visit Cooke City in summer, however, tourists can continue northward and westward on the famous Beartooth Highway (figure 1.6) that winds along Montana State Route 212 across mountain peaks above 10,000 ft. (3,000 m) before descending in dramatic fashion into Red Lodge and Billings, Montana. Alternatively, you can turn onto Wyoming State Routes 296 and 120 to Cody, Wyoming. This route takes you over Dead Indian Pass,

FIGURE 1.7 Sheepeater Cliff was named after the Shoshone (Sheep Eater) tribe by early park superintendent P. W. Norris in 1879.

which was traversed by Chief Joseph and the Nez Perce Indians on their poignant final trek through the Yellowstone region in 1877.

From Mammoth Hot Springs, park visitors can also take an alternate route along the Grand Loop Road to Swan Lake Flat above 7,000 ft. (2,100 m). Along this route toward the Norris Geyser Basin, you pass by Sheepeater Cliff, so-named because of a Shoshone (or Sheep Eater) camp observed at the location in the mid-nineteenth century. Numerous archaeological sites are present along Indian Creek and the Gardner River in this area. In advance of bridge and highway construction near Sheepeater Cliff and the Indian Creek Campground, archaeologists working for the state of Wyoming found archaeological sites dating back about 9,000 years.

Farther south is Obsidian Cliff and still farther south is the Norris Geyser Basin and campground. Obsidian Cliff is a significant outcrop of obsidian (glassy volcanic rock) that was used by Native Americans to make stone tools and hunting implements like projectile points. There are literally thousands of archaeological sites in the vicinity of the cliff. The obsidian was traded among Native American tribes, resulting in its distribution across much of North America in prehistory. Hopewell Indian mounds in Ohio, which are 2,000 years old, have yielded hundreds of pounds of obsidian from Yellowstone.

Mammoth Hot Springs and Obsidian Cliff are on the northern edge of the vast Yellowstone Plateau, which forms the heart of Yellowstone National Park today. The plateau's higher elevations were formed by uplift from active volcanism over the past two million years. Pine forests dominate the upland plateau, while aspen and willow occur in wetlands along Solfatara Creek, Obsidian Creek, Indian Creek,

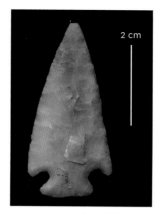

▲ FIGURE 1.9 I found this chert projectile point near Canyon Village in 2015. A Native American hunter left it there 2,000 years ago.

◀ FIGURE 1.8 The Norris Geyser Basin is the hottest geothermal area in the park, with most thermal features above the boiling point (212°F/100°C).

and the Gardner River, among others. High mountains surround the plateau, with peaks as high as 11,000 ft. (3 km) in all directions.

Norris Geyser Basin, just south of Obsidian Cliff, is made up of dozens of active thermal features and geysers. From Norris Junction south of Obsidian Cliff, you can turn eastward toward Canyon Village across a densely wooded highway along the headwaters of the Gibbon River. Another route to Canyon Village follows the Grand Loop Road from Tower Junction across the edge of Mount Washburn. Once you arrive at Canyon Village, you'll find a gas station, a museum, restaurants, and abundant lodging opportunities. This area offers spectacular scenic vistas along the Yellowstone River Canyon. During an archaeological survey near Canyon Village in 2015, I found a beautiful flaked chert projectile point (figure 1.9) left behind by a Native American hunter over 2,000 years ago.

FIGURE 1.10 Yellowstone Lake is North America's largest natural high-elevation lake. The Yellowstone River enters the lake at the south (shown here) and exits it 20 mi. (32 km) north at Fishing Bridge.

From Canyon Village, the Grand Loop Road continues southward to Yellowstone Lake. This portion of the road follows the beautiful Hayden Valley, so named after one of Yellowstone's first explorers in the early 1870s, Ferdinand Hayden. Here, along the shores of the winding Yellowstone River, vast herds of bison congregate in the summer. The wide-open sagebrush grasslands of this valley attract the bison and, in turn, predators like wolves and bears. Several hot springs are present in the Hayden Valley, as are dozens of prehistoric archaeological sites.

Following the Hayden Valley of the Yellowstone River southward takes you to Yellowstone Lake, which is North America's largest natural high-elevation lake. The lake, 20 mi. (32 km) long and 15 mi. (24 km) wide, dominates the central portion of Yellowstone. Thick stands of pines are common along the lakeshore, often interspersed by open meadows. Native Americans were attracted to these meadows for their diverse plant species, including such edible plants as camas and bitterroot, as well as grazing game animals, such as bison and elk. In 2013, my team of University of Montana archaeologists found a 1,500-year-old elk bone at an archaeological site on the Flat Mountain Arm of Yellowstone Lake, evidence that a Native American hunter may have killed and butchered the animal in the grassy meadow near the site.

The Yellowstone River flows into the lake at the south and out of the lake to the north at Fishing Bridge, where you'll find a gas station, a small museum, a restaurant, a store, and campgrounds. Fishing Bridge was one of the most densely populated areas of Yellowstone in prehistory; nearly any open meadow near the mouth of the Yellowstone River contains the remains of Native American camps. If you drive

FIGURE 1.11 Mummy Cave is the Yellowstone region's most significant archaeological site. It is located along the North Fork of the Shoshone River just east of the park.

to the east along the East Entrance road, you'll pass along the northern shore of the lake and up across Sylvan Pass (8,500 ft./2,590 m). This road follows tributaries of the Shoshone River past the park's East Entrance and eventually to the popular tourist town of Cody, Wyoming. North of the road, you'll pass one of the most important regional archaeological sites, Mummy Cave, tucked into the cliffs along the Shoshone River about halfway between the East Entrance and Cody. Mummy Cave was home to Native Americans for the past 9,500 years, with thousands of artifacts recovered during excavations in the 1960s. Artifacts include the remains of bighorn sheep, among hundreds of varieties of projectile points, scraping tools, and pottery sherds (pieces of broken fired clay pots).

Cody, with a population of approximately 10,000 people, is a Wild West sort of town with a nightly rodeo in the summer. Cody absolutely bustles with activity and offers abundant restaurants, hotels, and other tourist attractions. It is also home to several important Native American prehistoric archaeological sites. For example,

the Horner site is a location where Native Americans killed dozens of bison approximately 9,000 years ago along the Shoshone River. The spot is one of only three
Wyoming prehistoric archaeological sites on the National Historic Landmark list.
Similar artifacts to those found at the Horner site have been found at sites at Yellowstone Lake and along the Yellowstone River, indicating that Native Americans
migrated seasonally from the lowlands of the Bighorn Basin to the uplands of the
Yellowstone Plateau during the Paleoindian Period. Artifacts from Mummy Cave
and the Horner Site are on display at the Buffalo Bill Center of the West in Cody.

After traveling through the Hayden Valley, instead of turning east toward Cody,
you can travel southward from Fishing Bridge along Grand Loop Road. Here, as
you pass Yellowstone Lake to the east, you'll drive past the marina, where you
can take a boat tour across the lake in summer. At the lake, there are numerous
backcountry campsites, which are wonderful places to canoe or kayak to on a hot
summer day. The lake also provides outstanding fishing for both the lake trout and
the native Yellowstone cutthroat trout. On a typical summer day, dozens of boats
will be on the lake fishing in the inlets and bays of the lake. There is little evidence
that Native Americans fished at the lake, seeming to prefer to hunt for bison and
collect rich camas bulbs from the meadows next to the lake.

Driving southward eventually takes you to the West Thumb Geyser Basin at Yellowstone Lake's south shore. One of the most important archaeological sites in the
park—the Osprey Beach site—is located a few miles to the east of the West Thumb
Geyser Basin. The site is more than 9,300 years old, indicating that Native American hunter-gatherers were frequent users of the lake soon after the glaciers melted.

South of the West Thumb and Yellowstone Lake, the main artery toward Jackson, Wyoming, is the John D. Rockefeller, Jr. Memorial Parkway. This road takes
you past Grant Village, which has nice hotels, restaurants, gas, campgrounds, and
tourist facilities. The road continues southward across the Continental Divide
(around 8,000 ft./2,430 m) for a few miles before arriving at Lewis Lake. This
lake is wonderful for camping and canoeing. Across Lewis Lake is the Lewis River
Channel, which connects Lewis Lake and Shoshone Lake. The Lewis Channel is
the only river in the park that allows travel by nonmotorized boats (e.g., canoes
and kayaks). From Lewis Lake, the highway dives into the Lewis River Canyon, a
deep, stunning gorge with several falls offering outstanding photographic opportunities. The upper rim of the gorge was an active travel route for Native Americans
between the Snake River in the south and Yellowstone Lake in the north.

Continuing southward for 15 mi. (24 km), you will come to the South Entrance
of the park along the Snake River. Another well-used area by Native Americans in

FIGURE 1.12 The Lewis River Canyon provides a stunning backdrop for visitors entering the park at the South Entrance.

prehistory, the Snake River Valley winds southward toward Grand Teton National Park and the small town of Jackson, Wyoming (population 9,700). The Snake River eventually winds for over 1,000 mi. (1,600 km) to the west through Idaho to its confluence with the Columbia River in Washington State. In the Jackson area, the Snake River provides ample opportunities for whitewater rafting and fly fishing.

The town of Jackson is one of the most popular park entryways; it is also the only Yellowstone entrance city that offers abundant downhill skiing opportunities

in winter. The area south of Yellowstone is a must-see, including John D. Rockefeller, Jr. Memorial Parkway and Grand Teton National Park. The majestic peaks of the Teton Range are among the most striking in North America.

At Grant Village near Yellowstone Lake, instead of heading south to Jackson, you can turn westward toward the famous Old Faithful geyser and the Upper Geyser Basin. After traversing the Continental Divide near Isa Lake at Craig Pass (elevation 7,250 ft./2,200 m), you'll descend to the popular area around Old Faithful and the numerous hot springs of the geyser basin. Several lodges there, including the architecturally notable Old Faithful Lodge, accommodate tourists during all seasons; the only way to get there in winter, however, is by motorized snow vehicles from West Yellowstone, Montana, or from Mammoth, Wyoming. The Firehole

FIGURE 1.13 The Teton Mountains are among the most picturesque in the Yellowstone region. *Molly MacDonald photo.*

River flows through this area, and the Grand Loop Road follows the river valley. Via the road, you travel westward through the Midway Geyser Basin and to the largest and one of the most spectacular thermal features in the park, the Grand Prismatic Spring.

Farther north and west along the road, you come to the Upper Geyser Basin near the park's West Entrance. Here, the westward-flowing Firehole River and the southerly flowing Gibbon River join to form the scenic headwaters of the Madison River. This river, in turn, flows through West Yellowstone, Montana, and eventually to the north past Hegben and Earthquake Lakes and Ennis, Montana. Farther north, the Madison River joins the Jefferson and Gallatin Rivers near the town of Three Forks, Montana, to form the vast and majestic Missouri River up which Lewis and Clark

FIGURE 1.14 To visit Old Faithful in winter, you travel by snow coach from West Yellowstone, Montana.

explored in 1805–6. At Madison Junction, you can travel northward back to Norris Junction along the Grand Loop Road through the steep canyons and by the falls of the Gibbon River to complete your park loop, or you can head westward to the park's West Entrance at the town of West Yellowstone, Montana.

West Yellowstone has become the most popular entry point for park visitors and is the home of about 1,500 permanent residents. The small western-style city contains numerous hotels, restaurants, and shops. In the winter, West Yellowstone continues to be a hub of activity for snowmobilers and cross-country skiers. In that season, the entrance road to the park is open only to licensed snow coaches; the trip from West Yellowstone to Old Faithful in winter by snow vehicle is a memorable one. Native American hunters took advantage of the presence of winter game in this area, as indicated by the many archaeological sites present in the Madison River Valley.

11,000 YEARS OF NATIVE AMERICANS IN YELLOWSTONE

Nearly every American at some point in their lives yearns to see the wilds of Yellowstone, with millions of them completing the trip each year. Whether they choose to enter from Gardiner, Cooke City, West Yellowstone, Jackson, or Cody, their visit is mostly focused along the main highways, like the Grand Loop Road, looking out

FIGURE 1.15 The Grand Prismatic Spring is one of the most beautiful thermal features in the park. *Molly MacDonald photo.*

of their car windows for grizzly bears, wolves, bison, elk, pelicans, and trumpeter swans. They might hike to see mighty falls and golden cliffs of the Grand Canyon of the Yellowstone River or to watch geysers shoot scalding-hot water some 125 ft. (38 m) into the air at Old Faithful. Or they might simply stay at the grand Yellowstone Hotel and peer across Yellowstone Lake at the undisturbed wilderness. For good reason, Yellowstone is often referred to as America's largest outdoor zoo and waterpark. Most tourists know little about the park's early use by Native American peoples.

Unbeknownst to most tourists in the park, no matter what route you take through Yellowstone, you'll pass hundreds of camps and other sites that were used by Native Americans over the past 11,000 years. With the exception of a small handful of these sites that are marked by roadside signs (e.g., Obsidian Cliff and Sheepeater Cliff), they are invisible to visitors traveling by car.

FIGURE 1.16 A sow grizzly and two cubs nibble on flowers along State Route 26 north of Jackson, Wyoming.

Since their earliest arrival about 11,000 years ago, Native Americans have lived in Yellowstone, indicated by the archaeological sites that dot the park, such as the stone circles that mark the bases of ancient Native American tipi lodges (figure 1.17) near Gardiner, Montana. Archaeological sites, as well as interviews with living Native Americans, document the presence of Native Americans at places such as Yellowstone Lake until as recently as 100 years ago.

THE NATIVE AMERICAN TRIBES OF YELLOWSTONE

Prior to the formation of Yellowstone National Park and before the reservation era of the late 1800s, Yellowstone was a popular summer hunting and gathering area for numerous Native American tribes, including the Shoshone, Crow, Salish, Nez Perce, and Blackfeet. The Shoshone, or Sheep Eaters, are the Native American tribe most commonly linked to Yellowstone. Two other Shoshone groups—the Lemhi (Northern Shoshone) and the Eastern Shoshone—comprise the three major bands of Shoshone that frequented the Yellowstone region. These three Shoshone bands, along with the Northern Paiute and Bannock tribes, were often referred to collectively as the Snake Indians by early fur traders and settlers of the region because of their active use of the Snake River region.

The three Shoshone groups speak mutually intelligible Shoshone languages within the Numic family, most common to tribes of the Great Basin region today. A related tribe—the Bannock—speak a similar Numic language and share common cultural attributes with the Shoshone. The Shoshone were hunter-gatherers prior

FIGURE 1.17 This stone circle near Gardiner, Montana, marks the location of a Native American tipi built along the Yellowstone River hundreds of years ago.

to the reservation era, subsisting on a wide variety of wild resources available in the Greater Yellowstone Ecosystem. The Shoshone ventured into the upland valleys of the park to procure a variety of plants and animals, especially bighorn sheep.

The precise date of the arrival of the Shoshone to the Yellowstone region is a source of much debate (and is discussed further in chapter 8). Some archaeologists suggest that it wasn't until the past 1,000 years or so that the modern Shoshone peoples actually became permanent residents of the Yellowstone region. Numic language speakers are hypothesized to have expanded their ranges from the Great Basin northward into the Rocky Mountains of Montana, Idaho, and Wyoming during the past millennium. However, sites like Mummy Cave along the Shoshone River east of Yellowstone National Park suggest longer use of the region dating back nearly 10,000 years. Today, descendants of the Sheep Eaters and Eastern Shoshone live on the Wind River Reservation south of Cody, Wyoming, while Idaho's

FIGURE 1.18 This photo of a Shoshone camp in Yellowstone was taken in 1871 by an unknown photographer. *National Park Service photo.*

Fort Hall Reservation is home to the Lemhi Shoshone, the Bannock, and other bands of the Shoshone, including some Sheep Eaters.

Another Native American tribe that lives in the Yellowstone region is the Crow. They speak a Siouan (a family of North American Indian languages spoken by the Sioux and related peoples, including Crow, Dakota, Hidatsa, Lakota, Mandan, Omaha, and Yankton) language that is similar to that of the Hidatsa people of North Dakota. The two tribes split sometime in the past two millennia, with the Crow moving from North Dakota to their homelands in central and southern Montana and northern Wyoming. The Crow hunted and gathered within Yellowstone over the past several hundred years, especially along the park's eastern and northern areas.

When Yellowstone National Park was first established in 1872, part of it was within the Crow reservation boundaries. At that time, the Crow reservation measured approximately 8 million acres (3.2 million hectares) in Wyoming and Montana, as established in the Fort Laramie, or Horse Creek, Treaty of 1851. Today, the Crow Reservation occupies a smaller area of about 2.3 million acres (930,000 hectares) in Big Horn, Yellowstone, and Treasure Counties of south-central Montana.

FIGURE 1.19 A Blackfeet camp in Montana (1931). The northern portions of Yellowstone are part of the Blackfeet traditional territory. *James Willard Schultz photo. Courtesy of Montana State University's Special Collections and Archives.*

The Blackfeet also traveled to the northern edges of Yellowstone during the past 2,000 years. According to archaeological evidence, the Blackfeet likely originated from midwestern North America and established their traditional homelands in Alberta, Canada, and Montana 2,000 to 3,000 years ago, if not earlier. With their territories in northwestern and north-central Montana and southern Alberta, near what is today Glacier National Park, the Blackfeet expanded their ranges, especially after the introduction of the horse to the region in the eighteenth century. Known as a nomadic bison hunting people, the Blackfeet ventured southward in the Yellowstone region to exploit the vast herds of buffalo, elk, and other game.

According to tradition, another northwestern Native American tribe that ventured occasionally into Yellowstone were the Salish, or Flathead. Most closely related to other Salish-speaking tribes of the Columbia River Plateau of western Montana, northern Idaho, and eastern Washington and Oregon, the Salish homeland is northwestern Montana, but they ventured into the Rocky Mountains and Great Plains to hunt bison. These hunting trips brought them occasionally to the Yellowstone River Valley, or the Elk River as most tribes called it. Today, the Salish tribe shares the Flathead Reservation in northwestern Montana with the Kootenai and Pend d'Oreille tribes.

In total, 26 Native American tribes claim cultural association with Yellowstone National Park today. The tribal territories—the limits of each tribe's ancestral lands in which they hunted, gathered, traded, and socialized—extend well beyond the tribal governmental reservation boundaries. Today, cultural resource managers at Yellowstone National Park consult with all 26 different Native American tribes that have traditional territories or a cultural interest in the greater Yellowstone region. In addition to the tribes previously discussed, including the Shoshone, Crow, Blackfeet, and Salish, several other associated tribes include the Nez Perce, Northern Cheyenne, Sioux (10 different bands), Assiniboine, Gros Ventre, Chippewa-Cree, and Kiowa, among others.

In the late eighteenth century, the various indigenous Native American tribes hunted and traded with Euro-American trappers as they worked the region's many rivers to find furs. Lewis and Clark entered the region in 1805, getting to within 50 mi. (80 km) of what is today Yellowstone National Park. Soon after, early explorers such as John Colter (in 1807) and early trappers such as Osborne Russell (in 1834) encountered the Shoshone and other tribes in Yellowstone.

With the trapping era coming to an end in the mid-nineteenth century because of decreasing European demand for furs, Native Americans likely had the area of the park all to themselves for a couple of decades. It wasn't until the 1860s that the federal government sent explorers to map the region, including the Folsom-Cook-Peterson Expedition of 1869, the Washburn-Langford-Doane Expedition of 1870, and the first Hayden Expedition of 1871. These explorers all noted the presence of Native Americans in the park and vicinity.

In 1872, when President Grant signed 2.2 million acres (890,000 hectares) of land into existence as America's first national park in Wyoming, Montana, and Idaho, Native American hunter-gatherers were camped along the shores of Yellowstone Lake and along the Madison and Yellowstone Rivers. However, as is well documented in historic literature and the words of Native American elders, Native Americans were forced by the US government to abandon their traditional lifestyles, their religions, their languages, and their cultures. Tribes were pushed out of Yellowstone and onto reservations, where they were taught to use Western values, the English language, and Euro-American culture.

INDIAN WARS IN YELLOWSTONE

Each and every one of the tribes that frequented Yellowstone resisted this decision by the US government. Among them were the Nez Perce, or Niimíipu as they call themselves, who frequently hunted, gathered, and traveled in Yellowstone from their homeland of northeastern Oregon, southeastern Washington, and northern Idaho. In late summer 1877, the Nez Perce, under the leadership of Chief Joseph, fled their homeland to escape government-forced reservation life and to join the Lakota Sioux chief Sitting Bull in Canada. Chief Joseph led 700 of his fellow Nez Perce for three months through harrowing canyons and across high mountains on a daring journey over approximately 1,200 mi. (1,930 km), including about 84 mi. (135 km) through Yellowstone National Park. The Nez Perce War, as it was called, included several battles

FIGURE 1.20 A Nez Perce camp. *National Park Service photo, no date.*

between federal military forces—totaling as many as 2,000 individual US Cavalry soldiers—against as few as 200 Nez Perce warriors.

During their journey through Yellowstone National Park, the Nez Perce also had a few brief, deadly encounters with tourists and US Cavalry during that summer and early fall. Archaeological sites now mark the locations of some of those skirmishes. One of the most important archaeological sites in the Lower Geyser Basin marks the location where a group of Nez Perce warriors encountered a group of nine tourists now referred to as the Radersburg Party. Upon the initial encounter near the Grand Loop Road crossing of Nez Perce Creek today, the Radersburg Party quickly packed their belongings and headed northward toward the Madison River, escorted by several Nez Perce warriors on horseback. Many more Nez Perce eventually joined the procession until at one point several hundred people and as many as 1,500 horses made their way along Nez Perce Creek. Eventually, warriors looted the tourists' wagons, took their supplies, and killed two members of the party, as well as took three more hostages. Today, artifacts, including gun shells, horse bridle fragments, and an assortment of camping supplies, mark the location of the final stand of the Radersburg Party along Nez Perce Creek a few miles north of the Grand Loop Road.

The Nez Perce were viewed by the US government as the aggressors in this skirmish, but they were the rightful inhabitants of the park, given their long history of use. In the minds of the Nez Perce warriors, the early tourists were the invaders and threatened the success of their escape to join Sitting Bull in Canada and avoid reservation life. Yellowstone road signs mark the locations of some of these encounters between the Nez Perce and Euro-Americans, including one in the Hayden Valley identified as Nez Perce Ford, the location where Chief Joseph led his tribe across the Yellowstone River to get to Yellowstone Lake's north shore after their encounter with the Radersburg Party.

After camping at Yellowstone Lake, the Nez Perce traveled into the Sunlight Basin in the far northeastern corner of Yellowstone National Park and up over what is today called Dead Indian Pass and the Chief Joseph Scenic Byway. After traversing the 8,000 ft. high (2,440 m high) pass northwest of Cody, Wyoming, the US military chased the Nez Perce for several weeks, eventually capturing them in the snows of October within 50 mi. (80 km) of the Canadian border in the Bear Paw Mountains of north-central Montana. Here, Chief Joseph famously lamented, "Hear me, my chiefs. I am tired; my heart is sick and sad. From where the sun now stands, I will fight no more forever."

Another regional "Indian war" involved the Bannock and Shoshone against the US Cavalry. Dubbed the Bannock War of 1878, the two tribes revolted over Euro-American farming within traditional camas fields near Fort Hall, Idaho. Early in the war, most of the activity was focused in eastern Idaho near Fort Hall, southeast of Yellowstone. A group of Bannock and Shoshone eventually fled into Yellowstone, following much the same escape route taken by Chief Joseph a year earlier. The final skirmish of the Bannock War occurred within 20 mi. (32 km) of Dead Indian Pass. Here, along Bennett Creek, US Cavalry General Nelson Miles led his troops to

FIGURE 1.21 This pamphlet was produced by the Northern Pacific railroad in 1885 to increase tourism to the park. *Courtesy of the Yellowstone Research Library, Heritage and Research Center, Gardiner, Montana.*

victory over the Shoshone and Bannock warriors. According to Peter Nabokov and Lawrence Loendorf in their 2004 book, *Restoring a Presence: American Indians in Yellowstone National Park*, the Shoshone and Bannock peoples lost 80 lives, 250 horses, and 32 prisoners, while the US Cavalry suffered only 40 casualties.

To counteract the bad publicity of the Nez Perce and Bannock Wars of 1877 and 1878 in Yellowstone and to encourage tourism, early park officials initiated marketing campaigns to downplay the presence of Native Americans in the park and promote the natural beauty of Yellowstone. The eastern media outlets were rife with news of "Indian attacks" in the West, and early park officials wanted potential tourists to think that Yellowstone was safe from such activity. The Northern Pacific railroad also wanted to increase tourism, having built a rail line connecting Livingston and Gardiner, Montana, to transport tourists from their main rail lines to the North Entrance of the park. The railroad produced vacation brochures such as one in 1885 of Alice's Adventures in the New Wonderland (figure 1.21) to encourage visitors to the newly formed Yellowstone National Park.

FIGURE 1.22 Camp Sheridan at Mammoth Hot Springs (ca. 1900). *National Park Service photo.*

The US military then established a permanent presence in the park to discourage Native American hunting and gathering and to protect the burgeoning tourist trade. The cavalry also guarded against poachers who entered the park's boundaries to hunt animals for food and hides. From their barracks at Camp Sheridan (1886–1890) and, later, Fort Yellowstone (1891–1918), in Mammoth Hot Springs, the US Cavalry patrolled the park for 32 years. In 1918 many of the buildings constructed for the military at Fort Yellowstone were converted into park administration offices; they continue to serve this purpose today.

Since the establishment of the park, the preservation of wilderness has been the primary declared goal of the park. The Historic Sites Act of 1935 established the National Park Service as the government agency in control of Yellowstone and other national parks, with the main goal of preserving the park's natural wonders. Even today, the natural beauty of Old Faithful, the Yellowstone River, and grizzly bears, rather than the park's significant cultural resources, is the focus of most marketing campaigns.

Certainly, the significant cultural importance of the park to Native Americans was not considered during the park's formation. For most of the park's history, park officials have insisted that Native Americans never lived in the park out of their fear of the explosive geysers and scalding-hot thermal features. Today, because the National Park Service, among other entities, funded research into Native American presence in the park, we know this is not true. Native Americans frequented the park's thermal features for spiritual, medicinal, and subsistence reasons. Among other areas, thermal features and mountaintops mark the locations of important spiritual events for many Native American individuals. For example, the famous Crow shaman, the Fringe, brought tribal members to the thermal features of Yellowstone to heal them and to seek visions through fasting.

Over the past 20 to 30 years, the US government, including the National Park Service, realized that their treatment of Native Americans during the early years of the park was a tragedy. In the early 2000s, the park funded an important ethnographic study of Native Americans in the park, resulting in the 2004 *Restoring a Presence* book by Nabokov and Loendorf. The book finally established the roots of many regional Native American tribes in the park over the past 11,000 years.

As exemplified by the National Park Service's role in Nabokov and Loendorf's ethnographic project, relationships between the US government, including the National Park Service, and modern Native American tribes have improved in Yellowstone. Today, the 26 associated Native American tribes are routinely consulted by park officials when making important decisions regarding the management of bison or impacts to archaeological sites, among other issues. There still is occasional conflict between tribes and federal officials, but the active intergovernmental consultation in recent years has improved the management of natural and cultural resources in Yellowstone.

The Yellowstone area provided abundant resources—from plants to animals to rocks—that were harvested by Native Americans for 11,000 years in Yellowstone, allowing these hunter-gatherer peoples to survive and thrive in a wilderness that many of us view with trepidation today. They camped on the shores of North America's largest high-elevation natural lake—Yellowstone Lake—and traveled along the rugged canyons of the Madison, Firehole, Gibbon, Yellowstone, and Snake Rivers, among others. They explored mountain slopes to hunt bighorn sheep and elk. They gathered bitterroot and camas bulbs from alpine meadows. They procured obsidian from the numerous volcanic flows of the region, especially Obsidian Cliff, for tools and projectile points.

Native American hunter-gatherers watched their backs and feared grizzly bears and wolves like modern tourists do today, but that did not keep them away from the resources they needed in order to survive. The land and the rivers and the mountains and the animals and plants are all part of an integrated Native American worldview that is likely very different from the one shared by most visitors to Yellowstone today. Whereas the Fringe sought spiritual guidance at Yellowstone's thermal features, thousands of modern tourists seek photographs and experiences of the natural beauty to share with their friends and family.

ARCHAEOLOGY IN YELLOWSTONE

While the purposes of Yellowstone have changed dramatically in the past two centuries, most of the park has been preserved in much the same state as it was before 1805. This preservation of the natural setting has also protected many of its cultural resources, such as archaeological sites that mark the presence of Native Americans in the park for millennia.

Archaeological sites, such as one on the south shore of Yellowstone Lake (figure 1.23), mark places where Native Americans formerly lived in the park. At some of the major archaeological sites, such as Obsidian Cliff, there are literally millions of pieces of stone chipping debris, called scatter, from stone tool manufacture. Many of the sites are well known simply because of the abundant artifacts visible on the ground.

Archaeological information on the precontact use of the park by Native Americans is not widely known to the public. The use of the park by contemporary Native Americans has been well-documented by Nabokov and Loendorf's *Restoring a Presence*, which remains the most important book on the topic. It covers contemporary Native American use of the park, and discusses the various tribes that frequented the park in the past.

Nabokov and Loendorf offer limited coverage of the deep precontact history of Native Americans in Yellowstone. Instead, a wide array of academic and federal scientific data document the prehistoric use of the park by Native Americans, and that documentation is largely inaccessible to the public in an effort to protect sites.

Archaeological sites comprise the basis for knowledge of the precontact history of Native Americans in Yellowstone. Contemporary tribal oral narratives, such as those recorded by Nabokov and Loendorf, are extremely informative, and the scientific investigation of archaeological sites is also an important source of information for interpreting Native American history in Yellowstone. At the thousands of archaeological sites—places Native Americans lived—in Yellowstone National

FIGURE 1.23 University of Montana archaeologists Samuel White and Michael Ciani excavate a site on the south shore of Yellowstone Lake (2014).

Park, the evidence found usually includes a variety of artifacts and features that reflect the lives of those who lived at the location.

Archaeological sites in Yellowstone typically contain stone, or lithic, artifacts produced from various volcanic rocks, including obsidian. Other types of rocks, including chert, quartzite, quartz, petrified wood, and chalcedony, were used by Native Americans to make stone tools for use in their daily lives. In my numerous archaeological explorations across the park, we have found thousands of pieces of rock that are the by-products of stone tool manufacture. While we don't always find the finished tools, these waste flakes (often referred to as *debitage* by archaeologists) that are left behind after the tool is made allow us to reconstruct the tool's creation. From the waste flakes, we can tell what type of stone was used and where it was obtained, thereby telling us where those people traveled prior to living at the site.

FIGURE 1.24 The atlatl, or spear thrower, was used by Native Americans to hunt animals starting 11,000 years ago in Yellowstone. This technology was replaced by the bow and arrow ca. 1,500 years ago. *Illustration by Eric Carlson, 2016.*

Stone tools can provide many answers to questions about hunting practices, technology, and subsistence patterns. For example, did Native Americans hunt with handheld spears, throwing spears (or atlatls), or bows and arrows? While we rarely find the actual weapons, we do find the stone spear and arrow tips, which inform us greatly about Native American hunting technology. For example, we know that for about 10,000 years, Native Americans in Yellowstone threw spears or atlatl (spear thrower) darts with large stone projectiles on their tips for hunting. It was only within the past two millenia that Native Americans all across North America, including Yellowstone, used smaller point tips associated with the innovation of the bow and arrow. The sizes of the projectile points (figure 1.25) reveal their technology of use, with the arrow points considerably smaller than the atlatl dart points. According to Yellowstone National Park archaeologist Elizabeth Horton, bow and arrow technology was adopted in the nearby Columbia Plateau and Pacific Coast of Washington and Oregon by as early as 4,000 years ago, but it did not become widespread in the northwestern Plains, Rocky Mountains, and Yellowstone until 1,500 years ago.

The types of materials used to make the stone tools inform us about travel and trade patterns of Native Americans. For example, if we find an obsidian arrow point in the southern portion of Yellowstone along the Snake River, my first question usually is: What obsidian is it made from? If it is made from Obsidian Cliff obsidian, that tells me that a Native American individual traveled northward into Yellowstone to collect the rock and then returned southward to the Snake River. Alternatively, it could mean that the individual acquired the stone by trading with people who had traveled to Obsidian Cliff. In the end, we can discern a great deal about Native American settlement patterns, trade routes, and travel corridors by looking at the distribution of obsidian across the region.

Late Archaic
Atlatl Dart Point
ca. 2,000 years old

Late Prehistoric
Arrow Point
ca. 500 years old

2 cm

FIGURE 1.25 Atlatl dart tips (left) are two to three times larger than arrow tips (right).

Another common type of artifact found at Yellowstone archaeological sites is bone. It is well known that Native Americans hunted a lot in the park. On the face of a quickly eroding terrace escarpment on the shore of Yellowstone Lake in 2016, University of Montana archaeologists excavated a bison bone that marks the location where a Native American hunter killed a bison approximately 800 years ago. The bison was probably attracted to the nearby thermal features for warmth during the cold nights at Yellowstone Lake, thus making an excellent ambush location for Native American hunters.

We occasionally find bone at Native American campsites as well, in which hunters carried back portions of hunted animals to butcher and eat by the warmth of their campfires and shelters. An illustration by artist Eric Carlson (figure 1.26) shows a Native American camp near Yellowstone Falls, in which a family is conducting daily activities, such as processing an elk kill, which was no doubt a typical scene along the river during precontact times.

Even though such animal preparation activity was very common for Native Americans in Yellowstone, preserved animal remains are scarce because of the highly acidic soils in the park. Those corrosive soils erode and deteriorate bone quickly, so they are often lost to the archaeological record. While bone is scarce at sites, another good way to identify the types of animals hunted is protein residues left on stone tools. While bone may deteriorate over time, some protein residues from blood, fat, and other bodily material sometimes stick to the stone tools. Analysis of such proteins can tell archaeologists which animals were hunted and butchered by the stone tools. To date, dozens of stone tools have been tested for protein residues with bison, deer, bear, rabbit, and elk among the most common residues found on the tools.

Other types of artifacts at archaeological sites are largely too small to see. Microscopic plant remains and pollen, for example, provide much information about plants collected by Native Americans in the past. Native hunter-gatherers in Yellowstone collected hundreds of different plants for food and medicinal use in the park. Fields of camas and bitterroot provided abundant proteins and nutrients for Native American survival in Yellowstone and the vicinity. Archaeologists examine soil samples from sites and can identify trace remains of these plants in the dirt. Among the most common plant remains found in the park at archaeological sites are goosefoot (*Chenopodium* genus), sunflower, sagebrush, grasses, balsamroot, wild onion, prickly pear cactus, as well as a variety of wood burned in fires, including sagebrush, pine, spruce, ash, aspen, and mistletoe.

FIGURE 1.26 This illustration by artist and archaeologist Eric Carlson (2016) shows a typical scene of Native American life along the Yellowstone River in the past. A small family is shown at a camp; a woman is butchering an elk, while another makes a stone tool.

Archaeologists also occasionally find the remains of habitation structures, or lodges, of Native Americans. Prior to the mid- to late twentieth century, wickiups commonly were found in Yellowstone. Wickiups are timber lodges mostly used by the Shoshone and occasionally other tribes for temporary shelter while traveling. Over time, many of these wickiups have disappeared because of fires and other natural and human disturbances. Occasionally the remains of wickiups survive to modern times, such as one (figure 1.27) along Alkali Creek in northwestern Wyoming near Yellowstone.

Stone circles are another type of archaeological site that marks the remains of Native American living structures. Stone circles are the former bases of tipi lodges, usually comprised of 10 to 30 or more large round rocks in a circle from 10 to 20 ft. (3 to 6 m) across. (There are various spellings for the word *tipi* [e.g., tepee or teepee], but I use the traditional Lakota Sioux spelling of the term.) In our excavations at Yellowstone Lake, my archaeology crews from the University of Montana located the remains of a stone circle that dates to approximately 1,200 years ago. Near Gardiner, Montana, we excavated three stone circles that date to between 1,000 and 300 years ago.

A rare type of archaeological site in the park is one that yields ancient human remains. While it is certain that Native Americans laid their dead to rest in the park, few burials have been discovered by archaeologists. Some of the deceased probably were placed aboveground, on timber platforms that decay quickly over time. Even human remains placed in the ground are likely to decay rapidly because of the park's highly acidic soils. I think such remains should stay buried because of their sacred nature. But human remains can provide information to archaeologists about diet, culture, and the human condition, above and beyond the information provided by stone tools and animal and plant remains. Only a few Native American human remains have been found in Yellowstone. These individuals were buried along the shores of Yellowstone Lake likely within the past 2,000 years. Great care was taken during their analysis and, as per the 1990 Native American Grave Protection and Repatriation Act—commonly referred to as NAGPRA, regional tribes were consulted as to their disposition after their discovery.

One type of archaeological site that has not yet been identified in Yellowstone National Park is precontact Native American rock art. There are many different types of Native American rock art—from images "pecked" with stone tools on cave walls (petroglyphs) to painted images on cliffs (pictographs)—that are present across much of Montana, Wyoming, and Idaho. Other archaeologists and I have searched far and wide for examples of Native American rock art within the park boundaries, to no avail. We've done archaeological surveys in the north along the Yellowstone River, in the south along the Lewis and Snake Rivers, and in the east along the Madison, Firehole, and Gibbon Rivers. These places have rock walls, caves, and shelters upon which rock art could have been produced by Native Americans. But as far as we can tell, early Native Americans did not make such art in

FIGURE 1.27 The wickiup (left) and the tipi (right) were the most common types of living structures used by Native Americans in Yellowstone and vicinity.

the park, for reasons that remain a mystery. Perhaps we just haven't found it yet. One would think that in a place as remarkably beautiful as Yellowstone that Native American hunter-gatherers would have considered it a prime place to contact the spirits through art. Such is the practice of Native Americans in places not too far from Yellowstone.

One of the most amazing rock art sites in the region is located near Thermopolis, Wyoming, at Legend Rock State Park, only 60 mi. (100 km) southeast of Yellowstone. Here, hundreds of ghostly images are pecked into the rock faces. In interviews with Shoshone tribal members, they have identified many of the images as ghost people who lived in the waterways and rocks of the region. South of Livingston, Montana, red pictographs of humans are painted above the Yellowstone River approximately 25 mi. (40 km) north of the park. Red painted images are also present on the walls of Mummy Cave only 10 mi. (16 km) east of the park's East Entrance. In the south, rock art is present in some areas of the Teton Mountains. And in the west, the Madison and Gallatin River valleys have ample examples of rock art.

FIGURE 1.28 This petroglyph, or pecked image on a rock face, was found outside of Yellowstone near Thermopolis, Wyoming. Such rock art images have not been found within the park limits.

PROTECTING YELLOWSTONE'S ARCHAEOLOGICAL SITES

The destruction and looting of archaeological sites has long been a source of consternation for archaeologists, Native Americans, and others. Various federal laws have been passed by the US Congress over the years to protect archaeological sites on federal lands. As mentioned previously, NAGPRA is one of a handful of federal cultural resource laws that provide important protection to archaeological sites in Yellowstone. NAGPRA protects Native American human remains on federal and tribal land. Discovery of Native American human remains on these lands requires consultation with tribes, as well as the repatriation of burials and ceremonial items to tribes. If found in Yellowstone, human bones are to be left alone and the authorities (park rangers) should immediately be contacted to determine how to proceed with the care of the fragile and important remains.

Another important archaeological law in Yellowstone is the Archaeological Resource Protection Act, or ARPA, of 1979. This law updated the rather outdated federal protections of archaeological sites found in the original Antiquities Act of

HOW DO ARCHAEOLOGISTS IDENTIFY ARCHAEOLOGICAL SITES IN YELLOWSTONE?

Over the years, many different archae-ologists from across the region have conducted archaeological survey in Yellowstone. My own research has taken me across thousands of acres in the park to find archaeological sites. We use two main methods for archaeological site identification there: pedestrian survey and shovel-test survey. In areas of the park with good ground visibility —e.g., areas that are comparatively open with little vegetation—archaeologists can use pedestrian survey to identify sites. Pedestrian survey (figure 1.29) entails a team of archaeologists walking in a controlled and comprehensive manner across the survey area. The goal of this approach is to visually examine the exposed ground in the area of survey for the presence of artifacts. This method is by far the most common one used by archaeologists to find sites in the park. In the region, by pedestrian survey, we have identified sites in the Yellowstone River Valley, Yellowstone Lake, the Snake River Valley, and the Gibbon River Valley.

In some areas of the park, such as the upper Snake River Valley, thick ground vegetation and soil cover archaeological sites and make them impossible to spot just by looking. In these cases, we conduct shovel-test survey. This approach requires exca-vation of round holes every 50 to 100 ft. (15 to 30 m) or so in an area to find sites. The holes are approximately 1 to 2 ft. (30 to 60 cm) wide and 2 to 3 ft. (60 to 100 cm) deep, with all excavated dirt screened through quarter-inch mesh screens. This method requires more labor for the same amount of ground as pedestrian survey, and so it is more expensive and takes more time. But shovel-test survey often results in the discovery of amazing prehistoric Native American archaeological sites that otherwise would remain hidden under thick vegetation and soil.

After the identification of archaeological sites through survey, archaeologists often strive to determine whether the sites are significant—that is, important enough to be listed in the National Register of Historic Places (NRHP). If an archaeological site holds information that can contribute to a better understanding of past human

FIGURE 1.29 Archaeologists walk in evenly spaced transects to identify Native American sites along the shore of Yellowstone Lake (2010).

Subsurface Imaging

Test Unit Excavation

Site Mapping

activity in Yellowstone, it is considered to be important enough to be listed in the NRHP. To establish whether a site is eligible for listing in the NRHP, archaeologists conduct controlled excavations at the site. We excavate meter-square test units in areas where we expect to find artifacts or features. Sometimes we use advanced technology, such as subsurfacing imaging machines, to see features (such as fire pits) below the surface of the ground. As shown in figure 1.30, Professor Steven Sheriff collects information on the magnetic qualities of soils and then generates digital maps that show locations of possible prehistoric fire pits. The locations of surface artifacts can also help us determine the locations of additional archaeological features beneath the ground surface. Every artifact and feature is carefully mapped, using computerized technology and software, the results of which allow us to reconstruct the past activities at the site.

Within the boundaries of Yellowstone National Park, my teams of archaeologists have conducted excavations at hundreds of archaeological sites, including historic-period train stations and precontact Native American hunting camps. During excavations of Native American precontact sites, we might

FIGURE 1.30 Technology is helpful in all aspects of archaeology. Subsurface imaging can help identify Native American fire pits buried below the ground, while computerized technology improves the accuracy of archaeological site maps.

find fire pits or stone circles or animal remains, all of which would indicate that the site is important. For example, we excavated a Native American site (figure 1.31) on the shores of the Flat Mountain Arm in Yellowstone Lake that contained the remains of two fire pits, hundreds of stone tools and debris, and elk bone. Each artifact was methodically collected for analysis in our laboratory at the University of Montana. After analysis and reporting, the artifacts were curated at the Yellowstone Heritage and Research Center in Gardiner, Montana, where they are now available for other researchers to study.

Occasionally, archaeological excavations at sites result in the discovery of very few or no artifacts. In such cases, we might just find a few small pieces of stone tools, which would be insufficient to list the site on the NRHP. Through these excavations, we can determine the importance of the site so that Yellowstone National Park can manage the resources appropriately. Once a site is determined to be significant, great care is taken of the site to avoid impact from future development in the park.

Dozens of excellent archaeologists have conducted surveys and excavations to look for and evaluate archaeological sites for their significance in Yellowstone. Nearly 300 archaeological sites have been identified and studied around the shores of the lake alone. In total, approximately 1,800 sites have been recorded within the confines of Yellowstone National Park. Archaeological reports are produced to document these findings, with most of them growing dusty on the shelves of federal libraries and research facilities. Still, despite these many surveys and reports, only about 5 to 10 percent of the park has been appropriately surveyed and documented by archaeologists, leaving thousands of as-yet-undiscovered sites across the park.

FIGURE 1.31 The University of Montana excavated meter square test units at this Native American site on the shore of the Flat Mountain Arm of Yellowstone Lake (2014).

1906. With stronger mandatory penalties for violation, including large fines and imprisonment, ARPA protects any archaeological site older than 100 years on federal land. And so, anyone who finds any kind of artifact at an archaeological site in Yellowstone should leave it alone. Under ARPA, the federal court in Mammoth Hot Springs has convicted several individuals for collection of Native American artifacts in Yellowstone.

The National Historic Preservation Act (NHPA) of 1966 provides additional protection for Yellowstone archaeological sites. This law requires land-owning federal agencies to identify and preserve cultural resources on their lands. Yellowstone has archaeologists on staff, including a park archaeologist and a cultural resource manager, who can be contacted with questions about park archaeology. They also direct research and survey for archaeological sites in the park (and they approved the dissemination of information in this book). The NHPA law also requires that federal undertakings take into consideration their effects on archaeological sites. So if a new highway or a new rest area is constructed in Yellowstone, for example, the park archaeologist examines the area to ensure that no significant archaeological sites will be disturbed or destroyed during construction. Among NAGPRA, ARPA, the NHPA, and a few other laws, archaeological sites on federal lands such as Yellowstone have adequate protections that will hopefully allow them to survive well into the future.

CHAPTER TWO

HOW LONG HAVE NATIVE AMERICANS LIVED IN YELLOWSTONE?

APPROXIMATELY 13,500 YEARS AGO, long before Chief Joseph led his tribe on their harrowing attempt to escape from the US Cavalry along Nez Perce Creek, a half-mile-high sheet of glacial ice stood tall above Yellowstone Lake. There were no people; there were no animals; there were no plants. There was pretty much just ice and perhaps a few birds living off mosquitoes. Gradually, after the glaciers melted from all of Yellowstone except the tallest mountains, vegetation and animals began to migrate back into Yellowstone. By as early as 12,000 years ago, the first Native Americans entered the region and survived by hunting game and collecting edible plants. These first Americans, often referred to as Paleoindians, made their way to Yellowstone by about 11,000 years ago. These early Native Americans were the first people ever to see the natural beauty of Yellowstone. Imagine being the first people to ever walk along the Firehole River and encounter Old Faithful erupting, a scene vividly depicted in this illustration.

▶ FIGURE 2.1 This painting is a re-creation of the moment when the first Native Americans witnessed an eruption of Old Faithful geyser approximately 11,000 years ago. *Illustration by Eric Carlson (2016).*

THE CLOVIS PEOPLE

Evidence of this early human arrival in Yellowstone exists in the form of a Clovis projectile point found on the shore of the South Arm of Yellowstone Lake by my University of Montana archaeological team in 2013 (figure 2.2). Approximately 11,000 years ago, Clovis people were among the first Native Americans to arrive to the Americas from Asia. Clovis projectile points have been found in all 48 continental United States, Mexico, and all Canadian provinces. This Clovis point remains one of only two Clovis points ever found in Yellowstone National Park; in 2007, we also recovered a Clovis point along the Yellowstone River north of Gardiner, Montana. These Clovis points indicate that Native American hunters traveled to Yellowstone some 11,000 years ago.

Some of the most important Paleoindian archaeological sites in North and South America (map 2.1) are discussed in this chapter. The sites were used by early Native American hunters to process animals they had killed, including mammoths, bison, horses, camels, and other now-extinct megafauna.

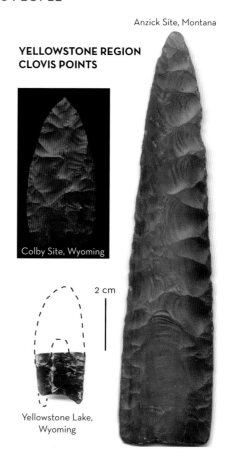

FIGURE 2.2 Clovis points from the Yellowstone region: from Yellowstone Lake (lower left), from the Colby site (upper left), and from the Anzick site (right).

A team of archaeologists from the University of Arizona excavated the oldest location of Clovis human habitation, or Clovis site, found to date in north-central Mexico, called El Fin del Mundo site. It marks the location where Clovis hunters killed a rare and now-extinct form of elephant—called a gomphothere—using Clovis points similar to the ones found in Yellowstone. The points found in Mexico and Yellowstone have a telltale flake removed at the base of the projectile point. This flake removal—called a channel flake—is unique to Clovis and subsequent Folsom

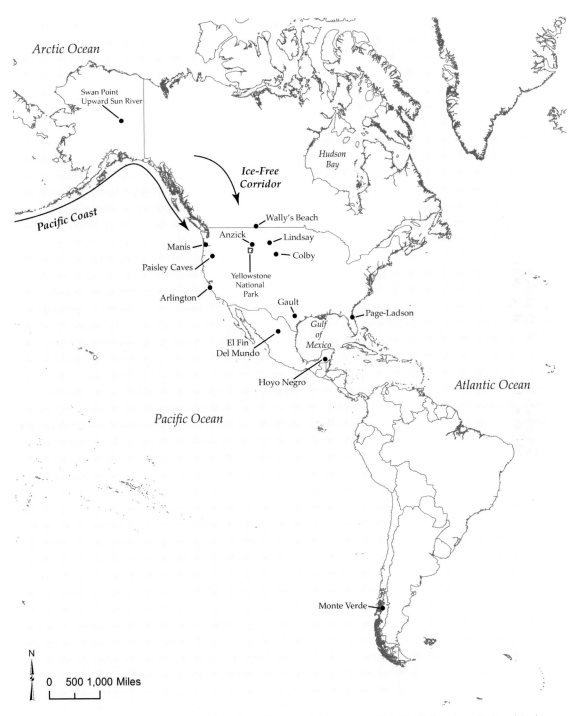

MAP 2.1 Important Paleoindian archaeological sites in the Americas related to Yellowstone National Park

points, and so it can be used to date the artifacts and the sites where points with this characteristic occur. The presence of Clovis points in Mexico about 11,500 years ago indicates that the ones found in Yellowstone are of a similar age, somewhere between 11,500 and 10,500 years old, the period in which Clovis Native Americans are known to have used the unique spear points in North America.

Still another Clovis age site, called Wally's Beach, was discovered on the shores of the St. Mary Reservoir near Medicine Hat, Alberta, approximately 50 mi. (80 km) north of the Montana state line. At the site in the late 1990s and early 2000s, a group of archaeologists from the University of Calgary excavated the remains of seven horses and a camel that were killed and butchered by early Native Americans. The site yielded radiocarbon dates of about 11,400 years ago in association with stone tools recovered there, which were used to butcher the horses and camels. It is unclear how the horses and camel were killed at the site—no projectile points were found in them—but Clovis points (with horse protein on two of them) were recovered nearby, suggesting that this site also represents very early evidence for Clovis people in the Great Plains region.

A large number of Clovis sites exist between Mexico and Alberta, but only a handful have been found in such high-elevation settings like Yellowstone. Clovis people apparently preferred the open plains and prairies that supported the large herds of mammoths, bison, horses, and camels. Most Clovis sites show evidence of megafauna hunting, while many also show that Clovis people hunted and gathered a wide variety of small game and plants. Due to the comparatively harsh environmental conditions in the high elevations of Yellowstone, Clovis people were probably infrequent travelers to the park area.

One of the Clovis sites nearest to Yellowstone, near Worland, Wyoming, is called the Colby site. The site is on a high terrace above a dry creek bed, which 11,000 years ago was a tributary of the Bighorn River. Located about 100 mi. (160 km) to the east of Yellowstone, the Colby site yielded the remains of seven mammoths killed by Clovis hunters over the course of several years. Hunters likely monitored small herds of mammoths in the area and took advantage of them when they neared their hunting areas along the creek. Two large bone piles at the site are the locations where Clovis hunters stacked meat for use, perhaps during winter. Led by University of Wyoming archaeologist George Frison and his colleague Lawrence Todd in the early 1980s, the team also found a beautiful red chert Clovis point (see figure 2.2, upper left) in association with the mammoths, indicating that their deaths were caused by human hunters.

Numerous other mammoth kill sites are present across the region. The Lindsay mammoth site near Glendive, Montana, dates to approximately 12,000 years ago, and may represent the earliest evidence of human hunting anywhere in the northwestern Great Plains. No projectile points were found at the site during excavations by Montana State University's Leslie Davis in the later 1960s, but a few large sandstone blocks there appear to have been used by early Native Americans for butchering the animal. In addition, cut marks and bone breakage patterns appear to have been produced by humans. While the site's human association is questioned by some because of the lack of associated stone tools, the site may represent the location where human hunters killed mammoths in Montana several hundred years before Clovis. If the human association is proven, the site would indicate a very long tradition—at least 1,000 years—of mammoth hunting in the interior of North America near Yellowstone. Remains of this mammoth from the Lindsay site are in the collections of the Museum of the Rockies in Bozeman, Montana.

THE ANZICK SITE

The Colby and Lindsay sites indicate that Clovis Native Americans preferred to hunt large game in the open prairies of the northwestern Great Plains. While the Yellowstone Plateau was likely not on the regular travel route of many Clovis people, they definitely frequented many of the river valleys that surround the park. In fact, the most important of all Clovis sites anywhere in North America is only 80 mi. (130 km) north of Yellowstone National Park along a small tributary of the Yellowstone River. Here, in 1968, at the Anzick site in the small town of Wilsall, Montana, two local men excavated rock from a cliff face to use for a construction project at the local school. As they dug into the cliff face with their backhoe, they saw a pile of red dirt and some shiny objects fall out of the rocky slope. They stopped excavating and discovered one of the most remarkable Clovis archaeological sites ever found in North America.

The Anzick site—named after the landowners—yielded more than 100 Clovis stone tools, several bone rods, as well as the skeletal remains of a two-year-old boy. A finely crafted Clovis fluted point (see figure 2.2, right) was among the artifacts found buried with the boy. His remains were radiocarbon dated to approximately 10,700 years ago, while an associated bone artifact was radiocarbon dated to 11,000 years ago. The remains and artifacts were covered with a thick red ochre dust. The Anzick site is believed to be the location where Clovis hunters buried an infant boy

FIGURE 2.3 The Anzick site is one of the most important Clovis sites in North America. The remains of a two-year-old boy with over 100 bone and stone tools were found here in 1968 near Wilsall, Montana.

with stone and bone tools he could use in the afterlife. The red ochre was believed to have been ceremonially sprinkled on the artifacts in some form of ritual to promote the boy's well-being in the spirit world. To this day, the Anzick site is the only Clovis site anywhere in North America that has yielded human remains.

In a 2014 issue of the scientific journal *Nature*, Danish geneticist Eske Willerslev and his colleagues (including one of my students, Samuel White, from the University of Montana) presented results of their analysis of the DNA of the Anzick boy that was carried out to determine his origins. Today, all Native American people can be placed into five mitochondrial DNA haplogroups: A, B, C, D, and X. These DNA groups trace their maternal lines back to ancient origins in northeast

Asia and Siberia. And so, most archaeologists believe that all Native Americans derive from people originally from these areas. If the boy from Anzick also came from one of these DNA groups, then it would prove that Clovis people in Montana descended from people in Asia.

Results of Willerslev's study indicated that the Anzick boy was descended from people that belonged to the mitochondrial DNA haplogroup D. The DNA also indicated that the boy was genetically connected to all modern Native Americans in North and South America. Willerslev's study also concluded that the Clovis boy was descended from people who traveled from northeastern Siberia at least 16,000 years ago. Similarly aged skeletons found in Mexico and Alaska share the same genetic mitochondrial DNA haplogroup D as the Anzick boy, suggesting a possible migration route along the Pacific Coast for the ancestors of the boy. Still, today, the origins of Clovis people, including the Anzick boy, in Montana and Yellowstone remain a point of fierce archaeological debate.

Willerslev and his colleagues' study of the Anzick site very close to Yellowstone National Park was remarkable for proving that Clovis people are in fact the ancestors of modern Native American people. Prior to Willerslev's DNA analysis of the Anzick boy, this idea had been in dispute because of archaeological discoveries found in the eastern United States. In Virginia, South Carolina, and Pennsylvania, stone tools from early Native American archaeological sites showed a possible technological and cultural connection between Clovis people in North America and the early Europeans of France and Spain called the Solutreans. Based on similar stone tools between the two cultures, Dennis Stanford of the Smithsonian Institution and stone tool expert Bruce Bradley reasoned that the two cultures must be related. However, ample evidence—including the fact that Clovis and Solutrean cultures are separated by 5,000 years of time and 3,000 miles of space—suggested that there was no connection between Clovis people in North America and early Europeans.

Doubt about Clovis origins persisted until the DNA study of the Anzick boy. Willerslev's study proved once and for all that the Clovis people that lived in Montana—and presumably Yellowstone—some 11,000 years ago were in fact Native Americans and that they are the genetic ancestors of the hundreds of Native American cultures that later spread throughout the Americas. Clovis people in Montana clearly descended from people from northeastern Asia and Siberia, not from France or Spain.

In addition to the human remains, archaeologists found over 100 stone tools and several bone rods at the Anzick site. The stone tools included dozens of bifaces produced from a variety of very high-quality stone sources found within a hundred

CLOVIS TOOLS AND PREY

Woolly Mammoth
Mammusthus primigenius
(Illustration by Eric Carlson)

Clovis Point
Anzick Site, MT

Clovis Bone Rod
Sheriden Cave, OH
(Lithics Casting Lab)

Clovis Point
Lange Ferguson, SD
(Lithics Casting Lab)

Clovis Point
Yellowstone Lake, WY

FIGURE 2.4 The Clovis tool kit was comprised of a variety of bifacial stone tools and cylindrical bone rods used to hunt mammoths, camels, horses, and other large prehistoric animals.

miles of the site. Interestingly, none of the artifacts were produced from Yellowstone obsidian. Bifaces, like those shown in figure 2.4, are stone tools that are finely flaked on both sides to produce a very thin tool that is perfect for killing and butchering animals. The stone tools found at the Anzick site indicate that their producers were among the best flintknappers (makers of stone tools) anywhere in the history of the world. They had truly perfected their technology in their pursuit of mammoths, horses, and camels.

The bone rods found at the Anzick site are similar to those found at sites across the country, including one found at a site in Ohio (see figure 2.4). The bone rods were likely used as foreshafts that connected the projectile points with a main shaft of a spear or atlatl (spear thrower) dart. Alternatively, the bone rods could themselves be projectiles used in the hunting of mammoths, horses, and camels. The Manis site in the state of Washington contained the remains of a mastodon that was killed by a bone (not stone) projectile point.

The entire assemblage of Clovis artifacts from the Anzick site is on display at the Montana State Museum in Helena. They are typical of the artifact assemblages at many Clovis sites across North America. The tool technology of Clovis people was quite sophisticated and was well suited for hunting large game animals, such as the woolly mammoth.

Based on the archaeological information recovered from the Anzick site, I find it probable that the two-year-old Clovis boy and his family traveled and traded widely in Montana and Wyoming. They hunted mammoth, horse, camel, and bison, but perhaps also collected a wide variety of plants and other small mammals for food in their travels throughout the region. Based on the few Clovis artifacts found in the park, they likely only occasionally traveled to the Yellowstone Plateau. Instead, Clovis people preferred to kill mammoths near Worland, Wyoming, and horses near Medicine Hat, Alberta. Somewhere in between, a family of Clovis people sadly lost a son, today called the Anzick boy. Their memorial was likely extremely heartfelt, so much so that they left dozens of fine stone and bone tools for him to use in his travels beyond this world.

The ancestors of the Anzick boy traveled up and down the Yellowstone River, the Madison River, and others in the region surrounding Yellowstone. Here, along the banks of the rivers, were herds of mammoths, horses, and camels, which provided for fairly easy living among hunter-gatherer peoples in the area. Occasionally, it seems, these Clovis people made their way into Yellowstone, as attested by the two Clovis points found in the boundaries of the park.

RADIOCARBON DATING

Radiocarbon dating of objects, which is calculated based on the decay of radioactive carbon in the item, is the main way archaeologists can establish when people lived at archaeological sites. We obtain radiocarbon dates from the remains of organic material, such as bone, wood, and plants, found at an archaeological site. If a Native American built a campfire at a site in Yellowstone, we can take a sample of the charcoal and learn how long ago the fire was made. If a bison was killed by a Native American hunter, we can learn when the animal was killed from a sample of its bone. Any once-living organism younger than 50,000 years old can be radiocarbon dated. Radiocarbon dating was invented in the 1940s, and since that time, it has become the principal way archaeologists date sites. Today, archaeologists can radiocarbon date

an 11,000-year-old site in Yellowstone within an accuracy of 30 years.

The process by which radiocarbon forms and is dateable is fairly simple, while the technology used to actually date the sample material is quite sophisticated. Radiocarbon is created in the atmosphere by the interaction of cosmic rays with nitrogen. Radiocarbon combines with oxygen to form radioactive carbon dioxide. This radioactive CO_2 becomes part of plants during photosynthesis, and animals and humans ingest radiocarbon by eating the plants. When the biological organisms die, they stop ingesting radiocarbon and it decays at a known rate that has a half-life of 5,730 years. As such, by measuring the amount of radiocarbon remaining in the dead organism—whether it is an animal or a plant—archaeologists can estimate the age of the material. This technology is very helpful since archaeologists find dead organisms at sites all the time. The most commonly dated material is charcoal (burned wood), which I am collecting from a fire hearth at a 2,000-year-old site on the Flat Mountain Arm of Yellowstone Lake (figure 2.5). In addition to charcoal, animal remains and other organic materials are also frequently radiocarbon dated to find out the ages of sites.

The sophisticated process of estimating the age of organic material by radiocarbon dating must be conducted at a laboratory with precise measuring instruments. I submit my samples to a specialized lab that does the dating for me.

While radiocarbon dating is fairly precise, the dates require calibration. Scientists calibrate the radiocarbon years to calendar years by comparing radiocarbon dates with tree rings. In so doing, archaeologists estimate that early people likely arrived in Yellowstone approximately 12,875 calendar years ago, or 11,000 radiocarbon years ago. For my research and the purposes of this book, I strictly use uncalibrated radiocarbon dates to eliminate confusion. Calibrations are constantly changing with the advances of technology and the refinement of tree ring measurements, but the actual radiocarbon dates don't change. Many archaeologists, however, use the calibrated calendar years measurement; so you'll often hear one archaeologist refer to Clovis as being nearly 13,000 years old, while others describe it as being 11,000 years old. In fact, both archaeologists are correct, but are simply using the two different dating systems, calibrated and uncalibrated years before the present.

◀ FIGURE 2.5 Radiocarbon dating of charcoal from fire pits, such as this one at Yellowstone Lake, is the main way to determine the age of an archaeological site.

YELLOWSTONE DURING THE CLOVIS PERIOD

The fact that only two Clovis projectile points have been found anywhere in Yellowstone National Park attests to generally low human populations in the region 11,000 years ago. The Anzick boy and his family were perhaps among the first to ever see Yellowstone, or any other part of Montana and Wyoming. What must these first people have thought when they first witnessed the Old Faithful geyser shoot scalding hot water 125 ft. (40 m) into the air?

While today we see these wonders of nature as a reason to visit Yellowstone, Old Faithful and other oddities of Yellowstone likely provided little in the way of attraction for early Native Americans to the area. Early people at Yellowstone would have encountered serious obstacles to exploration. Yellowstone, because of its high elevation and recently glaciated environment, was probably a mucky, wet, cold, and mosquito-ridden place for several hundred years after the glaciers melted. At the end of the Late Pleistocene, before Clovis people entered North America, the world was undergoing a dramatic global warming that caused glacial ice to melt all over the world. Glacial margins retreated northward, and mountain glaciers, such as those in Yellowstone, melted away in a matter of 1,000 years.

In Yellowstone, glaciers dammed the Yellowstone River, forming a lake north of Gardiner. As the glaciers melted, they released millions of gallons of water across the Gardiner Basin, scouring the valley and leaving behind abundant glacial debris. At Yellowstone Lake, the glaciers melted as well, forcing enormous amounts of water down the Yellowstone River Valley. As the glaciers decayed, meltwater emptied into the Yellowstone Lake basin, raising its levels significantly higher than today. Over time, lake levels subsided to their current levels. The formerly high lake levels are visible in the terraces that ring the lake.

During the Clovis period some 11,000 years ago, winters were probably longer than today. Yellowstone Lake, which currently freezes solid from December to May, likely remained ice-ridden for much of the year. River valleys were probably much fuller and wetter and buggier than today, making passage along and across them difficult. Rivers like the Yellowstone may have been largely impassable 11,000 years ago, when Clovis people first started to explore the region. Imagine a place like the Alaska Range, in which modern people struggle to cope with natural conditions even today with electricity, cars, planes, and other conveniences.

Imagine early hunter-gatherers—people that live off the land for their living—trying to traverse ice-covered mountains and swollen rivers. Why would they bother when places at lower elevations, like the Paradise Valley between Gardiner and Livingston, Montana, provided ample food supplies? Places around Yellowstone in

FIGURE 2.6 Today, Yellowstone Lake is frozen for six months of the year. During the Clovis period, the Yellowstone region likely experienced even longer and colder winters. *Jim Peaco photo, National Park Service.*

all directions—from Cody, Wyoming, to Gardiner, Montana, to West Yellowstone, Montana, and Jackson, Wyoming—likely were much better places to live 11,000 years ago than the heart of Yellowstone.

In fact, human populations in Yellowstone were very low during the Clovis period, as evidenced by only two projectile points having been found to date in Yellowstone. One was the obsidian Clovis point we found at Yellowstone Lake (figure 2.7, left). This fine projectile point was produced from Teton Pass volcanic glass from near Jackson, Wyoming. The point was already broken when the University of Montana found it on the beach of the lake in 2013; it probably was broken during a hunting trip by a Clovis hunter along the lake's shores. The complete

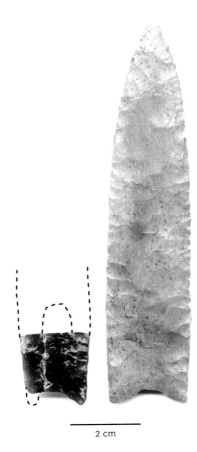

2 cm

FIGURE 2.7 Clovis technology was very similar across North America, as demonstrated by these two Clovis points, one from Yellowstone (left) and one from Missouri (right).

Clovis point next to it (figure 2.7, right) is nearly identical in the size and shape of its base, providing the possible length of the Yellowstone Clovis point. The intact point was found at the Kimmswick mastodon kill site near St. Louis, Missouri. As attested by these two very similar projectile points from sites hundreds of miles apart, Clovis stone tool technology was quite uniform across the Midwest, Great Plains, and Rockies. These people had perfected their craft so that an individual hunting a mastodon in Missouri used technology that was nearly identical to that used by a mammoth hunter in Yellowstone.

My archaeology team recovered a second fluted Clovis point just northwest of Gardiner, Montana, in 2007. It was produced from red porcellanite, a rock found commonly in coal seams of eastern Montana, a couple hundred miles east. Use of such an exotic material for points was not uncommon for Clovis people. Many Clovis projectile points show use of rare and exotic rock, evidence that they valued high-quality material and traveled widely to obtain it.

THE ORIGINS OF THE FIRST PEOPLES IN YELLOWSTONE

The origins of Clovis people in North America, and therefore, in Yellowstone National Park, has long been a mystery. Genetic data, such as those found in the young boy at the Anzick site, clearly indicate that all Native American peoples originated in northeast Asia and Siberia. But, how did these first Americans arrive at places like Montana, Wyoming, and Yellowstone? To answer this question, we must go all the way to the Arctic Circle in northeast Asia, Siberia, and Russia. According to archaeological and genetic research, this is the ancestral home of all Native peoples who came to North and South America.

The oldest archaeological sites in the northern reaches of Siberia are approximately 25,000 to 30,000 years old. For example, the Yana RHS site in northern Siberia has yielded hunting implements in association with many now-extinct animals such as mammoths and rhinoceros. This site is located near the Arctic Circle, clearly indicating that by at least 25,000 years ago, people in Asia had developed ways to survive the coldest climates on Earth. A comparison of the tools used by these people with those of the Anzick boy's family in Montana indicates a clear cultural connection. Willerslev's DNA linkage is the final piece of the puzzle, showing that the first peoples to places like Yellowstone, Montana, and Wyoming came from Siberia.

Farther to the east and closer to Alaska, Russian archaeologists have excavated several other sites that date to 13,000 to 11,000 years ago. People in this region used bifaces, such as those found at the Anzick site, and other hunting implements such as microblades (small multipurpose stone tools), which are not present at Clovis sites in the Americas. Most significant, Alaskan and Siberian hunters did not use Clovis points with the telltale missing channel flake at the base. And so, that Clovis projectile technology was likely invented by people after they left Asia and arrived in North America.

By 12,000 years ago, these mammoth- and rhinoceros-hunting Asian people continued to migrate northward and eastward, eventually making their way to Alaska. Today, the region that they traveled between Siberia and Alaska is marked by the 50 mi. (80 km) wide Bering Strait, which connects the Bering Sea of the Pacific Ocean with the Chukchi Sea of the Arctic Ocean. During the Late Pleistocene, however, the vast glaciers of the period contained a significant amount of the earth's water, reducing sea levels by as much as 150 to 300 ft. (45 to 90 m). And so, at this time, the Bering Strait was actually a land mass called Beringia that connected Asia and America.

Beringia was not covered by glaciers, and had a tundra-steppe environment and a wide variety of plants and animals, including many of the megafauna species found in the Americas that were eventually hunted by Clovis people.

The earliest archaeological sites in Alaska—such as the Swan Point site and the Upward Sun River site (see map 2.1)—contain artifacts suggesting subsistence

FIGURE 2.8 The northern interior of Alaska, such as the Brooks Range and vicinity shown here, has some of the oldest archaeological sites in the Americas, evidence that the earliest Native Americans traveled through the region to get to the rest of North and South America. *Lisa Smith photo.*

patterns that were similar to those of people living in Siberia. The sites are in the mountains, foothills, and river valleys of central Alaska, such as the Brooks Range.

At Swan Point in the Tanana River Valley, 12,000 years ago, early Native Americans made a fire out of birch wood and ate swan, goose, and moose meat for dinner. Another 11,000-year-old site in Alaska—the Upward Sun River site—has yielded the remains of three infants buried in a way similar to that of the boy at the Anzick site in Montana, with stone tools, bone rods, and red ochre. Although lacking the diagnostic Clovis point of cultures farther south, the similarity in hunting implements between Swan Point in Alaska, as well as the burial traditions at Upward Sun River, and those of Clovis people farther south in the Americas is probably not a coincidence.

We know that the first people to Yellowstone and to North America in general came from these areas to the north in Alaska, Siberia, and Asia. Archaeologists suggest that the first Native Americans, such as those who buried the Anzick boy in Montana, likely arrived by one of two routes from Siberia and Alaska: through an ice-free corridor in Canada (ice-free corridor theory); and/or along the Pacific Coast (the coastal migration theory). These approximate routes are shown on map 2.1.

The first hypothesis—the ice-free corridor theory—contends that the earliest peoples traveled from Alaska between two massive glacial ice sheets—the Laurentide and Cordilleran—that occupied much of Canada during the Late Pleistocene until 12,000 years ago. Until recently, the most common theory to explain Clovis origins was that these early Alaskans—at sites like Swan Point and Upward

Sun River—continued to migrate eastward and southward by traveling through an ice-free corridor between two glacial ice sheets—the Cordilleran along the Pacific Coast and the Laurentide in the interior of Canada—to reach the Lower 48 states, and, eventually, Yellowstone. In this scenario, Clovis technology, including its fluted spear point, was invented by people as they migrated southward into southern Canada 11,500 years ago.

The Wally's Beach site in southern Alberta near the Montana state line contained 11,400-year-old horse and camel remains. Nearby, archaeologists at Wally's Beach found Clovis points with horse protein residue. Based on this information, Clovis hunters killed horses in Canada more than 11,000 years ago. Wally's Beach is the oldest site in Canada and may be evidence of these early migrations through the ice-free corridor.

BUT WHAT ABOUT THE PACIFIC COAST ROUTE?

There is much dispute about the timing of the opening of the ice-free corridor between the two Canadian ice sheets and whether it was even open to travelers by 12,000 years ago. Scientists are certain that the corridor was open for travel at the time of the Clovis people and perhaps for a few hundred years before that. If this was the route that early peoples took to Yellowstone from Alaska, these hardy Native Americans traversed an extremely harsh landscape of wasting glaciers, swollen rivers, mud and muck within the ice-free corridor. Clouds of mosquitoes would have danced frantically around their heads. Nevertheless, it is at least conceivable and certainly plausible that Clovis people arrived in Alberta, Montana, and eventually Yellowstone National Park through the ice-free corridor from Alaska.

It is increasingly clear that there were already people living in other areas of North America before the arrival of Clovis. While it is still possible that the first people to Yellowstone and the northern Plains and Rockies came from Alaska via the ice-free corridor, there is now ample archaeological evidence of early Native Americans along the Pacific Coast before Clovis. Based on the presence of very old archaeological sites on the Pacific Coast (older than Anzick), we now know that early Native Americans lived on the coast earlier than the Clovis people who lived in the interior of North America, such as the Anzick boy in Montana. As such, the coastal migration hypothesis is now favored by most archaeologists to explain the earliest arrival of people to the Americas. While it is still conceivable that the first people to Yellowstone and the interior of North America came through the ice-free corridor, based on radiocarbon dates of sites recorded to date, the Pacific Coast route is definitely (without a doubt) how the first people came to the Americas. Whether these coastal people are also the ancestors of the Anzick boy and other interior Clovis culture is a question that remains unanswered. But, for now, let's entertain that possibility.

Research of paleoenvironments shows that the glacial ice sheets were interspersed along the Pacific Coast with a wide array of livable habitats, providing ample subsistence opportunities for early Native Americans. For example, mountain goat remains have been found in caves along the northwest Pacific Coast from the peak of the past glaciation more than 12,000 years ago. If mountain goats could survive on the Pacific Coast, then humans could have survived as well. From Siberia, the earliest Native Americans likely passed along the Alaska coast to British Columbia and to Washington and Oregon. We know that by 12,500 years ago, if not earlier, people had arrived at the southernmost extent of Chile in South America. And so it is clear that people must have traveled along the Pacific Coast of Alaska and California several hundred years before the first Clovis point was invented somewhere in the interior of North America.

As shown in map 2.1, there are five sites in North and South America that most archaeologists accept as being far older than Clovis: the Monte Verde site in Chile, the Paisley Caves site in Oregon, the Manis mastodon site in Washington, the Gault site in Texas, and the Page-Ladson site in Florida.

The Monte Verde site in Chile is arguably the oldest site in the Americas, dating to 12,500 years ago. The site has been excavated by archaeologist Thomas Dillehay from Kentucky over the past 40 years. He found the remains of mastodon meat, stone tools, houses, and medicines used by early Native Americans living within 20 mi. (32 km) of the Pacific Coast.

Washington and Oregon have yielded very early evidence of human migrations by Native Americans from Siberia as well, with two sites that are at least 1,000 years older than Clovis. The Paisley Caves site in the desert of south-central Oregon is the oldest-known archaeological site in North America, with human feces radiocarbon dated to 12,300 years ago. This puts people in the desert of Oregon earlier than a millenium before the Anzick boy lived in Montana. Another site in Washington—the Manis mastodon site—proves that early Native Americans killed a mastodon with a bone projectile point (not a Clovis point) near Puget Sound almost 12,000 years ago, nearly 500 years before hunters killed horses at Wally's Beach in Alberta and nearly a millennia earlier than Clovis people killed mammoths near Worland, Wyoming, east of Yellowstone.

Two additional sites, the Buttermilk Complex (including the Gault site) in Texas and the Page-Ladson site in Florida, are also widely accepted to be older than Clovis. Both sites have radiocarbon dates of greater than 12,000 years ago. Early Native Americans at both sites hunted big game, including mastodons and mammoths, but also subsisted on smaller game, including turtles.

Based on these five sites and a few others, archaeologists now believe that the earliest Native Americans arrived in North America before 12,000 years ago. Because continental coastlines have been drowned by ocean water since that time, few earlier sites there have been found. Archaeologists like Jon Erlandson from the University of Oregon have been looking for such early Native American sites among the California coastal islands and are beginning to find early evidence of human adaptation to these coastal waters perhaps prior to Clovis. The Arlington Springs site on the Channel Islands contains human remains dating to more than 11,000 years ago. This shows that people used boats to get to the offshore islands of the Pacific Coast at the same time that Clovis people hunted horses in the interior of North America.

Another set of Clovis-age human remains in Mexico—called Eva de Naharon—were found at the Hoyo Negro site in the Yucatán Peninsula. Eva shares the same DNA haplogroup D as that of the Anzick boy. Perhaps the earliest Native Americans migrated down the Pacific Coast and turned inland to the American Southwest and Mexico rather than northward to Montana and Yellowstone. In support of this theory, one of the oldest Clovis sites yet found, El Fin del Mundo, in northern Mexico in 2011 yielded the remains of gomphotheres (now-extinct elephants smaller than mammoths) in direct association with Clovis points dated to about 11,500 years ago. Is it possible that Clovis projectile point technology was invented in the southwestern United States and northern Mexico and then spread northward into Montana and Yellowstone? At this point, it is possible if not probable that Clovis technology was invented in Mexico, perhaps at El Fin del Mundo, or even in Alberta, at Wally's Beach, and then spread throughout the Americas quite rapidly.

So multiple migration routes were possible for the first peoples to Yellowstone. Research of Clovis origins is a major topic for archaeologists in the Americas, including those who work in Yellowstone and vicinity. Did the first Native Americans come from Alaska via the ice-free corridor, or did they migrate from the Pacific Coast? And if they migrated along the Pacific Coast, did they turn inland at a northern point, perhaps at the Columbia River Valley, or did they turn inland to the south, perhaps in northern Mexico?

FIGURE 2.9 The earliest Paleoindians to Yellowstone National Park likely traveled up the Snake River Valley from the Pacific Coast. The Snake River flows for over 1,000 miles from its headwaters in Yellowstone to central Washington State, where it joins the Columbia River.

While these early people may have continued southward along the Pacific Coast to Mexico before turning inland, it is now just as likely that Clovis people actually traveled up the Columbia River and its tributaries, including the Snake River. These rivers were natural travel corridors that provided abundant natural resources for early hunter-gatherers to survive. Following the Snake River all the way through Oregon, Washington, Idaho, and Wyoming to its source would have brought them eventually to Yellowstone National Park. The headwaters of the Snake River are in Yellowstone, only 20 mi. (32 km) south of Yellowstone Lake. It makes sense that the first humans would have eventually arrived at the lake to leave behind the now-11,000-year-old obsidian Clovis point found by University of Montana archaeologists in 2013. In either scenario, the distinctive Clovis technology was likely invented somewhere along the way, perhaps even near Yellowstone.

FIGURE 2.10 Comparison of an ancient bison, *Bison antiquus* (left), a contemporary American bison, *Bison bison* (center), and a human for scale (right). *Illustration by Eric Carlson (2016).*

YELLOWSTONE AFTER CLOVIS

The Clovis culture existed in the Yellowstone region until about 10,500 years ago, after which came a group of descendant people referred to as Folsom. Across the Great Plains and Rocky Mountains, numerous archaeological sites show that a new projectile point—called Folsom—replaced the Clovis point. Since much of the megafauna was extinct, Folsom Native Americans switched their hunting to another megafauna species, *Bison antiquus*. This ancient, now-extinct form of bison was 50 percent larger than the American bison (*Bison bison*) we know, and lived in large herds across the Great Plains of North America in Montana and Wyoming. These bison herds likely increased greatly with the demise of the megafauna, such as the mammoths. With all of the other large-bodied mammals gone, the bison flourished in the abundant grasslands.

While there are no known Folsom projectile points in Yellowstone, an Obsidian Cliff obsidian Folsom point was found in the Bridger-Teton National Forest south of Yellowstone in the mid-1990s. This finding indicates that a Folsom hunter traveled within Yellowstone to obtain the obsidian to produce the Folsom point. Also, the Folsom-age Indian Creek site near Helena, Montana, yielded Obsidian Cliff obsidian, indicating that Folsom individuals collected the stone in Yellowstone. Another type of projectile point—called Goshen—was also used by Native Americans around the time of Folsom. Goshen points are similar to Folsom points but lack the diagnostic channel flake. Goshen projectile points were found at a site along the shore of Yellowstone Lake in the early 2000s as well as near Lewis Falls in southern Yellowstone National Park by a University of Montana team in 2015.

One of these Goshen points is shown in figure 2.11 (bottom row), as are numerous other projectile points that mark time in Yellowstone. The figure shows the types of projectile points and the significant chronological changes over time of Yellowstone Native Americans.

THE CODY CULTURE IN YELLOWSTONE

The low numbers of Clovis and Folsom points found in the region indicate that these Paleoindian Native Americans traveled extensively throughout Montana, Idaho, and Wyoming between approximately 11,000 and 9,500 years ago but were not regular inhabitants of Yellowstone. They hunted mammoths in Wyoming, as well as horses in Alberta, and buried their deceased near Livingston, Montana, but did not regularly travel through Yellowstone.

All of that changed about 9,500 years ago when the Late Paleoindian Cody Culture—descendants of Clovis and Folsom peoples—started to camp regularly at Yellowstone Lake and in the rest of Yellowstone. These people lived in Yellowstone, as well as much of the northwestern Great Plains, for approximately 1,500 years. The culture is named after the town of Cody, Wyoming. Here, in the 1970s, the archaeologist George Frison excavated a bison kill site dating to 9,000 years ago. Bones and distinctive artifacts at the site revealed that Native Americans of the Cody Culture killed several bison (*Bison antiquus*) with Cody projectile points and butchered them with Cody knives. Cody projectile points have square-stemmed bases, while Cody knives have a distinctive asymmetrical blade and a square base. Because of the location of the archaeological site, Frison dubbed the remains from Horner to be evidence of the Late Paleoindian "Cody Culture."

Whereas only a small handful of sites in the Yellowstone region have yielded Clovis and Folsom points, archaeologists to date have found Cody artifacts at more than 50 different archaeological sites in the park. The Scottsbluff projectile point and the Cody knife (see figure 2.11, bottom row) are examples of the primary characteristic types of hunting and butchering tools used by Cody hunters.

Dozens of similar Cody points and knives have been found in Yellowstone National Park, especially at Yellowstone Lake. From Cody, Wyoming, these Paleoindian hunters likely traveled westward up the Shoshone River and across the high mountain pass by Sylvan Lake to the headwaters of Clear Creek, which they followed for about 20 mi. (32 km) to Yellowstone Lake.

▶ FIGURE 2.11 Projectile points we have found at archaeological sites help us to understand precontact Native American cultures in the Yellowstone region from 11,000 to 300 years ago.

LATE PREHISTORIC PERIOD

1,500 to 300 years ago

Period of technological innovation
First pottery used by Native Americans in Yellowstone
Bow and arrow replaces the atlatl
Bison hunting remains a staple of diet
Use of mountains intensifies for pine nut collecting

LATE ARCHAIC PERIOD

3,000 to 1,500 years ago

Peak period for Native Americans in Yellowstone
Climate is similar to modern
Human populations increase throughout
Great Plains & Rockies
Extensive use of the region by Native Americans
Hopewell Interaction Sphere brings traders from Midwest
Obsidian Cliff obsidian mining is extensive for trade networks
Mounds in Ohio have hundreds of pounds of
Yellowstone obsidian
Bison hunting increases in popularity
Wide variety of plants & mammals used by Native Americans

EARLY & MIDDLE ARCHAIC PERIODS

8,000 to 3,000 years ago

Middle Archaic Period (5,000 to 3,000 years ago)
Climate starts to become essentially modern
Bison bison herds start to grow in size
Bifurcate spear points are the most common atlatl dart tips
Native American populations start to grow in Yellowstone
Early Archaic Period (8,000 to 5,000)
Hot and dry climate (altithermal) & fewer big game to hunt
Increased use of high-elevation areas
Constricted mobility compared to Paleoindian Period
Large side-notched points used by hunters

PALEOINDIAN PERIOD

12,000 to 8,000 years ago

First Native Americans arrive
Clovis, Goshen, and Cody projectile points
Subsistence focused on megafauna
Large spear points & atlatls were main hunting weapons
Low populations until ca. 9,500 years ago
Wide-ranging mobility and diverse stone materials
Key sites: Osprey Beach, Fishing Bridge, Malin Creek
Key areas: Gardiner Basin, Yellowstone Valley,
Yellowstone Lake

Late Prehistoric
Rose Spring

Late Prehistoric
Side-Notched

Late Archaic Besant

Late Archaic Pelican Lake

Middle Archaic
McKean

Middle Archaic
Oxbow

Early Archaic
Side-Notched

Clovis   Goshen   Scottsbluff   Cody Knife

One of Yellowstone's most important Paleoindian archaeological sites is the Osprey Beach site (figure 2.12) on the West Thumb of Yellowstone Lake. Here, approximately 9,300 years ago, Cody Culture Native Americans camped on the shore of the lake, hunting and gathering a wide variety of plants and animals. In the 1990s, archaeologists Ann Johnson and Brian Reeves conducted archaeological excavations at Osprey Beach and found protein residue on Cody projectile points

DID CLOVIS HUNTERS WIPE OUT THE MAMMOTHS?

Within several hundred years of their arrival, Clovis people and their ancestors inhabited not just Yellowstone but all of North America. These early Native Americans entered a world void of people and killed game animals that had never seen human hunters before. Some scientists argue that this lack of human awareness led to the extinction of 30 or so species of big game at the hands of Clovis and related people. Paul Martin of the University of Arizona posited in the 1970s that Clovis hunters spread so quickly across the Americas that they annihilated these unaware animals. Studies by archaeologists Todd Surovell and Nicole Waguespeck at the University of Wyoming have revived the Pleistocene Overkill Hypothesis of Paul Martin. Surovell and Waguespeck provide data to indicate that Clovis hunters likely contributed to the demise of the megafauna such as mammoths, mastodons, horses, and camels 11,000 years ago.

Still other archaeologists, such as Donald Grayson and David Meltzer, strongly dispute the role that humans played in the extinctions. While humans may have played some role in the extinction, recent studies by Richard Firestone and colleagues have indicated that an asteroid might have impacted the earth, causing the extinctions 11,000 years ago. The presence of minerals such as nanodiamonds and other microscopic space debris at some sites from this age may support this hypothesis. The asteroid impact theory has come under tremendous scrutiny by researchers, including Todd Surovell, and is considered doubtful by most. Still, more study needs to be conducted to prove this theory true or false. Ideally, an impact crater from this age would need to be found to ultimately prove it to be true. So far, no such crater has been found.

Still further studies suggest that a more gradual extinction event occurred, likely tied to the climate changes of the time. In the Great Plains around Yellowstone, only mammoths and horses show significant hunting and knives, showing that Native Americans hunted bison, bear, rabbit, deer, and a variety of other animals.

And so, by about 9,500 years ago, Native Americans actively used the Yellowstone Park area. Yellowstone Lake, in particular, was especially appealing to Cody Culture hunter-gatherers. The lake provided a variety of resources for Native Americans, and may have provided a cool respite from the emerging hot, dry

by people, but not on a scale likely to cause extinction. Human populations were so low during these early days that it seems impossible that they contributed to the extinction of the mammoths, mastodons, sloths, and their now-extinct mega-predators, including saber toothed tigers, short-faced bears, and dire wolves (larger, stronger prehistoric wolves). But much more research needs to be done on the topic. It seems highly possible that early Clovis people contributed in some way to the extinctions, perhaps simply as the breaking point for an extinction event already started by the dramatic climate changes of the period.

There is no doubt that Clovis people were extremely good hunters. They were the descendants of people from Asia who had hunted large animals for thousands of years and whose ancestors hunted game in Africa thousands of years before that. The long history of human hunting does in fact link Africa and Asia to Yellowstone National Park in a direct chain of human colonization of the globe. Whether these Clovis hunters helped to cause the extinction of the mammoths is a fascinating research question for future archaeologists to answer, with Yellowstone in the geographic center of the debate. Someday, I fully expect that archaeologists will find more evidence of Clovis people in Yellowstone that will help to clarify just how Clovis people arrived there and how the animals became extinct. As it stands today, though, Clovis people likely were only rarely in Yellowstone, perhaps passing through occasionally to get from the Snake River Valley to Obsidian Cliff or from the Bighorn Basin of Wyoming to the Paradise Valley of Montana. Because of the sparse nature of the archaeological debris they left behind, it appears that Clovis people did not spend much time at the rough and rugged Yellowstone Plateau, preferring the lower-elevation areas that were home to their megafauna prey.

FIGURE 2.12 The Osprey Beach site on Yellowstone Lake is among the most important Cody Culture sites in the park. Radiocarbon dates indicate that Native Americans lived at the site approximately 9,300 years ago.

conditions of the lower-elevation areas surrounding the park. Whereas during the Clovis and Folsom periods, Yellowstone may have been somewhat harsh, cold, wet, and mosquito-ridden, by 10,000 years ago, the climate in the region had warmed sufficiently to facilitate more regular occupation by Native Americans. Cody people clearly enjoyed their summer migrations to Yellowstone, likely following the bison and other game that also preferred the cooler air of the Yellowstone Plateau (average elevation 8,000 ft./2,400 m).

Since the excavations at Osprey Beach, many other archaeologists have surveyed and excavated dozens of archaeological sites at Yellowstone Lake, finding Cody Culture artifacts at more than 20 of them. Cody Native Americans also lived in many other areas of the Yellowstone Plateau, including the Yellowstone River Valley. In total, more than 70 Cody projectile points and knives have been found in Yellowstone, a dramatic increase from the two Clovis points and zero Folsom points.

Cody Culture Native Americans were the first to use Yellowstone on a regular basis. They likely traveled to and from Yellowstone frequently to hunt and to gather plants, among the wealth of resources available. From that time more than 9,000 years ago, Native Americans became regular inhabitants of the area. They lived throughout the park.

After the Paleoindian Period and the Cody Culture, between approximately 8,000 and 1,500 years ago, Early, Middle, and Late Archaic hunter-gatherers lived in the Yellowstone region, using a variety of side-notched projectile points as tips for atlatl darts. They were predominantly bison hunters, but also hunted and collected wide varieties of plants and other animals. Approximately 1,500 years ago, Native Americans adopted the bow and arrow, and started to produce small arrow points that were used for hunting until the time of European American contact some 300 years ago.

The projectile points shown in figure 2.11 were found by my team of archaeologists as they worked (between 2007 and 2016) in various areas of the park, including Obsidian Cliff, Yellowstone Lake, the Yellowstone River, and Old Faithful. The remainder of this book examines Native American precontact archaeology in these well-known areas of Yellowstone, starting with Obsidian Cliff.

CHAPTER THREE

OBSIDIAN CLIFF

WHILE THERE ARE still many unresolved mysteries about the first peoples in Yellowstone, one thing is for certain: ever since they arrived, they really liked Yellowstone obsidian for making stone tools.

Rocks, such as the obsidian cobbles from Obsidian Cliff (map 3.1) in Yellowstone National Park (figure 3.1), are important to people that hunt and gather their food. All over the world, hunter-gatherers have collected and used rock to facilitate their survival, and the peoples of prehistoric Yellowstone were no exception. Certain types of rock—like obsidian—became crucial to hunter-gatherer people, because with it they could make effective tools to hunt, gather, and process their foods. Using stone tools, humans could kill and butcher animals, and cut and process plants. And they could also produce other types of tools from other rocks, as well as from bone, antler, wood, and ivory.

Particular stone tools require specific types of rocks. The best types of rock for hunting, gathering, and processing tool manufacture are ones that contain a lot of silicon dioxide, or silica (SiO_2). The higher the silica content, the sharper you can make the edges of the stone. Some volcanic rocks, like basalt and gabbro, have very low silica content and would not make good stone tools. In contrast, obsidian, or volcanic glass (figure 3.2, upper left), is more than 75 percent silica and is ideal for stone tool manufacture. Fortunately, for the early Native Americans of Yellowstone, obsidian is abundant there. Obsidian forms when magma cools rapidly. The low density of impurities (e.g., formation crystals and other trace minerals) in some

▶ MAP 3.1 Important stone sources and archaeological sites in Yellowstone

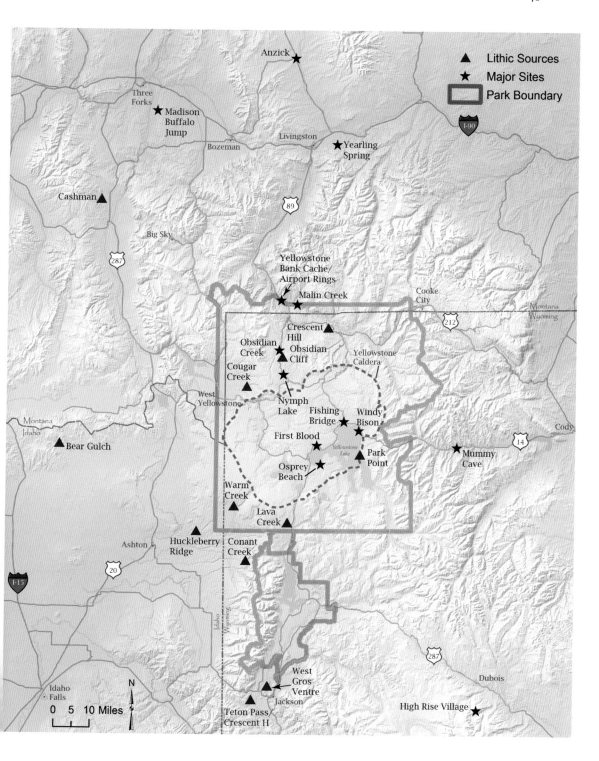

Lithic Sources

Major Sites

Park Boundary

Anzick

Three Forks

Madison Buffalo Jump

Livingston

Bozeman

Yearling Spring

Cashman

Big Sky

Yellowstone Bank Cache/ Airport Rings

Malin Creek

Cooke City

Montana Wyoming

Crescent Hill

Obsidian Creek

Obsidian Cliff

Yellowstone Caldera

Cougar Creek

West Yellowstone

Nymph Lake

Montana Idaho

Fishing Bridge

Windy Bison

Cody

Bear Gulch

First Blood

Yellowstone Lake

Park Point

Mummy Cave

Osprey Beach

Warm Creek

Lava Creek

Ashton

Huckleberry Ridge

Conant Creek

Idaho Wyoming

Idaho Falls

I-15

West Gros Ventre

Jackson

Dubois

Teton Pass/ Crescent H

High Rise Village

N

0 5 10 Miles

2 cm

FIGURE 3.1 Volcanic glass, or obsidian, provided the stone material for Native American tool manufacture in Yellowstone and beyond.

types of obsidian also means that the rock has very predictable breakage patterns. Because obsidian breaks in predictable ways, forming very sharp edges, it was perfect for Native American tools.

Obsidian is so sharp that it is used in modern surgery, because it cuts more deftly and cleanly than the best surgical steel, thus reducing scarring. Early Native Americans valued the material more than any other type of rock in Yellowstone. They used it to make arrowheads and spear points for hunting, to make knives for butchering bison, and to make scraping tools to remove gristle and meat from hides for tipis, blankets, clothing, and other items.

In addition to obsidian, other types of stone—several of which are shown in figure 3.2—were also used by early Native Americans to make stone tools. Within Yellowstone, chert, chalcedony, orthoquartzite, quartzite, and silicified (or petrified) wood were all used to make stone tools. First, a variety of cherts, or cryptocrystalline silica, are found in the park and vicinity. One major source of chert—called Crescent Hill chert—was popular for stone tool manufacture in the northern part of Yellowstone near Gardiner along the Yellowstone River. Another type of rock—orthoquartzite—is found as large cobbles around some portions of Yellowstone Lake. Yellowstone and vicinity have a fair amount of silicified wood that was also utilized by Native Americans to make stone tools.

2 cm

Obsidian Cliff
Obsidian

Red Park Point
Obsidian

Cashman Dacite

Chalcedony

Yellowstone Lake
Orthoquartzite

Yellow Chert

FIGURE 3.2 Different kinds of stone material were used by Native Americans to make tools in Yellowstone, including obsidian, dacite, chalcedony, orthoquartzite, and chert.

GEOLOGY AND DISTRIBUTION OF OBSIDIAN IN YELLOWSTONE

Several major obsidian quarries were used by Native Americans in Yellowstone. Obsidian Cliff was the major source of obsidian in the region. Among the Crow Indians, elders still talk about the rich source, Obsidian Cliff, as Shiiptacha Awaxaawe, translated roughly as Ricochet Mountain. Within the park boundary, other smaller sources of obsidian were used occasionally, including Park Point (at Yellowstone Lake), Conant Creek Tuff, Warm Creek, and a few smaller obsidian outcrops in remote areas of the park.

Several other volcanic stone sources outside of Yellowstone were also actively used by Native Americans within the park and vicinity, including Bear Gulch obsidian in Idaho and the Cashman dacite source near Ennis, Montana. South of the park, there are several obsidian locations near Jackson, Wyoming, and farther west near Idaho Falls, Idaho, including Teton Pass, West Gros Ventre Butte, and Packsaddle Creek.

As most visitors to the park know, Yellowstone is extremely active volcanically and could explode at any moment. Over the course of more than two million years, active and violent volcanism has completely reshaped the topography of Yellowstone National Park. Before that, the Yellowstone Plateau and adjacent areas had topography like the nearby Madison, Gallatin, Teton, and Absaroka Mountains of the Rocky Mountain region.

These explosive events transformed the region from a rugged, mountainous landscape to a high-elevation volcanic plateau covering an area of 10,500 sq. mi. (17,000 sq. km), or much of southern Yellowstone National Park. Over the geologic history of Yellowstone, there have been three major periods of volcanic eruptions within the past two million years, with many of the obsidian sites forming on the immediate edges of the volcanic calderas. These eruptions are marked by volcanic tuff formations that are visible across the park, including Huckleberry Ridge Tuff, Mesa Falls Tuff, and Lava Creek Tuff. They are called tuff formations because the various eruptive detritus, including magma, rock, and ash, consolidates into a rock, called tuff, because of the intensive heat of the volcanic eruption. Large calderas formed from each of these eruptions as the magma chambers emptied across the park. Yellowstone Lake comprises a portion of the Lava Creek Tuff caldera.

The Huckleberry Ridge volcanic eruption, about 2.1 million years ago, was the first in the Yellowstone area. It ejected material that is now mostly buried and deeply stratified below younger rocks from succeeding eruptions. The old caldera is thought to extend from Big Band Ridge, west of Island Park, Idaho, into the central Yellowstone Plateau of Wyoming, but much of it underlies younger rocks, making it difficult to map. This eruption ejected approximately 600 cu. mi. (2,500 cu. km) of magma and spewed enough ash to bury nearly 3,800 sq. mi. (16,000 sq. km).

The second period of active volcanism in Yellowstone, about 1.3 million years ago, was a smaller eruption called the Mesa Falls Tuff flow. The most famous landmark from this eruption is Henry's Fork Caldera measuring 12 mi. (19 km) across in the southwestern corner of Yellowstone. The thickest section of ash flow from this eruption occurs on Thurman Ridge, measuring up to 450 ft. (150 m) deep. Deposits of this ash have been identified in both the southern Rockies and the Great Plains.

The third volcanic cycle, some 640,000 years ago, climaxed in a massive eruption that formed the Lava Creek Tuff. A somewhat easily accessed outcrop of

Lava Creek Tuff formation with poor-quality obsidian lies along the park's South Entrance road, just south of Moose Falls and the bridge across Crawfish Creek. At this location, Moose Falls tumbles over the remains of this lava flow. Along a trail south of the creek lie large boulders of rhyolite, another type of mostly nonglassy volcanic rock, some of which contain obsidian within the Lava Creek Tuff. The obsidian in this formation is relatively low quality, and there is little evidence that Native Americans used this stone for tools.

Since the formation of the Yellowstone Caldera, two resurgent domes within the caldera have occasionally released rhyolitic magma (within which formed most of Yellowstone's obsidians) over the past 600,000 years. The youngest volcanic eruptions to release the rhyolitic magma (forming obsidian) occurred between 180,000 and 70,000 years ago.

THE OBSIDIAN CLIFF SITE

Among the most recent rhyolitic magma flows, what has been geologically designated as the Roaring Mountain Member of Plateau Rhyolite was violently released north of the main caldera around Yellowstone Lake. Along the northern edge of these flows was the Obsidian Cliff flow, which occurred at the beginning of the most recent cycles of volcanism, around 180,000 years ago. The Obsidian Cliff flow spread rhyolite and extremely glassy obsidian in an area of approximately 3 mi. (5 km) north-south by 1 mi. (0.8 km) east-west (6 sq. mi./15 sq. km) in the north-central portion of Yellowstone between Mammoth Hot Springs and the Norris Geyser Basin. The flow occurred within the valley of what is now called Obsidian Creek, with the obsidian cooling very rapidly against the wall of the creek valley. Since that time, Obsidian Creek has downcut and eroded the edges of the rhyolitic flow, exposing the large wall of Obsidian Cliff (figure 3.3). The rapid cooling of the silica-rich, rhyolitic magma produced Obsidian Cliff's very glassy and extremely high-quality obsidian.

Today, as you wind along the Grand Loop Road north of Norris Geyser Basin toward Mammoth Hot Springs, the massive rhyolitic outcrop of Obsidian Cliff stands tall above the gently meandering Obsidian Creek. Massive boulders of rhyolite and obsidian are visible along the roadside at this location south of Sheepeater Cliff. At a small visitor area on the west side of the Grand Loop Road, a roadside display explains the importance of Obsidian Cliff in the history and prehistory of the park; it was the first of its kind in any national park and is itself listed on the National Register of Historic Places.

FIGURE 3.3 Obsidian Cliff is Yellowstone National Park's most important archaeological site. *Jim Peaco photo, National Park Service.*

Working for the US Geological Survey in 1879, William Henry Holmes was the first European American to document Obsidian Cliff in scientific detail. Holmes was in the park recording its geologic history soon after the park was formed in 1872. While recording his findings, he used the original dirt wagon road constructed by the park's first superintendent, P. W. Norris. An 1899 photo (figure 3.4) shows the dirt road that skirted the edge of the cliff, very near where Grand Loop Road travels today. Superintendent Norris describes Obsidian Cliff in this passage from his 1879 superintendent report: "Obsidian there rises like basalt in vertical columns many hundreds of feet high, and countless huge masses had fallen from

FIGURE 3.4 Obsidian Cliff, Beaver Lake, Yellowstone National Park (1899). *F. Jay Haynes photo. Haynes Foundation Collection, Montana Historical Society Research Center Photograph Archives, Helena, Montana (Catalog Number H-3940).*

this utterly impassable mountain into the hissing hot-spring margin of an equally impassable lake [Beaver Lake], without either Indian or game trail over the glistering fragments of nature's glass, sure to severely lacerate."

Since Norris and Holmes, many geologists have mapped the distribution and thickness of the obsidian deposits at Obsidian Cliff. Given the approximate thickness of the flow at 100 ft. (30 m) within an area measuring 6 sq. mi. (15 sq. km), the estimated volume of the obsidian is approximately 1.5 quadrillion cu. ft. (435 trillion cu. m), amounting to millions of pounds of glassy, high-quality obsidian. There is enough obsidian to fill 3,000 large sports stadiums that can seat as many as 100,000 people. Imagine 3,000 Rose Bowls filled to the brim with glossy black obsidian. Because of its abundance, easy access, and high quality, Obsidian Cliff volcanic glass became one of the most desirable commodities in North American prehistory. Even the first European American explorers in the park remarked at the abundance of Native American artifacts around the area, and they often picked up and even sold the artifacts. Today, the cliff is closed to pedestrians, except at its margin along the highway. And it is now illegal to take obsidian from this National Historic Landmark.

STONE TOOL MANUFACTURE AT OBSIDIAN CLIFF AND BEYOND

Archaeologists have long known the value of Obsidian Cliff to Native American peoples in the Great Plains and Rocky Mountains and beyond. In the late 1980s and early 1990s, Montana State University's Leslie Davis mapped the cliff to understand its use in prehistory. Davis and his colleagues, including former park archaeologist Ann Johnson, described the distribution of obsidian at the cliff within a 6 sq. mi. (15 sq. km) area bounded approximately by Obsidian Lake on the north, Obsidian Creek on the west, and Lake of the Woods on the south. A photograph of this original archaeological survey of the cliff is shown in figure 3.5.

Leslie Davis and his colleagues from Montana State University, Steve Aaberg and James Schmitt, produced a report of their findings in 1995 for the National

SOURCING OBSIDIAN FROM YELLOWSTONE

Each volcanic flow ejects magma with specific chemical attributes. And so the rocks that form within each volcanic flow are unique and can be finger-printed as to their precise chemical composition. When we find an obsidian artifact at an archaeological site, we can analyze that artifact by a technique called X-ray fluorescence (XRF) analysis. This way, we can match the chemical signature of the recovered artifact with its original volcanic flow. And we can know that someone collected that obsidian at a particular original source and transported it to the later archaeological site, where it was found by archaeologists thousands of years hence.

Over the past 2.1 million years, active volcanism, including obsidian-rich rhyolitic magma flows, have played pivotal roles in shaping Yellowstone. The most recent volcanic cycle began more than 640,000 years ago, with the eruption of the Lava Creek Tuff and was later frequented with massive eruptions of both rhyolitic magma flows from which came Obsidian Cliff obsidian. These remarkable and explosive geologic events provided prehistoric hunter-gatherers in Yellowstone with a diverse selection of volcanic lithic raw materials. These rock sources range from amorphous obsidians (such as the poor-quality obsidians found near Moose Falls) to silica-rich materials (such as those at Obsidian Cliff).

The chemical sourcing of obsidian artifacts, as well as those produced from other volcanic materials such as basalt and dacite (two other types of glassy volcanic rock good for stone tool production), is an amazing tool by which to understand the use and distribution of the various rocks in Yellowstone over the past 11,000 years. The study of obsidians in Yellowstone is quite new compared to the fifty-plus years of XRF

Park Service. In this remarkable report, they recorded 59 concentrated activity areas where prehistoric Native Americans quarried obsidian at the cliff. What they found during their survey was some of the earliest evidence of rock quarry mining in the region. They found hundreds of trenches and quarry pits excavated into the hillsides of the cliff. The prehistoric Native Americans at the cliff were in fact Wyoming's original hard rock miners. These were not casual efforts to pick up pieces of obsidian to make a simple stone tool. The extensive prehistoric mining at the cliff indicates the input of vast amounts of labor for the procurement of large quantities of the obsidian, likely to use in Native American trade networks.

While walking on the cliff, archaeologists from the National Park Service and the University of Montana observed large boulders of obsidian that were tested

analysis that started at the University of California Berkeley. Continuing the work he started at Berkeley, Richard Hughes still conducts XRF analysis for obsidians found in Yellowstone. Some of the first Yellowstone artifacts submitted for XRF analysis came from Montana State University's late 1980s to early 1990s project at Obsidian Cliff led by Leslie B. Davis.

For their 1995 Obsidian Cliff report, Hughes, along with Davis, and Yellowstone archaeologist Ann Johnson, among others, reported on the use and distribution of Obsidian Cliff obsidian and in doing so chemically sourced approximately eighty obsidian artifacts. These artifacts from within the park boundaries were compared to another eighty artifacts from at least a dozen prehistoric archaeology sites across Montana. Subsequent to the initial rounds of obsidian sourcing from Yellowstone, almost every major

archaeological report stemming from work in Yellowstone over the past twenty years documents the recovery of obsidian artifacts. To date, close to 3,000 lithic artifacts from within Yellowstone have been subjected to XRF analysis. In my work over the past decade alone, I have subjected more than 1,000 artifacts to XRF sourcing. Based on this analysis, we know that obsidian dominates stone tool assemblages from the park. Closest to the source, at sites like Sheepeater Cliff, Obsidian Cliff comprises nearly 100 percent of the obsidian. Use of Obsidian Cliff obsidian at sites begins to fall off with increasing distance from the source. The role of XRF analysis cannot be overestimated; it is absolutely an essential scientific tool for understanding the Native American prehistory of Yellowstone.

FIGURE 3.5 Under the leadership of Professor Leslie Davis, archaeological survey work was conducted at Obsidian Cliff by Montana State University and the National Park Service in 1989. The team mapped dozens of Native American obsidian quarry pits, the earliest evidence of hard rock mining in the region. *National Park Service photo.*

for material quality by Native Americans for export and use. Thousands of large obsidian cores and bifaces are strewn across the cliff, likely left behind because they had internal flaws that would cause unpredictable breaking patterns. With so much high-quality obsidian, they simply left behind the lower-quality material. In figure 3.5, see the massive quantities of obsidian among mining pits left behind by Native Americans excavating for obsidian at the cliff.

My team from the University of Montana surveyed the southernmost portion of Obsidian Cliff in 2014. We observed millions of stone artifacts that attest to the vast amounts of stone tools produced at Obsidian Cliff by Native Americans over the past 11 millennia. Rivers of worked obsidian are present at the cliff, with large obsidian boulders broken open by Native Americans to make their tools. The ground is covered with literally billions of flakes, the by-products of the manufacture of millions of stone tools. As shown in figure 3.6, the entire ground surface for thousands of acres at the cliff is covered by flakes from stone tool manufacture.

In every direction around the cliff, there are thousands of stone tool production sites. During our archaeological surveys of the area south of the cliff, our University of Montana team found dozens and dozens of prehistoric stone tool production sites within the valley of Solfatara Creek and the Gibbon River. Closest to the cliff, these sites had large cobbles and large flakes of obsidian, likely the locations of the primary processing of huge obsidian cobbles into blocks and forms that could more easily be carried away by mobile hunter-gatherers. We also found stone circles at Obsidian Cliff, evidence that Native Americans had erected tipis at the site to live in while they collected stone.

Farther from the cliff, perhaps 1 mi. (0.8 km) south on Solfatara Creek, we found secondary obsidian processing areas and flintknapping (stone tool manufacture) stations where individuals sat thousands of years ago and transformed the large obsidian cobbles into even more transportable bifaces (such as knives) and projectile points (such as spear tips and arrowheads) to use in hunting. On a high terrace approximately 3 mi. (5 km) farther south of the cliff along the Gibbon River, in 2015, my team found piles of hundreds of obsidian flakes, further evidence of the importance of Obsidian Cliff.

Still another site along Obsidian Creek to the west of the cliff contains an archaeological site that stretches for at least 2 mi. (3 km), with more obsidian flaking debris on the ground than dirt in some places. From these areas close to the cliff, Native Americans transported their knives, projectile points, and other finished products to base camps in places like Yellowstone Lake to the south, along the Gibbon and Madison Rivers to the south and west, and along the Gardner and Yellowstone Rivers to the north.

PREHISTORY OF OBSIDIAN USE IN YELLOWSTONE

Since the first Clovis people arrived in the region, Native Americans have sought good-quality stone material for tool manufacture. While it seems that the earliest mammoth hunters of the Clovis period and the first bison hunters of the Folsom period did not use a lot of obsidian from Yellowstone, people of the subsequent Cody Culture some 9,000 years ago used it regularly. At the Cody Culture Osprey Beach site on the south shore of Yellowstone Lake, obsidian from Obsidian Cliff comprises about 20 percent of the entire stone tool assemblage at the site. Located approximately a hundred miles to the east, the 9,000-year-old Cody Culture Horner

FIGURE 3.6 In 2014, at Obsidian Cliff, my University of Montana team observed millions of waste flakes from the manufacture of obsidian tools by Native Americans.

site in Cody, Wyoming, also contained obsidian from Obsidian Cliff. In between, numerous sites have Obsidian Cliff obsidian, indicating that Native Americans used the Shoshone River and its many tributaries as travel corridors.

As a testament to this, Obsidian Cliff obsidian was also used extensively at the Mummy Cave site along the Shoshone River site near Cody, Wyoming. More than half of the obsidian used at the site came from Obsidian Cliff. Since 9,000 years ago, the Native American use of this site's obsidian increased and intensified across Wyoming, Montana, Idaho, and the greater region of the Rockies and Great Plains.

About 6,000 years ago, during a period called the Early Archaic (8,000 to 5,000 years ago), Native Americans at Fishing Bridge Point, on the north shore of Yellowstone Lake, used almost exclusively (90 percent) obsidian from Obsidian Cliff. So between 9,000 years ago at Osprey Beach and 6,000 years ago at Fishing Bridge Point, Native Americans escalated the use of the material from Obsidian Cliff. Archaeologists have found that Late Paleoindian hunter-gatherers (such as

FIGURE 3.7 Obsidian Creek flows along the western edge of Obsidian Cliff. Many Native American families camped along the creek during their visits to the cliff to collect the valuable obsidian.

the Cody Culture) incorporated a more diverse selection of lithic raw materials into their repertoire, reflecting a land-use and/or trade network encompassing much of the greater Yellowstone region. In contrast, during the 6,000-year-old Early Archaic occupations at Fishing Bridge Point, Native Americans emphasized use of a single source of obsidian—Obsidian Cliff—over all others. This supports an ever-increasing reliance on the high quality and abundant obsidian from the most important source in the park, Obsidian Cliff.

This escalating use of obsidian over time continued during the subsequent Middle Archaic period (5,000 to 3,000 years ago). At the Yearling Spring site near Livingston, Montana (40 mi./65 km north of Yellowstone), archaeologist Scott Carpenter and his crew excavated a cache of large obsidian bifaces and knives in 2010 (figure 3.8). The cache included 62 total artifacts, buried in a pit and covered by red ochre. The artifacts were all produced from Obsidian Cliff obsidian. This scene is eerily similar to the one we described in chapter 2 at the nearby Anzick site, approximately 20 mi. (32 km) to the north. However, radiocarbon dates from the Yearling Spring site indicate that the cache of red-ochre-covered Obsidian Cliff bifaces was placed in the pit only 3,680 years ago, some 7,000 years after the Anzick site!

No human remains were found in the pit at Yearling Spring (unlike the Anzick site). Such caches likely served as remote sources of lithic material in case of

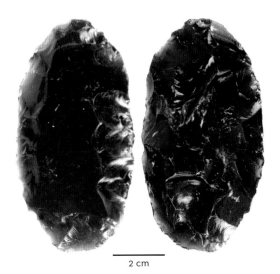

2 cm

FIGURE 3.8 These two large bifaces were among 62 obsidian artifacts found (in 2010) at the Yearling Spring site near Livingston, Montana. All of the artifacts were produced from Obsidian Cliff obsidian. *Scott Carpenter photo.*

emergency for mobile hunter-gatherer peoples. Perhaps someone needed to undertake a long trip and did not want to carry all the obsidian on the journey. To preserve and protect them for future use, the Native American individual buried the obsidian artifacts, in anticipation of a return trip to get them at a later date.

The individual had used some of the tools. Several of the pieces showed wear from cutting and scraping activities. To establish how they were used, Scott Carpenter had a few of the artifacts tested for protein residues. The results were amazing. One biface tested positive for Salmonidae protein (likely trout), one tested positive for Cervidae (likely deer or elk), while a red ochre fragment tested positive for Ursidae (grizzly or black bear). Whoever placed the tools in the cache had been awfully busy prior to arriving at Yearling Spring. They had hunted a bear, killed an elk or deer, and fished for trout along the Paradise Valley south of Livingston. Such was the life of Native American hunter-gatherers in Yellowstone 4,000 years ago.

Since all the bifaces at Yearling Spring were produced from Obsidian Cliff obsidian, it is clear that one or more individuals had traveled approximately 100 mi. (160 km) to the south, collected stone at Obsidian Cliff, and transported it back to the north along the Yellowstone River (they would have passed directly through today's town of Gardiner, Montana). The entire trip was over 200 mi. (322 km) and would have taken the individual many days to complete. The journey was probably conducted during the warmer months, since Obsidian Cliff was frozen and buried under snow above 7,500 ft. (2 km) during the winter.

The assemblage of artifacts from Yearling Spring weighs approximately 19 lb. (8.4 kg). The obsidian tools were likely transported in a leather bag on the back of a Native American hunter who walked northward from Obsidian Cliff, along the Yellowstone River toward Livingston. Along the way, they carried out primary and secondary processing of the obsidian, so that by the time they arrived at Yearling

Spring, the obsidian was in the form of nearly finished bifaces, a few of which had been used for a variety of hunting and fishing activities. Once the person arrived at Yearling Spring, the bifaces were placed within the pit, covered by red ochre, and left, presumably for future use. However, for some unknown reason, they were never collected or used again, lost to time and to their original makers.

OBSIDIAN CLIFF AND THE "LITTLE BIGHORN ON THE SCIOTO"

By the Late Archaic period, between 3,000 and 1,500 years ago, Native Americans increased their reliance on Obsidian Cliff. During this period, Obsidian Cliff obsidian became not just a local and regional commodity, but a continental one. More Yellowstone obsidian is present at Hopewell archaeological sites across the Midwest, Rockies, and Great Plains from this time period than any other type of obsidian used by Native Americans.

Obsidian Cliff obsidian has been recovered at scores and scores of prehistoric sites across Montana and Wyoming as well. In my research in Yellowstone, approximately 70 percent of the volcanic materials we have found are from the cliff. The remainder of the obsidian is from a variety of other obsidians, including Bear Gulch obsidian to the west and Jackson-area obsidians to the south. In addition to its dominance in Yellowstone, Obsidian Cliff obsidian was traded across a huge area during the Late Archaic period, about 2,000 years ago. Because of its incorporation as a commodity in what is called the Hopewellian Interaction Sphere, Obsidian Cliff obsidian has been found at archaeological sites in the Mississippi River Valley and many of its tributaries, including the states of Ohio, Iowa, Illinois, Wisconsin, Michigan, and the Canadian province of Ontario.

This intensity of use of Obsidian Cliff obsidian is noted at archaeological sites within Yellowstone as well. University of Wyoming archaeologist Paul Sanders states that obsidian use escalated in Yellowstone during the Late Archaic period. In the Hayden Valley of the Yellowstone River, as well as throughout the park area, human occupation increased during the Late Archaic period, between 3,000 and 1,500 years ago. In my own research in all corners of Yellowstone, Obsidian Cliff obsidian far and away dominates artifact assemblages at Late Archaic sites in the region.

The increase in obsidian use by Yellowstone Native Americans likely corresponded with the intensity of bison hunting during this period. The Late Archaic period marks the onset of the Plains Bison Hunting culture, which persisted from this time to the historic period. Late Archaic Plains bison hunters ran thousands of animals over cliffs and into corrals, thus requiring proportionately more stone tools to hunt and butcher the animals. In addition to bison hunting, the escalation

FIGURE 3.9 Sunrise over the Mound City site in Chillicothe, Ohio (unknown date). *Tom Engberg photo, National Park Service.*

of Obsidian Cliff obsidian use during this period corresponds with its commoditization by Hopewell people of midwestern North America.

One of the most remarkable occurrences of Obsidian Cliff obsidian during the Late Archaic period is far removed from Yellowstone in the state of Ohio. There, at the Mound City site on the Scioto River south of the city of Columbus, Ohio, archaeologists have excavated a series of mounds built by the Hopewell culture some 2,000 years ago (figure 3.9).

In his 2004 publication about the site, which he called "Little Big Horn on the Scioto," Warren DeBoer describes the presence of copper pounded into bighorn shapes and bighorn sheep motifs on Hopewell pottery, possibly suggesting that Hopewell Native American people traveled on foot nearly 2,000 mi. (3,200 km) from Ohio to the Rocky Mountains. American archaeologist James Griffin goes so far as to suggest that they carried back pounds and pounds of obsidian from Obsidian Cliff as part of a trade network of exotic goods from all over North America. He cites as evidence the presence of approximately 300 lb. (135 kg) of obsidian in Mound 11 at the Hopewell site in Ohio. Here, and at dozens of other midwestern sites, obsidian and other exotic goods were buried with the remains of important Hopewell Native Americans upon their deaths. Richard Hughes has sourced the obsidian in these mounds, and more than 90 percent of it came from Obsidian Cliff, with most of the remainder from Bear Gulch, west of the park.

Inside one Hopewell Mound at Mound City in Ohio, there is a platform upon which was found Obsidian Cliff obsidian bifaces, a copper sculpture in the shape of a bighorn sheep horn, as well as mica from North Carolina, shark teeth from the Gulf of Mexico, and strips of copper from the Great Lakes region. At still another site from the same time period in Wisconsin, one Hopewellian individual was buried holding large obsidian bifaces in each hand. The illustration at right is a re-creation of the Hopewell individual interred in the mound, based on a similar depiction in DeBoer's 2004 article.

BIGHORN SHEEP
HORN MADE OF
COPPER

FLAKED-STONE KNIVES MADE OF
OBSIDIAN FROM YELLOWSTONE

FIGURE 3.10 Illustration of a Hopewell individual buried at Mound City, Ohio, with Yellowstone obsidian bifaces and a copper bighorn sheep horn. Illustrator and archeologist Eric Carlson based this depiction (2016) on one that appeared in DeBoer's "Little Big Horn on the Scioto" article in *American Antiquity*, 2004.

DeBoer writes: "A parsimonious account would have peripatetic Sciotons actually venturing to bighorn and obsidian country [of Yellowstone]. On this adventurous junket, a horn was acquired, later to be rendered in copper, and an actual ram was seen, perhaps on a distant crag. . . . Unlike the Lewis and Clark expedition that struggled up the mercurial and often difficult course of the Missouri fifteen hundred years later, this extraordinary journey is more likely to have followed well-worn copper routes to Lake Superior and then overland trails across the Dakotas. . . . Judging from the large, bark-wrapped block of obsidian from the Riverside cemetery in Michigan's Upper Peninsula, the latter stretch was already trafficked [during the Late Archaic period]." DeBoer goes on to state that the purpose of collection of the exotic materials was to obtain spiritual power from the remarkable items for use by important religious persons, or shamans, in Native American ceremonies some 2,000 years ago. Upon their deaths, their religious items were interred in their graves within the famous mounds of the Hopewell culture of Ohio.

It is almost inconceivable to think that people actually walked 2,000 miles from Ohio to get obsidian in Yellowstone National Park, only to turn around and walk 2,000 miles back home. Averaging 20 mi. (32 km) per day, this 4,000 mi. (6,400 km) journey would have taken approximately 200 days or the better part of a year. Perhaps the ancient Ohioans started the journey in March when the snow began to melt and took the better part of the summer and fall to finish the trip before snow fell again in November. On the trip, they apparently saw bighorn sheep and collected obsidian for use in religious ceremonies. Today, even driving that distance, instead of flying, would cause consternation among most people. To think that Native Americans actually walked it is a remarkable feat of human desire, navigation, and stamina. During this period, contemporary tribes in the southeastern United States along the Mississippi River used large canoes to travel up and down the rivers; it is altogether likely that boats may have been helpful in the transport of such large quantities of obsidian from Yellowstone to Ohio. By following the Yellowstone River, the Missouri River, and the tributaries of the Mississippi River, Hopewell Native Americans could have canoed and walked the entire round trip to and from Obsidian Cliff.

In 2009, my crews from the University of Montana found a very large obsidian corner-notched knife on a high terrace above Yellowstone Lake (figure 3.11). The obsidian of this artifact was sourced to Obsidian Cliff. More important, however, is the fact that the very large biface is dissimilar to any known to have been used in this region of Wyoming. While it somewhat resembles Late Archaic projectile points in terms of its overall shape, the large biface we found is at least twice as big as most Late Archaic points typically observed in the park. Instead, the artifact more closely resembles in its size and shape the ceremonial bifaces interred in the burial mounds of the Hopewell of Ohio during the Late Archaic period (such as the ones shown in figure 3.11). It is not far-fetched to believe that the biface we found at Yellowstone Lake was lost at the site by a long-traveling member of the Hopewell culture, more than 2,000 mi. (3,200 km) from home more than 2,000 years ago.

Since the first Native Americans visited the cliff more than 11,000 years ago, dozens of tribes from across America, including the Hopewell culture of Ohio, realized the importance of the stone in their daily lives for both subsistence and spiritual purposes. On June 19, 1996, Obsidian Cliff was officially designated a National Historic Landmark by the National Park Service. Within the state of Wyoming, Obsidian Cliff is one of only two landmarks of 25 total in the state that are associated with a Native American archaeological site. Based on this recognition, it is fair to say that Obsidian Cliff is one of Wyoming's, and America's, most important prehistoric Native American archaeological sites.

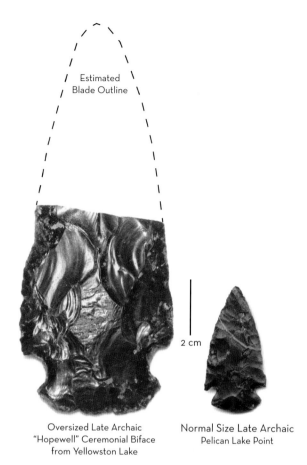

Estimated Blade Outline

2 cm

Oversized Late Archaic "Hopewell" Ceremonial Biface from Yellowston Lake

Normal Size Late Archaic Pelican Lake Point

FIGURE 3.11 Comparison of a large Hopewell-style obsidian biface (left) with a "normal size" Late Archaic projectile point (right). Both points date to approximately 2,000 years ago and were found at Yellowstone Lake.

OTHER ROCK USED BY NATIVE AMERICANS IN YELLOWSTONE

In addition to Obsidian Cliff obsidian, several additional sources of stone material were important to Native Americans in the vicinity of Yellowstone. Three primary obsidian sources dominate among a dozen or so other small sources of the rock.

Near Jackson, Wyoming, south of Yellowstone, Native Americans collected obsidian at Teton Pass. Farther to the west of Yellowstone on the Idaho-Montana state line, Native Americans collected obsidian at a place called Bear Gulch. Finally, northwest of Yellowstone, Native Americans collected large quantities of another type of volcanic rock—dacite—at the Cashman Dacite Quarry near Ennis, Montana.

Studies of obsidian use in the greater Yellowstone region by Scheiber and Finley in 2011 indicate that 40 percent of the more than 2,300 artifacts at nearly 250 archaeological sites derived from Obsidian Cliff. The next most popular sources of obsidian near Yellowstone were Bear Gulch (22 percent) and Teton Pass (9 percent). In our studies at Yellowstone Lake and the Gardiner Basin of northern Yellowstone, Obsidian Cliff obsidian dominates the stone tool assemblages, but minor percentages of Cashman dacite and Bear Gulch obsidian are also commonly found. By tracing the origins of stones, archaeologists can track human movements on the landscape in prehistory. In other areas of the Rockies, such as western Montana, Bear Gulch obsidian dominates artifact assemblages from sites. Near Jackson, Wyoming, Teton Pass obsidian was very popular. Proximity to the source, quality of the stone, and its abundance at the source were the key factors instigating Native Americans to select a certain type of rock over another for stone tool manufacture.

Another important type of rock used by Native Americans in Yellowstone is chert. Chert is a cryptocrystalline silica rock that, because of its high silica content, is also quite good for making stone tools. Some Native Americans preferred chert for making certain stone tools because it holds an edge longer, and breaks less frequently than the more brittle obsidian. One of the most popular sources of chert in Yellowstone is found today close to the Grand Loop Road between Mammoth Hot Springs and Tower Junction on the northern edge of the park near the Montana-Wyoming border.

Here, at a place called Crescent Hill, Yellowstone National Park archaeologists Robin Park and Ann Johnson first observed in 2005 that Native Americans collected this chert to make stone tools. They called the area Robin's Quarry after the park archaeologist. After their discovery, my University of Montana team revisited the site in 2010 and conducted a full survey of the chert outcrop. We renamed the stone Crescent Hill chert after the geologic formation of which it is a member. We extensively surveyed and mapped the Crescent Hill chert quarry, and the bulk of our results is presented in a University of Montana master's thesis by Jacob Adams. We identified more than 20 separate exposures of the chert across an area measuring approximately 2,000 acres (800 hectares). We found chert in a variety of colors, including purple, red, orange, black, and green. Unlike at Obsidian Cliff, we observed no quarry pits. Instead, the material was worked by Native Americans from the faces of bedrock exposures on or above the ground. In 2007, we found two Late Archaic projectile points from Yellowstone that were produced from red Crescent Hill chert (figure 3.12).

Crescent Hill chert formed within the Crescent Hill basalt formation and occurs in two contexts: eroding from hilltops or knobs, and as chert lenses within the Crescent Hill columnar basalt formation. The basalt formation is from the Eocene period (55.8 to 33.9 million years ago). Most cherts form in deep-sea environments and shallow water contexts, and so Crescent Hill chert presents an interesting scenario, with the chert having been formed within the basalt formation. Geologically, Crescent Hill cherts are extremely heterogeneous in appearance and morphology. Cherts, including Crescent Hill, range from extremely high-quality fine-grained materials to coarse-grained, inclusion-ridden materials.

2 cm

FIGURE 3.12 These two Late Archaic (3,000 to 1,500 years ago) projectile points were produced from Crescent Hill chert in Yellowstone National Park.

The Crescent Hill chert is scattered across an area primarily north of the Grand Loop Road and south of the Yellowstone River, in a place called the Blacktail Deer Plateau. Tourists can access the area at a pull-off on the road at Phantom Lake. You can park here and walk northward across the road up the hill. You will find the Crescent Hill chert exposures in the sagebrush meadows there. The outcrop areas are patchy across the landscape, and locating the high-quality raw materials would have been difficult for prehistoric hunter-gatherers. Since there is no evidence of quarrying raw materials at Crescent Hill, the stone was likely collected by Native Americans directly from the bedrock itself or from exposures of the bedrock eroding on the ground surface. Because of exposure to the elements and the vagaries of time, the quality of the chert there is highly variable, with most of it being of a low to moderate quality and not very amenable to making good stone tools.

Still, despite its scattered and limited abundance, and comparatively low quality, Crescent Hill chert was utilized by Native Americans. During the Late Prehistoric period, between 1,500 and 300 years ago, Native Americans living in the Yellowstone River Valley collected the stone and used it to make stone tools. At the Airport Rings site from 2007 to 2008, we excavated the remains of three stone circles, the locations where tipi lodges had been built by Native Americans north of Gardiner, Montana. We compared the use of Obsidian Cliff obsidian with

FIGURE 3.13 These stone circles are evidence that Native Americans built tipis while they camped at the Airport Rings site near Gardiner, Montana. Here, they also produced stone tools from both Obsidian Cliff obsidian and Crescent Hill chert.

that of Crescent Hill chert, with the goal of establishing whether Native Americans showed a preference for one stone over the other. In this study, we were able to hold the distance to source as a constant because the two sources—Crescent Hill and Obsidian Cliff—are about the same distance from the archaeological sites. Obsidian Cliff is located approximately 25 mi. (40 km) south of the stone circles and was most easily accessed following the Yellowstone River upstream through Gardiner, Montana, then heading south following the Gardner River past Mammoth Hot Springs and Sheepeater Cliffs to Obsidian Creek, near what is today the Indian

Creek campground area. This route required a hunter-gatherer to hike up more than 2,000 ft. (600 m) for 25 mi. (40 km) from what is today Gardiner, Montana, into the area of Obsidian Cliff.

Alternatively, to gain access to Crescent Hill chert, Native Americans likely followed the Yellowstone River eastward from Gardiner through the Black Canyon of the Yellowstone for approximately 20 mi. (32 km) until they reached the Blacktail Deer Plateau. Today, a hiking trail winds along the Wyoming-Montana state line following the Yellowstone River along more or less the same route believed to have been used by Native Americans. To gain access to the chert, Native Americans probably followed the very steep ravines of Blacktail Deer Creek, Oxbow Creek, or Geode Creek to the south and up onto the high plateau above the river. This requires a very steep elevation gain of about 1,500 to 2,000 ft. (450 to 600 m) within less than ½ mi. (0.8 km) to get to the Crescent Hill chert outcrops.

Both Obsidian Cliff and Crescent Hill required a hunter-gatherer to walk through steep terrain for approximately 20 to 25 mi. (32 to 40 km) from the Yellowstone River Valley. However, mile for mile, of the two sources, Crescent Hill was probably slightly easier to access by hunter-gatherers from near Gardiner than was Obsidian Cliff. Based on the results of our archaeological excavations at the Airport Rings stone circle site, Native Americans collected the chert and made stone tools from it. Nevertheless, despite the seemingly easier travel route to obtain the chert, our stone tool analysis at the Gardiner stone circle site indicates that the Late Prehistoric Native Americans greatly preferred Obsidian Cliff obsidian (80 percent of stone artifacts found) over Crescent Hill chert (13 percent of stone artifacts found).

Despite the slightly longer distance to Obsidian Cliff, the obsidian at that location was more abundant and easier to find on the landscape and, perhaps most important, was of an overall higher quality than Crescent Hill chert. As suggested by archaeologist Robin Park in *Yellowstone Archaeology: Northern Yellowstone*, the aesthetic qualities of Obsidian Cliff obsidian likely promoted its use as well. It is a beautiful black glassy rock, with some shades of orange, red, and even green. Native peoples probably went out of their way to go to Obsidian Cliff to collect the rock for several reasons, including its abundance, quality, and beauty. In addition to local people, the Hopewell culture of Ohio liked the looks of it enough to travel a total of 4,000 miles to get it and bring it back for their religious ceremonies. In contrast, there is no evidence that these same people collected Crescent Hill chert. Instead, collection of Crescent Hill chert was likely embedded in other activities of locally based hunter-gatherer peoples. While out hunting for deer, elk, or bison, or during the collection of plants or other resources, they perhaps made a side trip to one of the small outcrops of Crescent Hill chert to make a stone tool. Our excavations at another Gardiner, Montana, archaeological site in 2011, the Little Trail Creek site, showed a similar Native American preference for Obsidian Cliff obsidian over Crescent Hill chert in the production of stone tools.

Clearly, the use of Obsidian Cliff obsidian was quite common in Yellowstone and was greatly preferred over Crescent Hill chert for making stone tools. Over time, Obsidian Cliff obsidian exhibits an overall use-trend line that goes ever upward among Clovis, Folsom, Cody Culture, Early Archaic, Middle Archaic, Late Archaic, and, finally, to a peak in the Late Prehistoric period. Without the obsidian from Obsidian Cliff, Native Americans would have struggled to find enough quality stone by which to make their tools to survive in the wilds of the Yellowstone region. While the smaller sources of obsidian and chert—such as Crescent Hill—were likely important, Obsidian Cliff provided one of the most abundant and high-quality stone sources imaginable for a group of hunter-gatherers in any part of the world.

CHAPTER FOUR

YELLOWSTONE LAKE

ON THEIR WAY to or from Obsidian Cliff to collect obsidian for stone tools, many Native Americans likely ventured an additional 25 mi. (40 km) to the southeast to visit Yellowstone Lake. As North America's largest, high-elevation natural lake, this 20 mi. (32 km) long, 15 mi. (24 km) wide body of water has played an important role in the lifeways of Great Plains, Great Basin, and Rocky Mountain Native Americans for 11,000 years. As many as 10 different tribes likely lived around the lake to exploit its vast resources in the recent past. Just as tourists flock to the park today, Native Americans traveled on foot for many miles to camp at the lake as well.

At an elevation of nearly 8,000 ft. (2,400 m) above sea level, the freshwater Yellowstone Lake is the heart of Yellowstone National Park. The lake is easily accessed today by the Grand Loop Road from Canyon Village to the north, via the South Entrance road from the Tetons, and from the East Entrance of the park at Cody, Wyoming. Many facilities are available for tourists at Yellowstone Lake, including stores and camping on the north end at Fishing Bridge, a marina and campground at Bridge Bay, as well as a hotel, restaurants, and a large campground at Grant Village on the southwest end of the lake. The only portions of the lake not accessible by car are the eastern and southern shores, such as the southern inlet of the Yellowstone River. These areas can only be accessed by foot or by boat (figure 4.1). Backcountry campsites are scattered along the east and south shores for intrepid canoers, kayakers, and backpackers.

I led my University of Montana archaeology crews on five years of archaeological research trips (2010 to 2014) along Yellowstone Lake's remote southern and eastern shores. Traveling from Missoula, we entered the park at West Yellowstone and

100

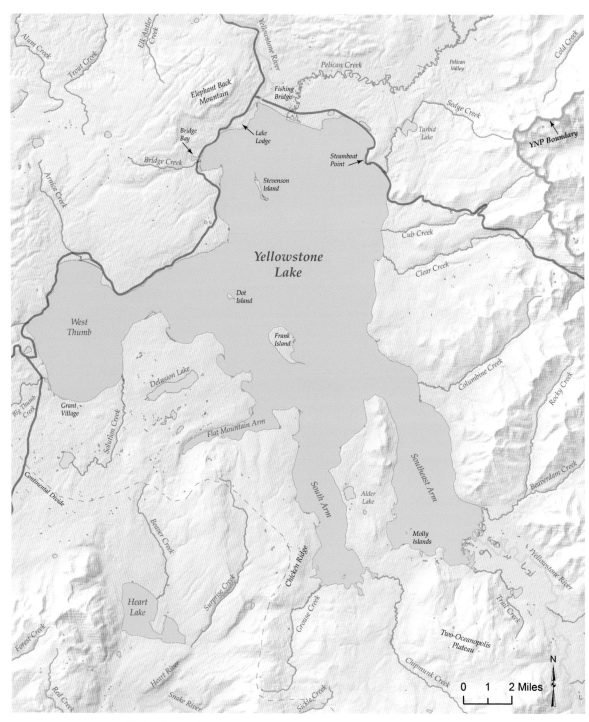

MAP 4.1 Yellowstone Lake

FIGURE 4.1 University of Montana archaeology crews conducted archaeological excavations at dozens of sites along the south shore of Yellowstone Lake between 2012 and 2014. The only way to access these areas is by canoe. These two canoes held all of our camp and archaeology gear, as well as four archaeologists.

drove along the Grand Loop Road past Old Faithful to Grant Village and our base camp, or we traveled the Grand Loop Road from Gardiner in the north through Mammoth Hot Springs, past Obsidian Cliff, through the Norris Geyser Basin, Canyon Village, and the Hayden Valley, arriving at the north end of the lake at Fishing Bridge. From either of these two base camps, our four-person team would travel along the western shore of the lake, past the National Historic Landmark Lake Hotel and an array of beaches and fishing and picnic areas, to the Bridge Bay Marina. Once at the marina, we loaded our equipment and supplies into a motor-boat piloted by Johnnie Player, a longtime Bridge Bay marina boat captain. Johnny dropped us off at the boundary of the no-motor zone on the lake, we transferred our supplies to two canoes, and we paddled to our backcountry camps.

FIGURE 4.2 Yellowstone Lake, which is North America's largest high-elevation natural lake, can sometimes resemble an ocean with big waves.

These trips were some of the most remarkable of my career as an archaeologist. Some days were scenic, peaceful, and calm, while others were filled with dread, near-swampings of our canoe, and lightning storms. Because the lake is so large, some days it can be a placid wonder, while other days it can rock like an ocean. Once we arrived at our camp, we set up our tents, loaded the canoes with archaeology gear, and paddled to many archaeological sites to conduct excavations.

Just as we did, Native American hunter-gatherers traveled up the valleys of the major rivers and creeks to get to the lake. Many of the camps we lived in for our archaeology work had been used by Native Americans in prehistory. Native Americans, however, walked to the lake and then around it once they got there. Based on our research, I don't think they used boats. For many of us today, such a long hiking trip with families (including grandparents and young children) would be unthinkable, but for hunter-gatherer people, the lure of Yellowstone Lake and its abundant wild resources was probably too good to pass up.

At its high altitude, the lake area averages about 70°F (21°C) in the summer, whereas the valleys outside the park can be as much as 20°F (6°C) warmer. Streams that flowed readily in the spring and early summer at the lower-elevation settings would dry up, as would many of the wild resources. As part of their mobile seasonal settlement pattern, Native Americans from the lower elevations focused upward starting in the early spring. They ventured to the higher elevations during the warmer months not only to escape the heat but also to follow the animals and the ripening plants they lived on.

The flow of the seasons is important in understanding prehistoric human use of Yellowstone Lake. May through October at the lake are the months with average temperatures around or above 50°F (10°C). From November through April, the lake area receives snowfall averaging 20 in. (50 cm) or more per month, with an accumulation of 3 ft. (90 cm) or more. Yellowstone Lake freezes up to 25 in. (63 cm) thick between about early December and early mid-May. In winter through early spring, Native Americans likely traversed the frozen lake surface to access the islands and other places more easily than they could other times of year. In the warm months, a variety of game animals migrate upward in elevation to places like Yellowstone Lake. And many of them move down from the lake area to lower elevations in winter. As many as 60 different mammal species live in the vicinity of Yellowstone Lake, including bison, elk, moose, bighorn sheep, deer, antelope, grizzly and black bear, mountain lion, coyote, cougar, bobcat, and wolf. The majority of Yellowstone's bison and other medium and large ungulates are seasonally migratory. Our archaeological research shows that Native Americans hunted all these large animals while they camped at the lake, and rabbit, deer, bison, elk, and bear were particularly popular prey species.

Another seasonally migratory food source in Yellowstone Lake is Yellowstone cutthroat trout (*Oncorhynchus clarkii bouvieri*), one of only two surviving original native cutthroat trout species left in North America. This trout species is abundant at the lake (and may have been in the past), especially in spring when it runs up the lake's creeks to spawn.

UNDERSTANDING PALEOENVIRONMENTS AND PALEO-SHORELINES IN YELLOWSTONE

Montana State University's Cathy Whitlock and other scientists are studying ancient environments in the region by examining plant pollen and plant fragments in sediment from lake bottoms in Yellowstone National Park and vicinity. Based on pollen samples in the southern portion of Yellowstone, the present-day ecozones (sagebrush steppe, montane conifer forest, and alpine tundra) were established sometime during the Late Pleistocene to the Holocene transition between 12,000 and 11,000 years ago. Associated with a warm, dry period called the Altithermal, steppe-dominating grasses were prevalent between 8,500 and 6,000 years ago, suggesting maximum dryness in the area during the period archaeologists refer to as the Early Archaic. After 5,000 years ago, during the Middle Archaic period, environmental conditions similar to what we experience today emerged across the northern Plains and Rockies, including Yellowstone. Native American use of Yellowstone Lake increased exponentially starting around 3,000 years ago during the Late Archaic period, until the late nineteenth century when the park was established and the US Cavalry pushed Native Americans out.

The water level of Yellowstone Lake, which sits within a caldera, has fluctuated during the past 11,000 years because of deglaciation, volcanism, and climate change, resulting in a series of old terraces, or paleo-shorelines, as defined by Kenneth Pierce of Montana State University. These paleo-shorelines have been well mapped and dated by Pierce, and University of Montana researchers Marc Hendrix and Michael Hoffman have refined some of the terrace formation chronologies. The ages of the terraces provide minimum timelines for prehistoric occupation, with the terraces closer to the modern lakeshore dating to as recent as 2,000 years ago and terraces farther from today's shore dating to the latest Pleistocene, about 12,000 years ago.

Generally, at Yellowstone Lake there is extreme variability in the elevation and location of ancient shorelines, as well as in the depth of cultural deposits, depending on the location at the lake. In the northern portion of the lake, such as Fishing Bridge, 10,000-year-old paleo-shorelines are about 26 ft. (8 m) above and 1,300 ft. (400 m) inland from today's shoreline, while modern shorelines reflect about 5,000 years of stability. In the southwestern portion of the lake, 10,000-year-old terraces are adjacent to and only 10 ft. (3 m) above the modern shoreline, while 3,000-year-old terraces are now submerged in the lake. In turn, the eastern shore of the lake outside of the caldera

FIGURE 4.3 These three scenes show the dramatic variation in locations and depths of Native American cultural deposits at archaeological sites at Yellowstone Lake. The West Thumb has 9,000-year-old sites within a couple feet of the ground surface, while Dot Island contained an 800-year-old bison bone more than 18 ft. (5 m) below the ground surface, and Fishing Bridge has 2,000-year-old artifacts on the ground surface.

has experienced significant uplift, resulting in paleo-shorelines as much as 2,300 ft. (700 m) inland and 80 ft. (25 m) above the modern shoreline.

Understanding the locations of paleo-shorelines is crucial to the identification of prehistoric Native American archaeological sites. For example, beachfront archaeological sites on the eastern shore of Yellowstone Lake are located as much as 650 to 2,300 ft. (200 to 700 m) inland from the current shoreline. Still other archaeological sites are completely submerged under the lake as a result of deformation resulting from volcanic activity.

Because of the dynamic volcanism and lakeshore uplift or submersion, rates of soil deposition also vary widely around the lake. Therefore, the depth of archaeological deposits differs dramatically on the different shorelines of the lake. Figure 4.3 shows the variability in terrace heights and cultural deposits at West Thumb, Fishing Bridge, and Dot Island. Along the West Thumb of the lake, 9,500-year-old Cody Culture sites are buried under only 2 ft. (60 cm) of sediment, while only a couple miles north on Dot Island, an 800-year-old bison bone was found more than 18 ft. (5.5 m) below the ground's surface. At the site near Fishing Bridge, we identified 2,000-year-old fire hearths only 2 ft. (60 cm) below the ground's surface. It is extremely challenging to understand the stratigraphy and geomorphology of these various lakeshores. For example, how can an 800-year-old bison bone be buried under 16 ft. (4.8 m) of sand and 9,500-year-old artifacts be buried under only 2 ft. (60 cm) of sand just a couple of miles away?

Because of the complexities of paleo-shorelines at Yellowstone Lake, archaeologists look for artifacts not only along the current lakeshores but also inland on the old lake terraces that could contain older sites. These paleo-shorelines provide a maximum age of a Native American archaeological site at Yellowstone Lake. For example, Pierce used radiocarbon dating to estimate that one of the Fishing Bridge area paleo-shorelines dates to no older than about 10,000 years ago; so, any archaeological sites on that landform should not be older than that. The University of Montana's archaeological excavations at the Fishing Bridge Point site in 2010 near the Yellowstone River outlet confirmed this landform age by discovering the only radiocarbon-dated Early Archaic (about 6,800 years ago) hearth in Yellowstone (but found no older materials).

FIGURE 4.4 Bears have been known to hibernate on the lake's islands, making them easy targets for Native American hunters wanting to take a bear for its power, wisdom, and sustenance. *Jim Peaco photo, National Park Service.*

Yellowstone Lake's shores contain several vegetative zones, including a subalpine spruce and fir zone, pine woodlands, riverine and marshland habitat, as well as sagebrush grasslands. These vegetative zones are the result of several transitions occurring in the park after deglaciation. Lodgepole pine stands are interspersed along the lakeshore terraces, with herbaceous plant communities making up the principal understory growth. Lakeshore terraces support silver sage, big sagebrush, as well as a variety of grasses, while the stream banks and marshy areas produce stands of willows, as well as sedges and rushes.

Interspersed among the extensive pine forests that surround the lake, there are abundant open meadows and riparian areas that contain an extremely diverse array of plants—as many as 400 different species. The ripening of these plants for food, like camas bulbs and bitterroot, likely drew people up to the lake in spring as well. During one of our archaeological field schools at Yellowstone Lake in 2010,

FIGURE 4.5 The meadows surrounding Yellowstone Lake provide dozens of plants used by Native Americans for food, medicine, and spiritual purposes.

two of my University of Montana students identified 52 different plant species used by early Native Americans in a 20-acre (8-hectare) meadow on the northwest shore of the lake near Lake Lodge, of which 15 species were recognized as food sources, 17 species as medicinal, and 8 species as spiritually important. For example, camas roots were collected in spring and baked for eating, while chokecherries ripen in fall and were mixed with bison meat and fat to make pemmican, a sort of Native American granola bar. Still other plants, including sage and sweetgrass, were collected and used for ceremonial practices, such as in sweat lodges to cleanse the body and spirit.

To get to the lake and the variety of wild resources, Native Americans followed the valleys of major creeks and rivers that cut through the mountain passes. The Yellowstone River is the major lake tributary and has two confluences on the lake, one flowing into it on its southeast corner and one flowing out of it about 18 mi. (30 km) to the northeast at Fishing Bridge. When the river exits the lake, it flows northeasterly for hundreds of miles through Wyoming and Montana. Among the 40 or so other smaller streams that flow into the lake, Clear Creek arrives on its northeastern shore and has its headwaters in the Absaroka Range, nearly meeting the Shoshone River, which flows eastward to the Bighorn Basin. Each of these three major waterways—the southern and northern Yellowstone Rivers and Clear Creek—were active travel routes in prehistory. Other major lake feeder streams include Pelican Creek on the north, Trail Creek on the southeast, Solution Creek on the southwest, and Arnica Creek on the west. The Madison River to the west of the lake and the Lewis River to the south were also major regional travel routes used by Native Americans to gain access to the resources of the Yellowstone Plateau.

ARCHAEOLOGICAL SITES AT YELLOWSTONE LAKE

The first survey for archaeological sites in Yellowstone National Park was conducted by Montana State University, Missoula (now the University of Montana). In the late 1950s and early 1960s, that original survey identified over 200 archaeological sites within Yellowstone National Park. The leader was Jacob Hoffman, who was the first professional archaeologist to identify the high density of prehistoric archaeological sites at Yellowstone Lake. In the early 1960s, Dee Taylor of MSU–Missoula performed additional archaeological excavations in the Fishing Bridge area on the north shore of the lake near the Yellowstone River. The National Park Service's Midwestern Archaeological Research Center and the University of Montana also conducted additional work there in the 1990s and 2000s, respectively. The National Park Service, together with a private archaeological consulting firm, Lifeways of Canada, led excavations at the Osprey Beach site in the early 1990s with its 9,300-year-old Cody Culture occupations. Between 2009 and 2016, Yellowstone National Park again provided funding to complete survey and testing of archaeological sites on the northwest, eastern, and southern shores of Yellowstone Lake by my University of Montana team.

These various studies have identified nearly 300 archaeological sites along the shores of the lake. Excavations by the University of Montana at dozens of sites from 2009 to 2016 confirm active use of the lake since the Clovis period. The University

FIGURE 4.6 The University of Montana excavated dozens of archaeological sites around the shores of Yellowstone Lake between 2009 and 2016, finding evidence of Native American use for 11,000 years.

of Montana found a Clovis projectile point on the south shore of Yellowstone Lake, indicating its use by the first Native Americans around 11,000 years ago. (See figure 2.11 for the various types of prehistoric Native American projectile points found in Yellowstone and the periods of time in which they were used.)

After the first ephemeral visits to Yellowstone Lake by Clovis people, Late Paleoindian Period Cody Culture people increased their use of the lake beginning about 9,500 years ago.

The Fishing Bridge site contained an Early Archaic hearth dated to nearly 6,000 years old, which remains the oldest radiocarbon-dated fire pit at any site at the lake. Early Archaic Native Americans used large side-notched projectile points that are often referred to as Mummy Cave points since several of them were found at the

Mummy Cave site near the eastern park boundary on the East Entrance road at Cody. Early Archaic hunter-gatherers sought the cool temperatures and reliable water supply of Yellowstone Lake during the altithermal, a hot and dry period that prevailed 6,000 years ago. The altithermal was so hot and dry at lower elevations that the modern form of bison (*Bison bison*) evolved at the expense of the large herds of the ancient, large-bodied bison (*Bison antiquus*).

Middle Archaic Native American camps are quite common at Yellowstone Lake as well. In the early 1990s, the National Park Service excavated several fire pits used by Native Americans dating to approximately 4,000 years ago at two sites on the lake's West Thumb near Arnica Creek. Here, as well as in Middle Archaic features at the Fishing Bridge Point site, archaeologists found several split-base McKean and Oxbow points that are diagnostic of the Middle Archaic period.

FIGURE 4.7 Native Americans built this campfire nearly 2,000 years ago on the eastern shore of Yellowstone Lake.

The Late Archaic period witnessed a significant increase in Native American use of the lake area between 3,000 and 1,500 years ago. Numerous archaeological sites around the lakeshore have fire features and projectile points that date to this time period. A hearth was excavated by my students from the University of Montana in 2010 at a site on the eastern shore of Yellowstone Lake (figure 4.7), with a radiocarbon date of the Late Archaic period, about 2,000 years ago, and was associated with Pelican Lake–type projectile points. Late Archaic Native Americans hunted large herds of bison like those visible today in the park.

Native Americans continued active use of Yellowstone Lake in the most recent Late Prehistoric period (1,500 to 300 years ago). We excavated the remains of several campfires used by Native Americans near the Fishing Bridge campground and

FIGURE 4.8 My team from the University of Montana (2014) excavated this stone circle on the southern end of Yellowstone Lake near the Molly Islands.

store in 2011, which were evidence that Native Americans lived along the shores of Yellowstone Lake around the time of Euro-American contact. For at least 10 millennia, Native Americans used a spear thrower (or atlatl) to hunt. About 1,500 years ago, the bow and arrow was introduced, changing the face of hunting in the Great Plains and Rocky Mountains. Bow and arrow hunting was superior to the atlatl for a variety of reasons, including increased stealth and reduced stone material requirements. The bow and arrow required use of very small arrow points, rather than the larger atlatl dart points. These small arrow points are present at numerous sites around the lake, including this site near the Molly Islands in the lake's southeast arm (figure 4.8). At that site in 2014, University of Montana archaeologists found the intact remains of a Late Prehistoric stone circle, or tipi lodge base, beneath a foot of dirt.

In addition to arrow points, sherds of small amounts of Late Prehistoric pottery that was used by Native Americans was found at the First Blood site in the West Thumb of the lake. National Park Service archaeologist Kenneth Cannon excavated that site in 1992, but most of the pottery was recovered in the late 1950s by Jacob Hoffman. The pottery was produced from local clay tempered with crushed rock, and it was used to both cook and store their food. The type of pottery found at the site is called Intermountain Ware, which is often associated with archaeological sites used by the Shoshone Indians within the past 1,000 years in Yellowstone.

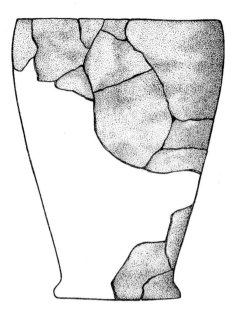

FIGURE 4.9 Illustration of an Intermountain Ware pottery vessel found at the First Blood site in the West Thumb area of Yellowstone Lake in the late 1950s. *Illustration by Janet Robinson. Courtesy of Kenneth Cannon.*

WHICH NATIVE AMERICAN TRIBES USED YELLOWSTONE LAKE?

Was Yellowstone Lake within the territory of one tribe or many? Some archaeologists suggest that Yellowstone Lake was at the center of a large territory used by a single group of Native Americans, perhaps the Shoshone or another tribe. Other archaeologists suggest that multiple tribes from different regions used the lake, a supposition supported in recent research by me and my colleagues.

Nabokov and Loendorf's research suggests that diverse groups utilized the region, including the Shoshone, Bannock, Crow, Blackfeet, Salish, Kiowa, Nez Perce, and many others. In particular, the Blackfeet and Crow are known to have used the northern tier of the lake, while Nabokov and Loendorf suggest that the Eastern (or Wind River) Shoshone mostly used the lake's southern tier. The Bannock and Nez Perce mostly used the northern tier of the lake as well, with the Nez Perce apparently using the Pelican Creek Valley as a main warm-season bison hunting area. With this approach, it is not reasonable to think that the Shoshone were the exclusive users of Yellowstone, even in later prehistory.

In support of the multi-tribe model of lake use, the archaeological data collected by the University of Montana and others at dozens of lake area sites suggest that a variety of Native American tribes used Yellowstone Lake before Euro-American contact. Based on lithic raw material source locations, it appears that each group of people likely utilized different travel routes to get to Yellowstone Lake, following similar routes that people use today to travel to the park. Except for sites on the southeast shore of the lake, Obsidian Cliff obsidian is common at most lake area sites. Therefore, nearly all the Native American people who lived at the lake (with the possible exception of tribes on the southeastern shore) also apparently traveled to Obsidian Cliff some 25 mi. (40 km) to the northwest of Fishing Bridge at the northern end of the lake.

Based on stone tool data, Crow, Blackfeet, Salish, Nez Perce, and, to a lesser extent, Shoshone were likely active on the northwest shore of Yellowstone Lake in the recent past. Because of extremely high densities of Obsidian Cliff obsidian and Crescent Hill chert at archaeological sites near Fishing Bridge, Native Americans living on the northwestern shore of the lake oriented their travel patterns toward Obsidian Cliff and the Yellowstone River, north of the lake. The low numbers of other types of obsidians from the south indicate infrequent travel and trade with people living south of Yellowstone Lake toward Jackson, Wyoming, and the Snake River Valley.

Crow, Northern Cheyenne, Arapaho, Kiowa, and Shoshone individuals likely frequented the northeast shore of Yellowstone Lake in recent history. They probably accessed the lake from the east up the Clear Creek and Shoshone River Valleys from areas such as Cody, Wyoming. Several other creek valleys push eastward through the Absaroka Mountains from the eastern shore of Yellowstone Lake. While Obsidian Cliff obsidian is very common at northeastern lakeshore archaeological sites, it appears in reduced quantities on the northwest shore, suggesting a falloff in Obsidian Cliff obsidian use with increasing distance to source. Instead, on the east shore, tools produced from Absaroka cherts and local Park Point obsidian (with a source on the east shore of the lake) are abundant in archaeological sites.

On the southeast lakeshore, the southern Yellowstone River and Snake River headwaters were the likely origin routes for Shoshone and perhaps Crow, Northern Cheyenne, Kiowa, and Arapaho groups in historic times. These Native American groups on the southeastern lakeshore probably didn't travel to Obsidian Cliff because it was more than 75 mi. (120 km) away, whereas Jackson, Wyoming, obsidian sources were only 30 mi. (48 km) away. Overall, at sites like the Donner site (figure 4.10) near the Molly Islands, excavated by Brian Vivian of Lifeways of Canada and colleagues from the National Park Service in 2007, obsidian densities are very low on the southeastern lakeshore, with cherts from the Absaroka Mountains east of the lake being dominant. The low densities of obsidian suggest that these southeastern shore Native Americans did not travel to Obsidian Cliff very often because of the long distance to walk around the lake to get to the cliff.

FIGURE 4.10 Native Americans cooked a variety of hunted and gathered foods in this large roasting feature at the Donner site on the southeastern shore of Yellowstone Lake. They also likely traveled mostly south of the lake, as indicated by very low amounts of Obsidian Cliff obsidian at the site. *National Park Service photo.*

The southwestern lakeshore appears to have been somewhat of a multiuse area for Native American tribes from the south, west, and north. The West Thumb of Yellowstone Lake appears to have seen active use by a variety of tribes, perhaps including those from the south (e.g., Shoshone), the north (e.g., Crow, Blackfeet), and the west (e.g., Shoshone and Nez Perce). Obsidian Cliff obsidian is among the more common obsidians at sites in the West Thumb area, but significant quantities of Absaroka cherts and Jackson-area obsidians are also present at West Thumb sites, suggesting multiple points of origin for Native Americans that camped there in the past.

These generalizations of lake use apply only to the recent past. As we go farther back in time, linking sites to tribes becomes very difficult, if not impossible, largely because of the similar types of material culture of Native American peoples across the region. In chapter 8 of the book, I discuss in more depth the longevity of Native American tribes in Yellowstone.

THE SUBSISTENCE SYSTEMS OF
NATIVE AMERICANS AT YELLOWSTONE LAKE

Another major question for park archaeologists is: How can we better understand the hunting, fishing, and gathering systems and the seasonality of Yellowstone Lake use by prehistoric Native Americans? In the 1980s, archaeologists from the National Park Service were the first to speculate as to the function of the lake in the prehistoric settlement and subsistence systems in the precontact period. They were mainly trying to figure out during which seasons Native Americans used the lake area. Those researchers proposed that the lake was used during the winter to hunt animals at volcanic hot spots or, alternatively, during the spring to fish for cutthroat trout as they ran up the lake's tributaries to spawn. However, their limited data resulted in inconclusive results. Their studies found no faunal remains to indicate winter hunting, nor fish remains to indicate spring fishing. Regardless, the researchers indicate that the locations of the hunting sites near thermal features and near stream confluences confirm their interpretations. In addition, they cite the presence of "notched flakes" as indication that Native Americans produced wooden sticks to be used for fishing. No detailed descriptions or illustrations of the notched flakes were provided, nor were blood residue analyses performed to confirm or refute the woodworking and fishing hypotheses.

Nabokov and Loendorf's work suggests that the various Native American groups that used the lake incorporated a wide variety of subsistence strategies in their survival repertoire. Various tribes hunted and gathered many mammals and plants. However, fishing appears to have been uncommon for tribes at the lake, despite the abundance of fish. Among the tribes, the Shoshone and Bannock are perhaps the only groups to have used the lake for fishing (if any did at all). In their 2004 book *Restoring a Presence*, Nabokov and Loendorf (on page 174) report that "[the Northern Shoshone] fished in Yellowstone Lake" although details and specific ethnographic accounts of fishing at the lake are not provided. Julian Steward's 1941 ethnographic report indicates that the Shoshone and Bannock fished extensively in the spring, mostly using brush dams and weirs. Shoshone and Bannock legends describe how coyote spilled mother earth's basket of fish (interpreted to be Yellowstone Lake), forming the various inland northwest river systems and establishing that the Shoshone were well aware of fish in Yellowstone Lake.

Therefore, since the Shoshone fished and were aware that the lake contains fish, it is reasonable to assume that the Shoshone fished at Yellowstone Lake. This activity likely occurred in spring, sometime between May through July, depending on the timing of the lake thaw and the spring fish runs up creeks. Nabokov and Loendorf's informants, including Dick Washakie (son of the Shoshone Chief Washakie), and early ethnographer Ake Hultkrantz, confirm that both the Northern and Lemhi Shoshone fished a lot and that there were no magical restrictions or other social limitations on who could fish, as there were with hunting activities. As with many hunter-gatherer groups, the Shoshone use a male-female division of labor that limits the role of women in hunting, whereas fishing does not have such restrictions.

Nabokov and Loendorf, however, do not provide specific ethnographic accounts of the Shoshone fishing at Yellowstone Lake, only saying that the Shoshone were known to have fished. The ethnographic data rule out fishing by both the Blackfeet and Crow at the lake, both of which focused on hunted and gathered resources, such as bison and camas, in their diets. Thus if the lake was used for fishing, it was by the Shoshone and Bannock in the spring, at least in recent history.

If there is some question as to the extent of Native American fishing at Yellowstone Lake, ecological data fully support the viability of hunting and gathering at the lake in recent history. Ethnographic accounts of recent use of the Yellowstone region include the collection of a wide variety of plants, including roots, seeds, and nuts. For the Shoshone, this plant material traditionally accounted for 30 to 70 percent of their diet. Ethnobotanical studies have identified more than 1,200 species of plants around Yellowstone Lake and vicinity, many of which are edible and/or have medicinal qualities. Blue camas bulb was especially used by the Bannock and Shoshone; it is one of the key edible plant species present today in the lake's shoreline meadows. Other researchers in Yellowstone speculate that camas was likely the most important spring root crop for Native Americans at Yellowstone Lake and vicinity.

Mammal hunting was also vital to lake area subsistence during recent history. As noted above, more than 60 species of mammals inhabit the lake's environs, including elk, bison, deer, bear, rabbit, and sheep, all of which were hunted. Bears are still active at the lake, although Nabokov and Loendorf do not provide data by which to address Native American bear hunting in the Yellowstone uplands. Bear hunting is common to a host of northern-latitude hunter-gatherer groups across the globe, including the regionally pertinent Cree in the northwestern Great Plains. All of these hunter-gatherers, including those from Asia, Europe, and the Americas, hunted bear (grizzly and black) in the late winter and early spring. During the spring, with snow still on the ground, bears emerging from hibernation were easier targets as they lounged outside of their dens. Dens were typically marked by hunters in the fall and winter or were otherwise located by hunters, who would then return in the early spring.

It is certainly reasonable to speculate that Native Americans in prehistory were attracted to Yellowstone Lake and its surrounding environs to hunt bear. The lake does not thaw completely until late May or early June. And so bear hunters likely were at the lake at a time when ice was still thick enough to walk on to reach the islands (all of which have archaeological sites) between January and early May.

In support of this supposition, Yellowstone National Park's bear management officer told me that he has observed bears on three islands and recorded one (Stevenson Island) with a bear hibernation den. The hunting of hibernating bears on the islands certainly would have encouraged native hunters to walk across early spring ice, especially if the hunter had pre-scouted the presence of a den. This supposition could easily explain the presence of archaeological sites on the lake's islands and would not require construction of boats to make the trip.

ARCHAEOLOGICAL EVIDENCE FOR HUNTING, GATHERING, AND FISHING AT YELLOWSTONE LAKE

Paul Sanders from the University of Wyoming has explored the seasonal use of the park by Native Americans within the nearby Hayden Valley, just north of the lake along the upper Yellowstone River Valley. Following the work of Ann Johnson at the Osprey Beach site at Yellowstone Lake, Sanders suggests only warm-season use of the higher-elevation portions of the Yellowstone Plateau, including Yellowstone Lake, with movement downslope into lower-elevation river valleys in winter. Sanders also refutes the earlier speculation for fishing, suggesting that "although preservation of fish bones is a problem, fishing-related artifacts (e.g., net weights or sinkers) have not been clearly identified at any site in the lake area or upper Yellowstone River."

More recently, archaeologists Ann Johnson and Brian Reeves have speculated that the lake was exclusively used during warm months because of the lack of available resources at the lake in winter. However, they also fail to provide information to support these ideas, admitting in their site report on the Osprey Beach site, "We have not found any seasonal indicators for sites around the lake."

Because of the intense winters and deep snow, most interpretations of Yellowstone seasonality posit a late spring to early summer start of the tribal-use cycle. However, I think individuals traveled to the lake earlier in the seasonal cycle, perhaps in March or April. These early trips to the lake were likely oriented around finding possible bear dens on the islands of Yellowstone Lake or in the hills above the lake. At the same time, these intrepid winter travelers surely scouted snow conditions to estimate the timing of plant availability and even perhaps the timing of cutthroat trout runs up creeks.

Excavation of numerous archaeological sites at the lake also provides good data by which to interpret how Yellowstone Lake was used in the past. Analysis of animal and plant remains, as well as protein-residue analysis of stone tools, provides insight into the nature of fishing, hunting, and gathering at Yellowstone Lake. Subsistence information has been recovered at 22 sites at Yellowstone Lake, including 13 excavated by University of Montana crews and 9 excavated by others. The sites are in all areas of the lake and date to a variety of time periods.

Based on animal bones and protein residue on stone tools excavated at archaeological sites, elk, bison, deer, bear, sheep, beaver, rabbit, cat, and squirrel were hunted by Native Americans at the lake in the past (figure 4.11). Animal, or faunal, remains are rare at Yellowstone Lake sites because the highly acidic soils deteriorate bone quickly. In fact, only four archaeological sites have yielded identifiable bone fragments at lake area archaeological sites. The Late Prehistoric Windy Bison site is located on the northeast-

FIGURE 4.11 Archaeological sites at Yellowstone Lake reveal bone and protein residues that indicate the types of animals hunted by Native Americans, including bison. *Neal Herbert photo, National Park Service*

ern lakeshore near Steamboat Point. This site yielded the remains of bison, elk, and sheep during excavations by Kenneth Cannon in the early 1990s. Unidentifiable bone fragments (possibly bison) were also found at the Donner site in a Middle Archaic occupation on the southeast arm of the lake. In 2016, my crew from the University of Montana also recovered a large bison leg bone dated to about 800 years ago in association with obsidian flakes eroding from the edge of Dot Island in the middle of Yellowstone Lake. One of the obsidian flakes was sourced to Bear Gulch in Idaho, while another was sourced to Obsidian Cliff. Finally, in 2014, my crew from the University of Montana recovered an elk toe bone from near a Late Archaic hearth dated to 2,000 years ago. This site was located on the Flat Mountain Arm of the lake, a few miles east of the West Thumb.

In addition to animal remains, 13 lake area sites have yielded lithic artifacts with positive blood protein signatures. Fish was identified on a single flake from an unknown north shore site. The fish species was identified as rainbow trout, not native to the lake. I interpret this to mean that someone used the flake to process rainbow trout somewhere else and carried the tool to the lake, or the flake may have been contaminated by one of the site excavators who fished for rainbow trout recently and touched the flake. Of the dozens of lake area tools tested so far for proteins, no others have yielded positive signatures for fish.

Deer protein was identified on tools at six lake area sites, with bear identified at five sites. Rabbit was identified at four sites, with three each of bovine (bison), cat (bobcat, lynx, or cougar), and bighorn sheep. Dog (coyote, fox, or wolf) was identified at two sites, with rat (squirrel) and guinea pig (probably skunk or beaver) also identified at single sites each. These protein identifications suggest a diverse hunting strategy at the lake, with the lithics dating from the Paleoindian to Late Prehistoric periods (9,500 to 300 years ago). The presence of bear protein on lithics from five lake area sites supports the hypothesis of active bear hunting at Yellowstone Lake in prehistory. That evidence also supports the idea of early spring trips to the lake by Native American hunters looking for bears waking up from hibernation.

Ethnobotanical plant remains and plant pollen have been identified at seven Yellowstone Lake sites, all excavated by my team from the University of Montana between 2009 and 2016. These plant species include buckwheat, goosefoot, sagebrush, Jacob's ladder, sedge, grass, sunflower, lily, and bitterroot. These species have edible and/or medicinal qualities and support the warm-season model of lake use because of their ripeness between May and September. Features in which these plants were found date variably to the Early Archaic, Middle Archaic, Late Archaic, and Late Prehistoric, suggesting long and consistent use of plants by lake area hunter-gatherers during the most recent 8,000 years of prehistory at a minimum.

Most significant in the subsistence data is the lack of any positive identification of fish remains or proteins on any of the tested materials at the dozens of sites studied at the lake. Presumably, this means that Native Americans did not fish at the lake very much, perhaps because of the abundance and ubiquitous availability of many other types of animals and plants.

In 2015, one of my University of Montana students, Cathy Jo Beecher, reviewed the results of our archaeological studies at Yellowstone Lake with the goal to establish whether whole families, including women and children, were at the lake in the past or whether the lake was only the domain of widely mobile male hunting parties. The analysis of botanical remains was conducted by our team's ethnobotanist, Jannifer Gish. As shown in figure 4.12, Beecher's analysis of the plant remains and feature types concluded that women (and presumably their children) accompanied men on their journeys to the lake.

In archaeological features at the lake, we found the remains of sagebrush leaves, which she thinks might have been used by women in a tea that helped with menstrual issues. She also notes that the presence of juniper in archaeological features may indicate that women collected the plant to use in a tea that helped with childbirth. We also found pine needles in some of the site features, which were used by tribal women to help deliver the placenta after childbirth. Finally, one of the site fire features that dated to the Late Prehistoric period contained mustard family plant remains, which were occasionally used by Native American women to end pregnancy, but were more commonly used as a flavoring in cooking.

FIGURE 4.12 A variety of plants were used by Native Americans at Yellowstone Lake for food, medicine, and spiritual purposes. *Data from Cathy Jo Beecher's University of Montana master's thesis (2015).*

Yellowstone Plants Used by Native Americans

FOOD/COOKING	MEDICINAL	OTHER PLANT USES
Nightshade	Willow	**Sunflower** (adornment/anointing oil)
Prickly pear	Subalpine fir	**Sorrel** (yellow dye)
Pine (ponderosa/lodgepole)	Sagebrush	**Prickly pear** (dye fixing agent)
Cottonwood	Juniper	**Pine** (glue, hair pomade, torches, tipi poles)
Goosefoot	Aspen	
Arrowleaf balsam root	Wild strawberry	**Cottonwood** (scent, firewood, dyes, paint)
Pine nut	Sunflower	**Willow** (ceremonial, adornment)
Spruce	Sorrel (*Rumex*)	**Subalpine fir** (incense, hair tonic, perfume, deodorizer, ceremonial)
Subalpine fir	Yellowstone whitlow grass (*Draba*)	
Jacob's ladder	Nightshade fruit	**Spruce** (incense, smudging, basketry)
Geranium	Prickly pear	**Alder** (dyes, hair dye)
Aspen	Pine	**Sagebrush** (incense, ceremonial, paintbrush, adornment, firewood)
Oak	Cottonwood	
Draba-type mustard	Arrowleaf balsam root	**Juniper** (incense, firewood, ceremonial)
Parsley	Pine nut	**Parsley** (incense, hide preparation, ceremonial)
Wild mint	Spruce	
Groundcherry	Alder	**Wild mint** (perfume, incense, aphrodisiac, insect repellent)
Wild strawberry	Jacob's ladder	
Sunflower	Parsley (family)	
Sorrel (*Rumex*)	Wild mint	

Data from Beecher, 2015

DID NATIVE AMERICANS USE BOATS AT YELLOWSTONE LAKE?

Another fishing-related research question that needs answering is: Were canoes or other types of boats used by Native Americans at Yellowstone Lake? In their 2004 report on Osprey Beach, Johnson, Reeves, and Shortt explain how the lake's islands contain archaeological sites, pushing forward the notion that Native Americans used canoes to access the islands. They state that "although direct evidence is lacking, we suggest seasonally resident Cody bands at Yellowstone Lake . . . probably fished, fowled, and perhaps used skin-covered boats on Yellowstone Lake." Their speculation of boat use is further confirmed in illustrations produced for the Late Paleoindian Osprey Beach site by Johnson for public presentations on that important site. But she largely disregards access to the islands when the lake was frozen because she believes that the frigid winter conditions were too harsh for Native Americans.

Boats certainly would have facilitated travel around the lake's shores and to its islands, as well as facilitated the transport of lithic raw material and other goods to the various lake areas. The ethnohistoric record provides little information by which to address this question or whether the lake's shores and islands were accessed only by pedestrian hunter-gatherers.

The ethnographic and ethnohistoric literature is deficient of any accounts of Native American boat use at Yellowstone Lake. Norris's 1880 superintendent report indicates the casual observation of a dugout canoe downriver on the Yellowstone River (well downstream of the lake) and another on Beaverdam Creek near the southeast corner of the lake. However, these canoes are just as likely to have been used by historic period trappers and do not necessarily support the hypothesis of Native American boat use at the lake. Nevertheless, among the tribes that used the lake, the Shoshone are known to have used skin boats (but not canoes) in their collection of riparian resources in lower-elevation lakes of the Great Basin (south of Yellowstone), as recorded by the anthropologist Julian Steward. There are no ethnographic accounts available to suggest that any of the tribes that used Yellowstone Lake had canoes.

If boats, especially canoes, were built and used at Yellowstone Lake, we should expect to see evidence of their manufacture in the archaeological record. But in all the excavations by the University of Montana around the shores of the lake, only one woodworking tool was recovered. On the southwestern shore of the lake, Ann Johnson and her colleagues noted the presence of two adzes from the Osprey Beach site, although it is unclear whether wear indicated woodworking for those tools. I am unaware of any other lake area sites yielding adzes or heavy-duty

LOCATION OF ARCHAEOLOGICAL SITES AT YELLOWSTONE LAKE

Using geographic information systems, two of my University of Montana students—Jordan McIntyre and Matthew Nelson—have studied the distribution of archaeological sites at Yellowstone Lake based on their locations relative to current and past habitats, paleo-shorelines, and proximity to stream confluences. Both students produced excellent studies of site locations at Yellowstone Lake to better understand how Native Americans used the lake in the past. Analysis of site locations relative to modern and past ecological zones and habitats is helpful in understanding the function of the lake in settlement and subsistence systems. These two students compared site locations relative to modern forest and open and riparian habitats. They also compared site locations by time period relative to pollen types attributable to open and riparian habitats for those periods.

Their studies show that open meadows on lakeshore terraces (such as those shown in figure 4.5 near Lake Lodge) were the most popular locations for Native Americans to build their camps at the lake. Statistical evaluation of those site location data confirms that open and riparian habitats predict prehistoric archaeological site locations for a minimum of 83 percent (Late Archaic period) to a maximum of 94 percent (Late Prehistoric period), with a mean prediction rate of 86 percent. This result is a very high success rate, which suggests that Native Americans in prehistory deferentially selected open and riparian habitats at Yellowstone Lake.

The students also evaluated whether site locations correlated well with proximity to streams. If so, it might indicate that fishing was a key factor in site placement. In other words, if sites were near the confluence of the lake with streams, it might indicate that Native Americans camped there to exploit trout in spring as they spawned up tributary streams. Their data do not show a strong correlation between stream proximity and site location, indicating that Native Americans did not fish extensively at the lake.

woodworking tools. If boats were utilized, it does not appear that they were of the dugout canoe variety, but could have possibly been of the skin-boat (umiak) variety, as were known to have been used by the Shoshone in the Great Basin. Since the Shoshone frequented Yellowstone Lake, it is conceivable that they used skin boats (but not likely canoes) there as well. However, no boats or boat parts have ever been identified to date at any lake area site.

Stone artifact data can be used to evaluate boat use as well. Presumably, if boats were used to transport people around the lakeshore, it is reasonable that they would have also transported stone by boat to save energy and maximize stone material availability in tool manufacture. Stone can serve as ballast in boats. In the often rough waters of Yellowstone Lake, ballast is essential to keep boats afloat. So my prediction is that amounts of rock at sites should be more or less similar around the different areas of the lakeshore if boats were used for travel, assuming that Native Americans would have carried lots of stone with them as ballast. In contrast, if foot travel was emphasized, I predict that we should see significant reductions in the amount of stone in different areas of the lake. Under the walking option, Native Americans would have also reduced their stone tool kits to minimum levels to save energy as they walked around the lake.

In summary, the stone tool data do not support a hypothesis that boats were used by Native Americans at the lake. The best example of this is to compare stone tools at sites on two areas of the lake that aren't that far apart, the northwest (near Fishing Bridge) and southwest shores (along the West Thumb). These areas are about 10 mi. (15 km) apart by boat, or about 30 mi. (45 km) by foot along the undulating shoreline. If boats were used anywhere, this would presumably be the place since it would have saved a great deal of time and effort. So we should see similar amounts of stone artifacts in the two areas, with the distance falloff curve flat. In contrast, if humans walked between the two areas, we would expect there to be a significant falloff in the amount of stone at sites in the two areas. The major presumption here is that the north shore sites are closest to the main source of material in the area, Obsidian Cliff. So, presumably, Native Americans traveling from Obsidian Cliff to the lake would have stopped first at Yellowstone Lake's north shore. We should expect to see fairly large amounts of Obsidian Cliff obsidian at sites on the north shore. And if canoes were used, we should see similar quantities of stone at sites on the southwestern shore; but if people walked between the two areas, we should expect to see a large drop-off in the amount of stone between Fishing Bridge and the West Thumb. Logically, people would have carried less stone with them if they had walked than if they had taken a boat.

On the northwest lakeshore from 2009 to 2012, the University of Montana excavated 70 1 m. sq. excavation units at seven sites, yielding 13,995 stone tools and flakes for a mean of 200 artifacts per excavation unit. On the southwest shore along the West Thumb and vicinity, archaeologists excavated 94 1 m. sq. excavation units at eight sites, revealing only 2,178 tools and flakes (with a mean of 23 artifacts per excavation unit). Both of these areas yielded Obsidian Cliff obsidian and/or cherts from northern lithic sources. Therefore, while people moved regularly between the northwest and southwest shores, the conservation of material (as shown in the reduced numbers of artifacts) supports the hypothesis that they traveled on foot, rather than by boat, to get from Fishing Bridge to the West Thumb.

The overall character of all sites along the north shore of Yellowstone Lake is of lithic abundance, whereas on the southwest shore it is one of lithic scarcity. The amount of stone recovered during excavations at sites on the south shore is about 42 lithics per excavation square (5,557 lithics; 131 1×1m test units; 11 sites) compared to 164 lithics per excavation square at sites on the north shore (18,809 lithics; 115 1×1m test units; 13 sites). The sheer volume of lithics from test units on the north shore (18,809 lithics) compared to the south shore (5,557 lithics) is even more striking considering that 16 additional excavation squares were conducted on the south shore compared to the north.

The weights of artifacts are also significantly different for those found on the northwest and southwest shore sites. Artifacts at north shore sites are bigger than those at south shore sites, supporting the hypothesis that south shore hunter-gatherers used and produced fewer lithics of smaller sizes, likely to conserve material as they walked around the lakeshore.

These stone artifact data suggest a significant falloff in lithic use in locations farther from sources, suggesting that Native Americans walked around the lakeshore and did not actively travel along the lakeshore using boats. I propose that this pattern of stone tool use supports my supposition that boats were not used by hunter-gatherers at the lake. If they were, such significant falloffs in the amounts and weights of lithic material use would not be evident since Native Americans would simply have filled their boats with stone material as they canoed around the lake.

CHAPTER FIVE

RIVERS

TO GET TO YELLOWSTONE LAKE, the first Native Americans walked along the more than 40 creek and river drainages that fill the lake from the surrounding hills and mountains. The most prominent routes to the lake include the Yellowstone River on both the north and south ends of the lake. On the north end of the lake, Pelican Creek also provided a prominent corridor toward the Lamar River. On the east shore of the lake, Clear Creek, Columbine Creek, and Rocky Creek all flow from Absaroka Mountain passes that likely helped Native Americans make their way to and from the Shoshone River and the Bighorn Basin of Wyoming. From the south near Jackson, Wyoming, the Snake River and its feeder streams, including the Lewis and Heart Rivers, led hunter-gatherers to the lake. And from the western hills along the Continental Divide, several small streams flow into the lake; following them, as well as numerous creeks and rivers, including Nez Perce Creek, the Firehole River, and, eventually, the Madison River, would have provided pathways toward the geyser basins.

Once on the plateau, Native Americans would have found Yellowstone Lake, Obsidian Cliff, and a host of other resources for their daily survival. For hunter-gatherers, the Yellowstone Plateau perhaps was a bit like Eden, a bucolic landscape with rich resources, at least during warm months. The high-elevation plateau, formed by the Rocky Mountains and active volcanism, provides the water for these creeks and rivers—thousands and thousands of gallons of the freshest,

▶ MAP 5.1 The rivers of Yellowstone

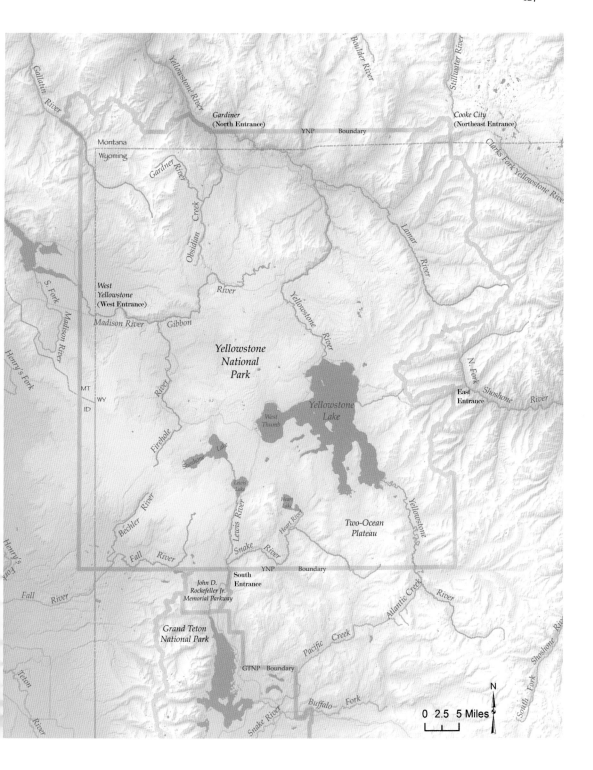

FIGURE 5.1 By traveling up the Snake River, seen here with the Tetons in the background, among hundreds of other water courses, Native Americans could reach the interior of Yellowstone country.

purest water found anywhere on Earth. The presence of such an enormous amount of vital freshwater must have also inspired Native Americans to journey to these areas.

The plethora of freshwater from Yellowstone's rivers and creeks eventually makes its way into the Atlantic and Pacific Oceans. For example, Flat Mountain, south of Yellowstone Lake, is situated on the Continental Divide, with water on its south slope draining into the Snake River and on to the Pacific Ocean, while streams on its north face drain into Yellowstone Lake and eventually to the Atlantic Ocean.

The vast majority of the creeks and rivers in Yellowstone drain into the Gulf of Mexico and the Atlantic Ocean, including the Yellowstone River, Pelican Creek,

FIGURE 5.2 At Flat Mountain on the Continental Divide, water on the north slope of the mountain flows into Yellowstone Lake, the Yellowstone River, and ultimately, the Atlantic Ocean, and water on the south slope of the mountain flows into the Snake River drainage, the Columbia River, and finally, the Pacific Ocean.

the Lamar River, the Gallatin River, the Madison River, the Gibbon River, and the Firehole River. These rivers and creeks are north and east of the Continental Divide, which traverses the park across its southern tier, and all meander toward the Missouri River. Most of the creeks and rivers in the western and northwestern portion of the park fill drainage basins of either the Gallatin or Madison River, and join the Jefferson River to form the Missouri River near Three Forks, Montana.

In the northern and northeastern areas of the park, the creeks and rivers feed the Yellowstone River, which subsequently flows for 691 mi. (1,112 km) northward from the park to join the Missouri River just across the Montana state line near Williston, North Dakota. The Yellowstone River (figure 5.3) is the Lower 48's longest undammed river. From its headwaters in Three Forks, the Missouri River flows for 2,341 mi. (3,767 km) to join the Mississippi River just north of St. Louis, Missouri. The Mississippi then flows southward to the Gulf of Mexico and the Atlantic Ocean. It is amazing to think that the crystal clear waters of Yellowstone Lake, the Yellowstone River, the Madison River, and the steaming waters of the Firehole River all end up in the same place, thousands of miles away, near New Orleans, Louisiana.

South and west of the Continental Divide, in the southwestern corner of Yellowstone National Park, creeks and rivers are tributaries of the Snake River. The Snake River forms in the far southern portion of Yellowstone National Park and

FIGURE 5.3 The Yellowstone River flows out of Yellowstone National Park for over 690 miles to its confluence with the Missouri River in North Dakota.

the adjacent Teton National Forest. Dozens of creeks drain southerly and westerly from the Continental Divide to form the Snake River, which flows westerly and then southerly toward the South Entrance of the park. The Snake River flows for more than 1,000 mi. (1,600 km) through Idaho to its confluence with the Columbia River near Kennewick, Washington. The Columbia River in turn flows westerly to the Pacific Ocean near Astoria, Oregon.

The headwaters of both the Yellowstone and Snake Rivers are in an area of southern Yellowstone National Park aptly dubbed the Two Ocean Plateau. There, you can stand in water that will be making its way to two different destinations.

Native Americans used Yellowstone's rivers as their lifelines, both as travel routes and as sources of freshwater. Literally thousands of archaeological sites along these waterways mark locations where people camped in Yellowstone over the past 11,000 years.

THE NATIVE CUTTHROAT TROUT IN YELLOWSTONE LAKE

Yellowstone's mammals—bears, bison, moose, elk, cougars, and wolves, among dozens of others—also used (and still use) the park's creeks and rivers as a means of passage and a source of freshwater. Birds flock to the shores of the creeks and rivers, with bald eagles among the most spectacular, to exploit the food resources of the waterways. Abundant fish inhabit the rivers and lakes of Yellowstone as well. In total, 11 native species of fish and 5 non-native fish species are present in the park. Among these species of fish, however, only 2—Yellowstone cutthroat trout (*Oncorhynchus clarkii bouvieri*) and longnose dace *(Rhinichthys cataractae)*—are native to Yellowstone Lake (figure 5.4). It took a great deal of effort for these fish to make it to Yellowstone Lake. Just as humans walked up the creeks and rivers to the lake over the past 11,000 years, these 2 species of fish managed to jump and squirm their way up hundreds of miles of creeks and rivers to become Yellowstone Lake's only native fish species.

Yellowstone cutthroat trout is the most significant of the native fish species in Yellowstone National Park. These trout are an important resource

FIGURE 5.4 Yellowstone Lake is a refuge for a significant population of native cutthroat trout. All "cutties," such as this one caught by Bureau of Land Management archaeologist C. J. Truesdale, must be released immediately upon capture at the lake.

for a variety of birds and mammals that feed on them, and today fishers come to the lake to catch them more than any other fish. Early historic accounts describe abundant cutthroat trout in the lake and in the feeder streams of the lake. Fish biologists report that this species in prehistory was widely distributed across the Snake, Yellowstone, and even the Columbia River basins; but as a result of competition and other threats, its range has been reduced to its current area of the Snake River north of Shoshone Falls, Idaho, and west of the mouth of the Tongue River in Montana, with Yellowstone Lake as the center.

At a conference at Mammoth Hot Springs in 2012, I gave a presentation on Native American cutthroat trout fishing at the lake. I stated that it does not appear from the archaeological record that Native Americans fished for cutthroat trout at the lake. Archaeological excavations have been extensive at Yellowstone Lake, and not a single site has yielded any evidence for fishing: no fish lures, fish weirs, fish protein on any stone tools, or fish bones. Nor are there any known ethnographic accounts of Native Americans fishing at the lake. Based on this information, I conclude that Native Americans didn't fish that much (if at all) at Yellowstone Lake.

Since the conference presentation, I began to wonder just how long cutthroat trout have been in the lake and how they got there. I thought perhaps the reason that Native Americans did not fish for them is because the species has not been in the lake very long, so I reviewed what fish biologists have documented on this issue. I discovered that the fish biologists don't really know, except in a general way. Genetic testing and visual comparisons show a clear relationship between Snake River fine-spotted cutthroat trout (*Oncorhynchus clarkii behnkei*) and Yellowstone Lake cutthroat trout. Research by the Idaho Department of Fish and Game showed significant genetic similarities between Yellowstone cutthroat trout and the Snake River fine-spotted cutthroat trout, indicating an ancestral relationship between the two species.

INVASIVE LAKE TROUT ·

Yellowstone cutthroat trout are endangered in Yellowstone and all surrounding regions. Their overall numbers have declined dramatically in the past century, especially at Yellowstone Lake. Three other species of fish were introduced to the lake in the 1920s: the redside shiner (*Richardsonius balteatus*), lake chub (*Couesius plumbeus*), and longnose sucker (*Catostomus catostomus*). Another non-native species, lake trout (*Salvelinus namaycush*), was introduced to Yellowstone Lake in the 1980s, and these large lake trout outcompeted the native cutthroat trout to the extent that they now far outnumber them. Significantly, native Yellowstone cutthroat trout comprise a large portion of the invasive lake trout's diet. Yellowstone fish biologists estimated that more than 40 native cutthroat trout would be saved by the elimination of one lake trout.

So to rejuvenate the native trout populations, since the mid-1990s the park has funded a large effort to eradicate the invasive lake trout. With gillnetting, the National Park Service has removed nearly two million lake trout to date, resulting in annual increases in the cutthroat trout populations. The goal of the park is to completely eradicate the invasive lake trout so that the native cutthroat trout populations can rebound to their early twentieth-century levels.

But these studies do not indicate when Yellowstone cutthroat trout emerged as a separate species from the Snake River trout. One early effort at explaining this was by Oliver Cope in 1957. Based mainly on geography, he suggested that the most likely origin was from the south and west of Yellowstone Lake in the Two Ocean Plateau. Matthew Campbell and colleagues from the Idaho Department of Fish and Game confirm a southern origin for Yellowstone cutthroat trout, stating that a northern origin via the northern Yellowstone River was impossible because of several large falls. This southern, Snake River origin for Yellowstone cutthroat trout makes sense given regional geography, DNA similarities between Snake River and Yellowstone Lake trout, as well as the visual features of the two species; but Cope and Campbell do not provide a timeline for this origin. Both concede that it was after the retreat of glacial ice from the Yellowstone region approximately 12,000 years ago, but they provide no more specific dates.

Robert Behnke's 1992 study of cutthroat trout in western North America remains the most significant study on the timing of this origin. He estimates that Yellowstone Lake cutthroat trout originated from the Snake River population sometime after the last glacial period. After the melting of the mile-high glaciers at Yellowstone Lake 12,000 to 11,000 years ago, the existing river and creek systems eventually formed their current trajectories in southern Yellowstone. Following Cope's earlier suggestion, Behnke proposed that Yellowstone cutthroat trout derived from the Snake River cutthroat trout population that existed in the Snake River drainage south of the glaciers prior to 12,000 years ago.

In one area of Teton National Forest, just south of Yellowstone National Park, the headwaters for the Snake and Yellowstone River systems are connected at the Two Ocean Plateau. Behnke hypothesizes that after deglaciation, Snake River cutthroat trout eventually moved upstream to the Two Ocean Plateau and the Continental Divide. Here, they entered North Two Ocean Creek and spawned there. North Two Ocean Creek splits, with one of its forks heading westward into Pacific Creek and another splitting to the east into Atlantic Creek. A portion of these early offspring likely swam downstream in North Two Ocean Creek and returned to Pacific Creek and the Snake River, while still others swam eastward into Atlantic Creek. From Atlantic Creek, these adventurous early Yellowstone cutthroat trout swam northeasterly for approximately 9 mi. (14 km) into the Yellowstone River and then northerly for another 30 mi. (48 km) to reach Yellowstone Lake.

While Behnke is likely correct about this origin story for Yellowstone Lake cutthroat trout, the exact timing of this migration event is uncertain. Campbell's genetic studies indicate that the Yellowstone Lake cutthroat trout have been genetically isolated from the Snake River trout for at least a few thousand years, although estimates are vague regarding the precise timeline. It is clear that this migration route occurred after 12,000 years ago (with the melting of the glaciers) and probably even after 10,000 years ago when the current stream systems became established (although the precise dates for the formation of these Two Ocean Plateau streams is uncertain as well). Then, it would have taken time for the fish to eventually make their way from the Snake River, to Pacific Creek, to North Two Ocean Creek, to Atlantic Creek, to the Yellowstone River, and finally to Yellowstone Lake. How long did this take? Hundreds of years? Thousands of years?

At this point, no one seems to know the answer to these questions. But perhaps the lack of evidence of Native American fishing for cutthroat trout at the lake provides some indication that this migration was much more recent than anyone thinks. If Yellowstone cutthroat trout were abundant in the past, it seems likely that Native Americans would have fished for them and that we'd find some evidence for such fishing in the archaeological record. But since no such evidence exists for now, perhaps by the time the cutthroat trout reached the lake several thousand years ago, humans already had a well-established diet based on the collection of bitterroot, pine nuts, and camas, as well as the hunting of bison, bear, elk, and mountain sheep.

NATIVE AMERICAN USE OF THE SNAKE RIVER IN YELLOWSTONE

Much like cutthroat trout migrated northward up the Snake River to get to Yellowstone Lake, Native Americans probably traveled a similar route on their way to Yellowstone Lake in prehistory. Given the evidence of early archaeological sites on the Pacific Coast of North America as early as 12,000 years ago, we have reasonably hypothesized that early Native Americans traveled up the Columbia River to the Snake River and eventually to Yellowstone. The recovery of a Clovis projectile point on the south shore of Yellowstone Lake has indicated that Native Americans ventured to the park as early as 11,000 years ago. The fact that the Clovis point was on the southern lakeshore and that it was produced from obsidian from the Jackson, Wyoming, area has indicated that these Clovis people migrated from the south up the Snake River and perhaps up the Lewis or Heart Rivers, or even the Pacific and Atlantic Creeks, to get to the lake.

We know that Native Americans enjoyed living in the southern portion of Yellowstone along the Snake and Lewis Rivers by 9,500 years ago. In 2014 and 2015, my team of archaeologists conducted an archaeological expedition to look

FIGURE 5.5 My University of Montana team surveyed the headwaters of the Snake and Lewis Rivers in 2014, looking for evidence of Native American archaeological sites. Justin Pfau (far left) wrote his master's thesis about the archaeological survey results.

for prehistoric Native American sites in the headwaters region of the Snake and Lewis Rivers in southern Yellowstone Park. In 2014, we forded the Lewis River just north of the park's South Entrance Ranger Station (figure 5.5). With water rushing forcefully, we locked arms and crossed from the west shore to the east shore of the Lewis River, near its confluence with the Snake River. We then walked north along the bank of the Snake River. There we found dozens of archaeological sites that showed active use of this area by Native Americans in the past.

Among the artifacts we found were three Paleoindian projectile points, including a 10,500-year-old Goshen point (see figure 2.11). Two of the points were found at a site near the confluence of the Snake River with the Lewis River, while another was found upriver along the Lewis River near Lewis Falls. One of these three points, a red stone projectile point, was produced from Park Point obsidian, which has its geologic source several miles upstream of the site on the Snake River. We know because several days later, we surveyed farther upstream and found the obsidian source.

All along both banks of the Snake and Lewis Rivers, we found evidence of prehistoric Native American sites. Most flat terrace landforms along both rivers contained significant prehistoric sites. One of the largest of the sites was approximately 10 mi. (15 km) upstream from the park's South Entrance. There, near the confluence of Coulter Creek, Wolverine Creek, and the Snake River, we found a stone tool production site, the location where Native Americans produced hundreds of stone projectile points, knives, and scrapers. Among the lithic raw materials from these sites were a wide variety of cherts and orthoquartzites: Obsidian Cliff obsidian accounted for only 9 percent of the obsidian artifacts and less than 5 percent of all stone artifacts found there. Instead, as we witnessed on the southern shore of Yellowstone Lake, Native Americans in this southern portion of Yellowstone clearly originated from the south, preferring to use obsidians from along the Snake River and its tributaries. They also used fair amounts of obsidian from western sources such as Bear Gulch, Idaho, about 60 mi. (100 km) to the west.

Our archaeological survey also included the Lewis River, a tributary of the Snake. The Lewis River has its headwaters in Lewis and Shoshone Lakes, approximately 18 mi. (30 km) north of its southern terminus near the South Entrance of Yellowstone National Park. My crew and I surveyed both sides of the Lewis River, including the extremely rugged, steep Lewis Canyon below the beautiful Lewis Falls. We found a large concentration of archaeological sites near the Lewis River's southern terminus at the Snake River, as well as a group of sites on the northern end of the canyon just south of Lewis Falls.

At one of these sites, we found the 10,500-year-old Goshen projectile point (figure 2.11, bottom), showing Native American use of the Lewis River as a travel route since the Late Pleistocene. This Goshen point was produced from Teton Pass obsidian, which has its source to the south near Jackson, Wyoming. The linking of

▶ FIGURE 5.6 Native Americans walked past Lewis Falls to get from the Lewis River to nearby Lewis Lake.

this site at Lewis Falls to the Jackson-area source is still another indication that these first Native Americans traveled from the south along the Snake and Lewis Rivers to get into Yellowstone.

NATIVE AMERICAN USE OF THE YELLOWSTONE RIVER

In addition to the Snake River, Native Americans also utilized the Yellowstone River as a major travel corridor during the past 11,000 years. Hunter-gatherers traveled along the banks of the Yellowstone River to get to Yellowstone Lake and as a stepping-stone to reach other destinations such as Obsidian Cliff. The Crow, among other tribes, referred to the Yellowstone River as the Elk River, and that name is seen on some early maps of the region. According to park historian Lee Whittlesey, Lewis and Clark are largely given credit for popularizing the name to the Yellowstone River during their 1805–1806 expedition in the region. While those early explorers never set foot in what would become Yellowstone National Park, they were among the first European Americans to explore the Yellowstone River and its major tributaries north and east of the park. Just northeast of the park, one of the feeder streams is dubbed the Clark's Fork of the Yellowstone River, so named by the early explorer.

As with the Snake River, the headwaters of the Yellowstone River are in the far southern reaches of Yellowstone National Park. In this region of the park, often called the Thorofare, multiple creeks and streams flow from the slopes of the Absaroka Mountains and the Two Ocean Plateau to form the southern Yellowstone River. This portion of the river flows northward for 30 mi. (48 km) before it enters Yellowstone Lake. There has been very little if any archaeological research on this southern portion of the Yellowstone River. My crew and I examined the mouth of the river as it enters the lake and found abundant evidence of Native American use, and we found numerous prehistoric sites on the banks of creeks and streams and the Yellowstone River itself.

At the northern end of the lake, the Yellowstone River flows out at Fishing Bridge. Today, Fishing Bridge is a tourist location, with a store, restaurant, and campgrounds, and in the past it was a popular camping spot for Native Americans. Archaeological sites in this area yield more than 80 percent of their obsidian from Obsidian Cliff, which is about 25 mi. (40 km) to the northwest. Native Americans likely incorporated a trip to Fishing Bridge after they ventured to Obsidian Cliff, then worked their way back north along the banks of the Yellowstone River toward the Grand Canyon of the Yellowstone and the Gardiner area. The Fishing

Bridge area contains archaeological evidence of human occupation dating back at least 9,000 years. In 2010, my crew
and I recovered a mustard-yellow biface at a site near Fishing
Bridge (figure 5.7), proof that Late Paleoindian Cody Culture
Native Americans lived in this area.

Between 2009 and 2010, my University of Montana crew
excavated five different sites just south of Fishing Bridge. At
the nearby Fishing Bridge Point site, we excavated the earliest radiocarbon dated hearth at the lake. Dated to 6,000
years ago, this hearth is the only one uncovered from the
Early Archaic period in all of Yellowstone National Park.
During our work there, my crew collected nearly 11,000 artifacts and excavated 15 prehistoric Native American hearths.
Among the five sites, Fishing Bridge Point not only contained
the Early Archaic hearth, but also evidence of abundant use
of the area during the subsequent Middle Archaic, Late
Archaic, and Late Prehistoric periods.

FIGURE 5.7 The confluence
of the Yellowstone River
and Yellowstone Lake was a
popular camp area for Native
Americans for 9,500 years, as
evidenced by this Cody knife
found there by my University
of Montana crew in 2010.

Comparison of stone artifacts from the excavated Native
American hearths at Fishing Bridge Point shows that Native
American travel patterns changed during the prehistory of
the region. Obsidian Cliff was the dominant source during
the past 7,000 years, accounting for more than 90 percent of obsidian recovered
at the site. Use of dacite from near Ennis, Montana (5 percent), and Bear Gulch
obsidian (5 percent), 90 mi. (145 km) west is consistent (but low) during all occupations at Fishing Bridge. The Middle Archaic period occupations, around 3,000
years ago, witnessed the widest variety of obsidian use, with 12 percent of the Middle Archaic artifacts deriving from the Crescent H and Teton Pass obsidian sources
near Jackson, Wyoming. Overall, based on artifacts sourced from their fire pits, the
Middle Archaic Native Americans used the most diverse array of obsidian and dacite sources at Fishing Bridge, with artifacts deriving from Obsidian Cliff (north),
Crescent H (south), Teton Pass (south), and Bear Gulch (west) obsidian sources.

Based on data from Fishing Bridge, material use was most constricted during
the Early Archaic. Selected lithic materials were oriented to the north-northwest.
During the subsequent Middle and Late Archaic, a heightened use of Crescent Hill
chert (located about 30 mi./70 km, northwest) and obsidians to the south near
Jackson (about 90 mi./210 km, south) suggests a relaxation of the constricted lithic
use that characterized the Early Archaic. While Early Archaic Native Americans

FIGURE 5.8 Sites like this one near Fishing Bridge along the Yellowstone River indicate long-term use of the area by Native Americans for thousands of years.

used local materials oriented toward northwest Wyoming and southwest Montana, Middle Archaic Native Americans appear to have widened their material use patterns to include the Gardiner Valley to the north and the Snake River Valley to the south. A constriction of lithic raw material use once again occurred during the Late Prehistoric period, as evidenced by a nearly exclusive use of Obsidian Cliff obsidian. These variations in tool stone use over time provide a window into the travel and trade patterns of Native Americans at Fishing Bridge for the past 9,000 years.

We can also learn about the types of animals and plants that were hunted and gathered from the Fishing Bridge archaeological sites. While no animal remains were recovered at Fishing Bridge Point, analysis of protein residues on stone tools suggests utilization of a wide range of animals by Native Americans. Thirteen lithic artifacts from Fishing Bridge Point were subjected to protein residue analysis, including three each from the Late Prehistoric, Late Archaic, and Early Archaic occupations, and four from the Middle Archaic occupations, including each of the stone tools shown on the following page. Of the three Late Prehistoric tested artifacts, one Late Prehistoric Rose Spring arrow point (see figure 5.9, top row, center)

FIGURE 5.9 Protein residues on stone tools provide information on the types of animals hunted by Native Americans near Fishing Bridge. Bear, cat, deer, bison, and rabbit were all frequent targets.

tested positive for deer. One of the Late Archaic artifacts—a multipurpose cutting tool—revealed bovine (bison) protein while another tested positive for rabbit. The large Late Archaic (Hopewell-like) projectile point (see figure 5.9, upper left) was used to kill and/or butcher bear, cat, and deer.

A Middle Archaic knife dated to about 3,000 years ago tested positive for deer and dog, while still other Middle Archaic artifacts yielded protein signatures of deer and cat. Finally, three Early Archaic artifacts yielded positive results during protein residue analysis. One Obsidian Cliff Early Archaic projectile point tested positive for bison, while one Early Archaic projectile point fragment tested positive for bear. A large Early Archaic Obsidian Cliff stone cutting blade (see figure 5.9, lower left) tested positive for deer.

Analysis of pollen samples from archaeological features provides information on hunter-gatherer plant use around Fishing Bridge. At the Fishing Bridge Point site, use of grass is indicated by high pollen values within the Early Archaic feature. As such, not only was the general environment of Fishing Bridge Point character-ized by a grassy meadow setting inviting to bison, elk, and deer, but people at the lake also apparently harvested grasses for cultural purposes, such as use in cooking, production of hairbrushes and brooms, and ceremonies (e.g., smudging to purify the soul), suggesting a warm weather (spring or summer) occupation.

Without a doubt, the headwaters of the Yellowstone River in the area around Fishing Bridge was an important camp location for Native Americans. At least by historic times and likely much earlier, tribes that used this area probably included the Crow, Blackfeet, Shoshone, and Nez Perce, among others. These tribes have tra-ditional territories that intersect in the northern portion of Yellowstone National Park, including the area of the Yellowstone River.

THE MALIN CREEK SITE ON THE YELLOWSTONE RIVER

Farther downstream from Fishing Bridge and the Hayden Valley, below the Grand Canyon of the Yellowstone, archaeologists excavated one of the most important Yellowstone River sites, Malin Creek. This site is located about 3 mi. (5 km) east of Gardiner, Montana, upstream on the Yellowstone River near its confluence with Malin Creek. Extensive excavations at the site in the mid-2000s by Brian Vivian, Brian Reeves, and Ann Johnson showed that Native Americans camped at the site seven different times. The earliest occupations dated from 9,800 to 9,400 years ago and were associated with the Cody Culture, similar to those that lived at Yellowstone Lake and at the Horner site in Cody, Wyoming. The association of Native Americans on the Yellowstone River with those that lived at Yellowstone Lake indicates early travel routes between the regions dating back more than 9,000 years. Results of protein residue and faunal remains studies indicate that a diverse array of animals were hunted by Paleoindians along the Yellowstone River,

From Fishing Bridge, the Yellowstone River flows northward through LeHardy Rapids as it descends through the Yellowstone Plateau toward Gardiner, Montana. Significant archaeological sites have been found throughout the Hayden Valley portion of the Yellowstone River north of LeHardy Rapids. University of Wyoming archaeologist Paul Sanders has conducted archaeological work within the Hayden Valley north of Fishing Bridge. During this work, he identified a wide variety of Native American prehistoric sites dating back to the Paleoindian period (more than 8,000 years ago), with increasing use over time.

Sanders's archaeological crews recovered Paleoindian artifacts at 4 sites in the Hayden Valley, as well as Early Archaic artifacts from 3 sites dating from 8,000 to 5,000 years ago. Nine sites contained Middle Archaic artifacts (dating 5,000 to 3,000 years ago), 13 sites had Late Archaic artifacts (3,000 to 1,500 years ago), while 17 sites contained Late Prehistoric artifacts (1,500 to 300 years ago). Native Americans increased their use of the Hayden Valley over time, likely becoming more and more familiar with the area and its wealth of resources. The large herds of bison and elk, among other animals, probably were a significant draw for Native American hunters in the Hayden Valley.

FIGURE 5.10 The Hayden Valley was a popular area for Native Americans to hunt and gather along the Yellowstone River.

FIGURE 5.11 The Malin Creek site was used by Native Americans for thousands of years as a base camp for hunting and gathering along the Yellowstone River. *National Park Service photo.*

including bighorn sheep, bison, beaver or marmot, and small birds. Another Paleoindian occupation of the site indicated procurement of bison, deer, bear, and grouse.

While there was not an Early Archaic occupation at Malin Creek, the upper component of the site yielded projectile points and fire hearths that span the past 5,000 years of prehistory, including the Middle Archaic, Late Archaic, and Late Prehistoric periods. During that period, the site was transformed from a small hunting camp into a large base camp. From that campsite, Native Americans ventured up and down the Yellowstone River and its tributary streams to hunt and gather, bringing their catches back for processing at the site. The site was primarily used in the spring, as animals and people began to migrate from the low-elevation winter camps in the Gardiner Valley southward and upward into the Yellowstone Plateau and eventually to Yellowstone Lake. Further support for this spring occupation is the presence of a fish hook at the Malin Creek site, one of the few sites that indicate that Native Americans fished as part of their subsistence strategy along the Yellowstone River. Spring was likely an ideal time to fish for spawning cutthroat trout at Malin Creek. This is among the only sites anywhere in Yellowstone to show evidence of fishing. Remember that Yellowstone Lake has yielded no archaeological sites with such evidence.

The Malin Creek site along the Yellowstone River also yielded bear remains, including a bear carpal bone, a mandible, and an astragalus dated to about 8,800 years ago. A bear toe bone was also found at Malin Creek dating to 9,500 years ago, while a Cody Culture Scottsbluff point tested positive for bear protein. University of Montana archaeologist Michael Ciani interprets the active bear hunting at the site to indicate that it might have been a winter or early spring occupation, the most common season to hunt bear.

ARCHAEOLOGICAL SITES IN THE GARDINER BASIN OF THE YELLOWSTONE RIVER

Approximately 5 mi. (8 km) northwest of the Malin Creek site is the confluence of the Gardner River with the Yellowstone River, an area often referred to as the Gardiner Basin. In this area, prehistoric Native American archaeological sites abound. My teams from the University of Montana identified more than 50 archaeological sites between the city of Gardiner and the northern border of the park at Reese Creek. This area is the lowest elevation (about 5,300 ft./1,615 m) of any in Yellowstone National Park. The valley of the Yellowstone River is characterized by sagebrush grasslands interspersed with several small tributary streams that derive from the mountains to the north and south of the Yellowstone River. Bison, elk, and pronghorn winter in this valley, as did Native American hunter-gatherers in prehistory.

Our work in the Gardiner Basin in 2007 to 2009 focused on the archaeology of the Yellowstone River northwest of the town of Gardiner. Among the more interesting finds was the red porcellanite Clovis point found there, which dates to more than 11,000 years ago. Nearby, our teams found two significant sites, the Late Archaic Yellowstone Bank Cache site, and the Late Prehistoric Airport Rings site.

Yellowstone Bank Cache Site

Local avocational archaeologist Tom Jerde identified the Yellowstone Bank Cache site during the summer of 1986 when he observed several concentrations of fire-cracked rock and lithic artifacts on the ground surface and eroding from the banks of the Yellowstone River northwest of Gardiner. He identified 58 artifacts from the site, several of which came from a cache of chert and obsidian stone tools. The University of Montana returned to the site in 2007 and found at least three prehistoric fire hearths eroding from the Yellowstone River bank. To salvage the remaining portions of the fire pits, we excavated them and found a fourth fire pit (figure 5.12).

Excavations within the four hearths indicate that Native Americans lived at the Yellowstone Bank Cache site during the Late Archaic period between 2,500 and 1,500 years ago. We were able to obtain four radiocarbon dates and three Late Archaic Pelican Lake corner-notched projectile points from the site. Late Archaic Native Americans conducted intensive stone tool manufacture activities, using both Obsidian Cliff obsidian and Crescent Hill chert. Assorted other tool production activities there were indicated by the presence of scraping and cutting tools. Each of the fire hearths was densely packed with fire-cracked rock and charcoal. Local vegetation, including sagebrush, juniper, pine, alder, and maple, was used for fuel in the hearths. Native Americans heavily processed medium- and large-size mammals at the site, including deer and several other indeterminate game, as well as plants, including goosefoot and pinecones (with pine nuts). While many Late Archaic sites in Montana show an increased reliance on bison 2,000 years ago, Native Americans at this particular site used a wide range of wild foods.

The Airport Rings Site

Nearby, in 2007 to 2008, our archaeology crews also excavated three stone circles at the Airport Rings site, also northwest of Gardiner along the Yellowstone River (figure 5.13). The stone circles mark the locations where Native Americans built a tipi lodge. Located near Landslide Creek, three fire pits were excavated at the site that provide a chronology of site occupation. One of the stone circles yielded evidence of a fire hearth dated to about 4,500 years ago. The rock-lined fire hearth was within the northeast corner of one of the stone circles and may represent one of the earliest examples of tipi structures in the prehistory of the northern Great Plains. Stone circles weren't actively used in the region until after 3,000 years ago. Another fire feature within the same stone circle dated to approximately 340 years ago.

FIGURE 5.12 In 2007, my University of Montana team excavated five 2,000-year-old hearths (including this one) used by Native Americans at the Yellowstone Bank Cache site north of Gardiner, Montana, along the Yellowstone River.

FIGURE 5.13 Native Americans camped 400 years ago at the Airport Rings site along the Yellowstone River north of Gardiner, Montana. Stone circles mark the locations where their tipis were set up.

Plant and animal remains indicate the possible cultural use of goosefoot by Native Americans in this tipi structure. Additional plant remains included charred monocot (such as wild onion), willow, birch, and small amounts of sagebrush. Wild onion was likely used as a flavoring in soup, while willow, sagebrush, and birch were likely burned in the fire to cook food. Small amounts of animal bones were found around the hearth as well, including several unidentifiable mammal tooth and bone fragments. Although the animal species could not be identified, the presence of the animal and plant remains in the hearth show that it was probably used for food processing by the Native American family that lived at the site.

The following narrative offers a fictional story of the lives of the people that built this tipi along the banks of the Yellowstone River several hundred years ago near Gardiner, Montana. I used the archaeological information from the site to create a picture of the lives of the Native American family that lived at the Airport Rings site. Keep in mind that my interpretations of the site are enhanced by knowledge of Native American lifeways in the region.

RAISING THE TIPI: A PREHISTORIC NARRATIVE
Elk River Valley, Montana, Late October, 400 Years Ago

The Native American family hunted and gathered in the hills above the Yellowstone River while nervously watching the black clouds roll in from the west over the red ochre streaks on the mountain. A small group of men hunted in the uplands for deer, pronghorn, elk, and bison, while a group of women collected driftwood for campfires from the banks of the Elk River, which today we call the Yellowstone. As soon as the black storm clouds inched over the red stripe on the mountain, both groups knew they had to hurry home.

Father, uncle, and son were on a steep slope above two small ponds on the pine tree line overlooking the Elk River Valley. A steep cliff loomed above them, a wall that provided initial protection from the winds that arose mightily in the west. Father had successfully killed a deer with his bow. The deer had stumbled to its knees almost immediately after impact, the arrow lodged in its neck. Father and son ran up to the deer and quickly dispatched it with their large obsidian knives hafted tightly by rabbit cordage to bone handles. They had collected the obsidian from Obsidian Cliff just a week ago and had fashioned the knives in a camp along Obsidian Creek, several miles south of the cliff. They had met family and friends at the cliff and had seen some old friends from the south, everyone there collecting the precious volcanic glass.

Father and son butchered the deer, packing the pieces of meat into leather bags. Uncle had been higher on the ridge and had run down to them, congratulating father and son. Uncle immediately began to process the skull for its antlers. Uncle used his obsidian knife to cut through the antler bases deeply enough that he could break them off. Uncle's knife blade was produced from a greenish obsidian from Grasshopper Knob west of Idaho Falls, Idaho, many miles to the south. At Obsidian Cliff, he had traded for the material with one of their friends, who in return gave him some Crescent Hill chert he had collected east of Mammoth Hot Springs. Uncle was an excellent maker of beautiful stone tools. He used the long, narrow tines of the antlers to control the removal of flakes from obsidian and chert. After he quickly removed the antler tines from the deer's skull, he handed father three of them and kept three for himself. Meanwhile, father and son continued to butcher the deer. The meat would provide enough food for a couple of days, while the hide would be processed by mother and grandmother into clothing. Son hoped he would get a new jacket out of this deer, but father needed leggings. In this cold weather and the coming snow, leggings would be vital for making it through the winter.

They descended the steep slope below the rock face, their bags heavy from the deer. At the base of the cliff, they crossed a muddy slope next to the two ponds. Bison had wallowed and walked in the mud to reach the ponds but were long gone now. The thick mud felt cool on their heavy fur and helped keep the bugs at bay. The rolling and wallowing bison had left behind a mucky mud flat filled with footprints and small puddles, some containing floating tufts of bison hair. The air was filled with the pungent odor of bison dung and stagnant mud.

Father, son, and uncle made their way down the steep sagebrush slope to the Elk River Valley a mile or so below them. A herd of pronghorn watched the men on a snowy slope to the west. Son took out an arrow and intended to fire, aiming his bow at the trailing animal of the herd. Both father and uncle laughed loudly at the arrogant son who thought he could kill a running antelope with an arrow from 150 yd. (137 m). "Son, the antelope is the fastest animal here. I know you are a good shot, but don't waste your arrow." Sulking, son lowered his bow, carrying it and the arrow together in his left hand as he proceeded downslope. He was only slightly dejected that he hadn't killed an animal that day, but he bitterly regretted not firing at the antelope.

Meanwhile, in the valley below, mother and her baby, grandmother, aunt, and daughter walked slowly along a high terrace next to the rolling river. As the wind howled, they edged up the terrace's steep slope toward their favorite campsite (a place that later would be called Airport Rings). Three wolf-like dogs followed behind them, scurrying to the tops of hills to scout for mice and rabbits.

FIGURE 5.14 Large herds of pronghorn migrate in winter to the Gardiner Basin in northern Yellowstone National Park.

Earlier that day, the entire family had walked four miles to their camp from the yellow canyon of the Elk River to the south. There, they had camped at the mouth of Malin Creek, where they had hunted, gathered, and even fished a bit in the final days of autumn. They had left Malin Creek in the early morning and arrived at Airport Rings by midday. They left their tipi poles, lodge coverings, and other equipment at the camp, and dispersed to collect food for dinner. While the men were high above them, the women collected driftwood from the river's rocky beach and a variety of plants that grew in the marsh along the river. The dry driftwood would burn nicely in their tipi's fire and the plants would provide fine flavor and powerful medicine to complement the meat brought by the men. A few times before, father, son, and uncle had been unsuccessful in their hunt. In early winter, animals were sometimes more difficult to find and kill than in summer. So the plants gathered by the women were crucial to their survival, especially if the men were unsuccessful. They could always delve into their bags of bison pemmican, but they didn't want to use their winter supplies if not necessary. They preferred to save that for the short days and long nights of January.

Luckily, there was little snow yet in the season and the frosts had not been heavy. As the women pulled upslope away from the river, the dogs startled a family of rabbits, causing them to scurry in multiple directions through the sagebrush. Daughter pulled her bow quickly and aligned an arrow with an obsidian tip. She favored obsidian because it was so sharp, even though she cut her fingers many times making the arrow tips. She also liked the obsidian because it glowed green in the sunlight, by far the prettiest of the stones. Even though the rabbit ran swiftly, its brown fur was easy to spot against the white snow that lightly covered the slopes. Daughter shot at the largest rabbit with her arrow, hitting it straight through its midsection. The rabbit would complement the vegetables in a stew. Daughter skinned and butchered the rabbit herself, with baby wailing on her mother's back from the cold wind and swirling snowflakes that delicately landed on her forehead and eyelids.

Grandmother continued up the hill away from the river. She was proud of granddaughter's success, turning back and praising her with a shout. She struggled occasionally up the steep slope, only stopping briefly at the top to catch her breath. She knew this terrain well, having lived her entire life among the sagebrush, pines, and willows. She missed grandfather and knew in her heart that she would be with him soon enough. In the meantime, she had things to do, things to teach her granddaughter and the new baby. She lamented that her other daughter and her husband had not had a child. Soon, she prayed, they would have daughter she could teach the many life lessons and skills she had learned from her mother, grandmother, and great-grandmother. She reached the terrace of the camp, with mother, baby, and daughter in tow, bags packed with dry willow and sagebrush branches, rabbit, and a variety of herbs and vegetables. Even if the men had not killed any animals, they would eat well tonight.

At this place, beginning as long as 4,500 years ago, Native American families built their camps on a high terrace above the Elk River. They built stone circles to hold down the edges of their hide shelters. The setting of the campsite was ideal, providing a high rocky ridge to the south, a fresh stream to the west, and a steep downslope to the Elk River to the north. It was protected on all sides and had a panoramic view of the wide Elk River Valley as it stretched northwesterly to the Plains and southeasterly to the great falls and steep canyon toward the great lake.

Today, this river is called the Yellowstone, so named after the bright yellow cliffs that line the river to the east-southeast.

But, on this late October day 400 years ago, the family struggled to beat the winter storm that rolled toward them. There was only a slight dusting of snow on the ground, but it was accumulating as they walked to their camp for the night. They had spent much of the summer and early fall in the uplands of the Yellowstone Plateau, among the pine and sagebrush hills that line the Elk River near the grand canyon of the Yellowstone. They had traveled all the way down to Yellowstone Lake in the warm days of summer, hunting bison and collecting bitterroot and chokecherries on their way. But with the dark storm clouds and the occasional frosts in recent mornings, they now returned to the lowlands of the Elk River for the winter. Depending on the weather and the locations of animals, they would stay in their camp for anywhere from one night to a few weeks.

Father, uncle, and son appeared above the ridge behind camp, while grandmother and the girls reached the camp. As daughter approached father, she shouted, "Look father, I got a rabbit." Father praised her, "Great shot! I told you that practice would make perfect!" Father smiled widely, and proudly hugged his daughter. Slightly jealous that his sister had killed the rabbit, son proclaimed loudly that their bags were packed with deer meat and hides. Daughter cheered for her older brother, whom she admired greatly. Uncle wrapped his arm around son and pushed him down the slope to camp, the boy tumbling and nearly falling on the slippery slope. Uncle jeered, telling the boy to learn how to walk and to stop taking so many mushrooms. Annoyed by uncle's comments, the boy quickly made a snowball and threw it at uncle, hitting him squarely on the leg.

In turn, uncle threw one of the antler tines toward his wife; it hit the ground with a puff of dry dust and snow at her feet. Aunt picked it up and threw it downslope toward the river, jokingly shouting for uncle to fetch it. Uncle, looking slightly amused at his wife's strong arm, didn't have to chase after it because all three dogs ran quickly for the antler tine, with the fastest one bringing it back to camp to chew on. The others two dogs pestered him as he ran away with the antler clutched tightly in his jowls. With loud barks and growls, the other two dogs tried to take the antler away to no avail, even nipping hard enough on the fastest dog's rear leg to cause a scrape of blood. Uncle went over and tore the antler from the mouth of the bleeding dog, causing it to growl angrily. Uncle reached into a leather bag on the ground and tossed a bit of bison pemmican to appease the angry dog.

As the Native American family entered the camp and rejoiced at their success, the wind whisked up a cloud of dust and snow around them in a vortex. They quickly built their shelter, hurrying to put up the hide structure in the midst of the early winter storm. The women began to gather rocks for the hide structure, while the men raised the poles above their heads. By the time the frame of the structure was raised, the snow was percolating from the sky. The family quickly removed their skin tent coverings from their bags that lay upon the travois. The dogs had pulled the small wooden travois behind them from the yellow canyon, greatly reducing the loads that the family had to carry on their backs. Grandmother pulled the leather skins from the bags, while mother and father threw the hides over the tipi poles. The tipi hides were decorated with painted images of the sun and buffalo, in yellow, red, and white pigments produced from crushed minerals, berries, animal fat, and other natural sources. Handprints outlined the bottom, marking the family's ownership. They placed the twenty or so large rocks on the lower edges of the hides to hold them down in the fierce wind. Father and son tied the poles together snugly at the top as the women continued to adjust the hides on the wood structure. Son had been helping his father with this task since he was old enough to walk. He probably could have raised a tipi in his sleep if he had to.

Just in the past ten days, they had raised and lowered the structure five times as they moved quickly off the high Yellowstone Plateau down to the Elk River toward their first winter camp. While father and son finished tying the poles, grandmother and aunt pushed the rocks over the bottom edges of the hides, making sure no wind or snow could enter the tent at night. The entire process took about an hour, and by the time they were done, two inches of snow covered the ground.

The family quickly went inside the lodge, hoping to get a fire going and warm themselves after the bitter cold tipi raising. Everyone's feet were cold. Father's hands were numb from tying the poles, while mother had accidently dropped one of the tipi hide rocks on her frigid toe. She was swearing a blue streak and yelling at uncle for not helping her with the heavy rocks. Uncle had wandered down to the Elk River to wash his hands, which had become muddy during the raising of the tipi poles. He had also gotten a splinter in his palm from one of the poles. Uncle looked up from washing his hands with a quizzical smile on his face, wondering what his sister-in-law was yelling about high above him at camp. He was sure he'd hear about it later from the sisters as they sat around the fire. He finished washing himself and looked up to the west to see the thick clouds of snow. Already, snow hugged the red stripe on the mountain and he imagined bear riding a hide down it to its depths. Perhaps he would tell the kids a story about the sliding bear tonight.

There were three children of various ages with the family. Daughter was ten years old and didn't venture far from her mother's side. As they entered the tipi, she quickly followed her mother to the north side and laid her bag down. Brother was thirteen and threw his gear down along the south side of the shelter. He got up to pee at night sometimes and liked to sleep close to the door, even though it was the coldest spot in the tent. His sleeping hides were the warmest, among them a thick bear skin grandfather had given him before he passed three seasons ago. The third child was a baby girl, strapped to the back of mother in a tight warm bundle. Daughter remembered those bundle days fondly and was jealous of baby. After she had set down her gear, she looked at baby and stuck her tongue out at her. This made the baby laugh, which irritated daughter even more. She made an angry face. Baby smiled widely. Daughter laughed too, anger dissipated by the baby's contagious chuckle. She reached up and took baby from the confines of the backpack and hugged her close, wiping baby's eyes to remove the accumulating snowflakes. She remembered that her little brother had passed from an illness four years before and she hoped he was okay with the great spirit and grandfather.

The family had camped at this spot on the Elk River at least three times before, and they always tried to use the same spot. There were several circles of stones on the ground, but they always picked the biggest one in the middle of the terrace. Chips of obsidian lay on the ground, and occasionally son picked up an old spear point left by his ancestors as he walked around camp.

The rest is history, or rather, prehistory. Left as circles of rocks. Left as fire pits. Left as bone and obsidian. Left for us, visitors to what we now call Yellowstone National Park, to find some 400 years later. We also found chips of obsidian and small fragments of arrowpoints, even the small flakes produced by father from the obsidian found 300 miles south near Idaho Falls. Another fire pit in the stone circle was 4,500 years old, showing that this family's ancestors had camped here for at least four millennia. Other stone tools the archaeologists found came from the west at a place near Bear Gulch, Idaho, while still more came from the volcanic dacite source near Ennis, Montana, along the Madison River Valley. Endscrapers were found inside the tipi structure, showing where mother and grandmother had prepared the deer hide for father's leggings. A small pile of Obsidian Cliff volanic glass flakes marked where daughter had made a small arrow point next to her mother to replace the one she had used to kill the rabbit. All of these discoveries were pieced together into a story told to the archaeologists by the family that had camped there 400 years before. We even found evidence of son's late-night pee.

Son had arisen from a deep sleep to the howls of the wind and the pelting of the snow against the hide. He was warm next to the fire and under his bear blanket, but he really had to go to the bathroom. He raised himself and pulled the hide around him as he left the tent. He walked a few more strides and emptied his bladder, quickly retreating back to his spot along the south wall of the tent. In his haste, however, he had forgotten to close the door tightly, and a strong wind entered the tent, blowing the fire and making smoke and embers fly against the northeast wall. Luckily, the family knew of the possibility of this happening and no one slept in that area. Everyone in the family knew that the winds were blowing from the southwest and that the northeast wall was nowhere to sleep with son's bad habit of forgetting to close the door tightly. Even though no one was covered by ash, grandmother coughed from the blowing smoke and father threw a shoe at son, telling him to close the door like he'd found it. An ember landed on the exposed arm of daughter and she scolded her brother. Son quickly arose from his bear blanket and placed rocks over the base of the hide door to shut it tight. He then placed three sagebrush arms on the fire and stoked it brightly, sending sparks up through the intercrossed arms of the tipi poles high above them. Son dropped to the floor and fell fast asleep, knees to his chest, comforted by grandfather's warm hide.

University of Montana archaeologists excavated that very same fire pit 400 years later and found the ash piled against the northeast wall of the shelter (figure 5.15). They even found pieces of the sagebrush in the fire, now only small bits of charcoal. Radiocarbon dating of that charcoal told us when the family slept there. Pieces of animal bone and plants were also found in the fire, remnants of the stew prepared by the mother. The rocks were still located near the door, pulled away slightly after the hide structure had been removed and packed during the family's next move of the camp.

The rest of the stone circle is still visible on the ground to this day, although it is hidden from curious visitors on the nearby road by a glacial moraine. My team of archaeologists working for Yellowstone National Park found the site in 2008, recording our results in reports and articles published in scientific journals and books like this one. Grandmother could have never thought that her family's story would end up on these pages.

FIGURE 5.15 This hearth was used at the Airport Rings site along the Yellowstone River nearly 400 years ago. The fire likely burned most of the night, providing warmth for a sleeping family in a tipi lodge.

CHAPTER SIX

MOUNTAINS

WHILE TRAVELING THROUGH Yellowstone country, Native Americans walked along river and creek terraces and through mountain passes to get to their destinations, such as the Gardiner Basin, Yellowstone Lake, or Obsidian Cliff. Just like today, nearly any trip to Yellowstone follows a meandering route across mountains that reach as high as 11,000 ft. (3,350 m) above sea level. Early Native Americans made their mountain journeys on foot, or on horseback after about 200 years ago. Their bags and supplies were on their backs and on travois (a two-pole sled) pulled by their dogs or horses.

Dramatic mountains, such as the Teton Range, provide the backdrop for much of Yellowstone. Despite the mountains' intimidating height, steep and rocky slopes, and their unpredictable weather, Native Americans weren't afraid to venture into them to get what they needed to survive. The tallest peaks in Yellowstone are Eagle Peak (11,372 ft./3,466 m), Electric Peak (10,969 ft./3,343 m) and Mount Washburn (10,243 ft./3,122 m). Yellowstone National Park has 39 peaks that are greater than 10,000 ft. (3,048 m) above sea level, with 31 of those in the Absaroka Mountains in the eastern portion of the park, as well as 7 of them in the northern portion of the park, mostly in the Gallatin Range. Ice and snow cover these mountains for most of the year, with ice patches present in shadowed, north-facing slopes for the entire year. Native Americans ventured for thousands of years to these high ice patches to hunt for animals that liked to gather on their cool expanses during the hot days of summer.

▶ MAP 6.1 The mountains of Yellowstone National Park

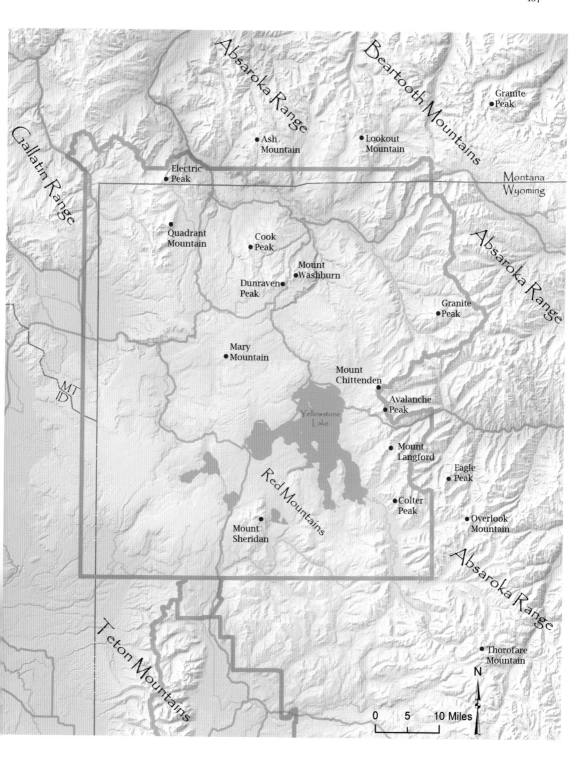

FIGURE 6.1 The Falling Ice Glacier and Skillet Glacier are on Mount Moran (left) in Grand Teton National Park. No glaciers remain on peaks in Yellowstone National Park.

While there are no glaciers in Yellowstone National Park today, all of Yellowstone's mountains were covered in glacial ice until approximately 12,000 years ago. In fact, 95 percent of Yellowstone National Park was covered by glacial ice during the peak of the last glaciation period about 17,000 years ago. After that time, the global climate started to warm and the glaciers melted away. By 12,000 to 11,000 years ago, most of the glacial ice was gone from Yellowstone except for the highest mountain peaks, and by 10,000 years ago, even that ice had largely melted away. Today, few mountains in the Yellowstone vicinity have glaciers. Teton National Park, south of Yellowstone, contains two glaciers, the Falling Ice Glacier and the

Skillet Glacier on Mount Moran (12,605 ft./3,842 m), which are visible to tourists from campgrounds and visitor centers near Jackson Lake, Wyoming. With global warming, these Teton Mountain glaciers will likely disappear completely, just as they are in Glacier National Park in Montana, approximately 375 mi. (600 km) northwest of Yellowstone.

Archaeological sites are not as common in these high-elevation mountains as they are along the shores of the lower-elevation lakes and rivers. Still, Native Americans explored these heights frequently, leaving remains of their activities behind for today's archaeologists. Four types of archaeological sites are found by archaeologists in the high-elevation settings of the Greater Yellowstone Ecosystem: religious structures (such as rock cairns, medicine wheels, and fasting beds) and three types of subsistence sites—pine nut processing villages, sheep hunting sites, and ice patches.

RELIGIOUS STRUCTURES

The high mountains of the Rockies contain several types of religious sites that were built and used by Native Americans for generations. These sites include rock cairns, large medicine wheels, and fasting beds. The rock cairns are present on some mountain peaks. These features are piles of between 5 and 30 rocks stacked atop one another, such as one in southwestern Montana (figure 6.2). The cairns mark trails or prayer sites for members of regional tribes.

Native Americans also organized rocks into large medicine wheels, like the notable one in the Bighorn Mountains east of Yellowstone (figure 6.3). The medicine wheels play an important role in religious ceremonies, dances, and prayers for regional Native Americans. The Bighorn Medicine Wheel has been used since at least the Late Prehistoric period as a sacred site by numerous northern Plains tribes, including Crow, Shoshone, Sioux, Arapaho, Kiowa, Blackfoot, Cheyenne, and Cree. The wheels are comprised of a central rock cluster, surrounded by several more rock piles arranged in the shape of wheel spokes. More than 135 of these structures have been found in the Rockies and Great Plains, mostly east and north of Yellowstone. To date, none have been recorded within Yellowstone National Park, although structures of possibly similar function are present near Mammoth Hot Springs.

The smaller rock pile features, or cairns, are more common than the larger medicine wheels. Most of the high mountain peaks in Yellowstone and vicinity, especially those with hiking trails, have cairns atop them. But it is difficult to

▲ FIGURE 6.3 The Bighorn Medicine Wheel, a high-altitude structure in the Bighorn Mountains of Wyoming, has been a sacred place to Native American people for thousands of years. *Richard Collier photo. Wyoming Historic Preservation Office, Department of State Parks and Cultural Resources.*

◀ FIGURE 6.2 Rock cairns, such as this one on a hilltop in southwest Montana, often mark the locations of Native American trails or prayer sites.

distinguish modern hiker and mountain climber rock piles from ancient Native American cairns. Today, it is common for hikers and climbers to place rocks in piles to acknowledge their successful walk to the summit of the mountain. Similarly, it is likely that many of the features on the peaks were originally established by Native Americans in the past. For example, the earliest European American mountain climbers of the Tetons humbly remarked at the presence of rock piles on the tops of the peaks, indicating that Native Americans had climbed them long before.

As with the larger medicine wheels, these smaller rock features in the high peaks of the Tetons, Absaroka, Gallatin, and other Yellowstone mountains likely are religious in nature, perhaps associated with Native American fasting and used to facilitate contact with the spirit world. Another type of Native American sacred site—fasting beds—are also present in the greater Yellowstone region. Fasting beds were used by numerous regional tribes, including the Crow, Blackfeet, and Shoshone, during vision quests. Native Americans travel to high elevations to facilitate contact with spirits through fasting. Sometimes referred to as the vision quest, this kind of fasting is usually completed by individuals who are seeking knowledge or strength for a significant life event. The goal is to seek a vision by depriving the body of water and food; it represents one of the most significant spiritual practices of many regional Native American tribes. The rock structure protected the fasting individual from winds on the mountain peaks.

In the early twentieth century, a Billings businessman and amateur anthropologist, William Wildschut, recorded the events that surround the fasting or vision quest experience among the Crow. From his interviews with dozens of Crow elders, Wildschut wrote the manuscript, *Crow Indian Medicine Bundles* in 1927 (published eventually in 1975) and described how the Crow prepared for a vision quest:

> Preparation for a vision quest required purification of both mind and body. The Indian cleansed his body by thoroughly scrubbing it, being careful that no dirt remained even under his fingernails and toenails. He prepared a sweat bath and prayed to "First Worker" to send him one of his powerful helpers. Then he purified his body again in the smoke of pine needles. From this moment he took no food or water until the completion of his vision quest. He believed that suffering would assist him in arousing the pity of a supernatural being, causing it to give him its medicine and thus to become his sacred helper. Abstinence from food and water also eliminated the odors of them, odors which the Crow believed were objectionable.

FIGURE 6.4 Fasting bed in the Pryor Mountains, Wyoming (2013). *Aaron Brien photo. University of Montana.*

These vision quests or fasting episodes are carried out in hills or mountains with dramatic views to better facilitate contact with spirits. Individuals hike into the mountains and construct a fasting bed from local rocks. Crow fasting bed features are common in the East Pryor Mountains of Montana at elevations between 8,300 and 8,700 ft. (2,529 and 2,651 m). This area has been the home to the Crow for several hundred years and they are known to have traveled frequently to Yellowstone. In his University of Montana master's thesis on the topic, Aaron Brien interviewed elders and conducted an archaeological survey to identify fasting beds in the Pryor Mountains (such as the one shown in figure 6.4).

Aaron's research resulted in the identification of 18 fasting beds used by Crow individuals over the past 500 years in the Pryor Mountains, approximately 90 mi. (145 km) east of Yellowstone. The fasting beds are most typically constructed on the edges of cliffs with panoramic views of surrounding areas. They are usually oval in shape, about 5 ft. (1.5 m) or so in length, and contain at least two to three tiers of rocks stacked atop one another. They are usually open on one end to allow for entry and exit. Pine trees are often found growing within the fasting beds, likely because

FIGURE 6.5 Possible fasting bed structure on a mountain peak in the southeastern corner of Yellowstone National Park. *Robin Park photo, National Park Service.*

pine needles (often with attached pinecones and seeds) were used by the fasters for cleansing during the vision quest. The beds provided a safe and secure place for the individual to peacefully seek spiritual guidance.

Based on this study, fasting beds are known to have been used by the Crow who also frequent the region of Yellowstone National Park. Other regional tribes, including the Shoshone and Blackfeet, also fasted in a fashion similar to the Crow. Since these three tribes frequently lived in Yellowstone, it seems reasonable that we should find such ceremonial features in the park. This possible fasting bed structure (figure 6.5) was recorded on a mountain peak southeast of Yellowstone Lake, although it appears to have been reconstructed in modern times. This reconstruction could suggest continued use as a fasting bed by regional tribes, but it could also indicate that hikers and climbers have maintained the structure.

Still other fasting beds used by Crow tribal leaders Long Bear and the Fringe are present in the northern mountains of the park, as communicated to Crow tribal archaeologist Timothy McCleary. This photograph from the Billings, Montana, Public Library Collection shows Long Bear in the early twentieth century. He was known to use fasting beds to seek visions in Yellowstone.

During my research near Yellowstone in 2014, my archaeology crews identified what we think are two fast-

FIGURE 6.6 The Crow leader Long Bear is known to have fasted in Yellowstone National Park. This photo of him was taken between 1898 and 1910 by Fred Miller. *Courtesy of Billings Public Library, Montana.*

ing beds. In the hills above the Madison River near Three Forks, Montana, we found two oval rock structures that measured approximately 5 ft. (1.5 m) in length with openings on the ends. Pine and juniper saplings grew within each one and both were located on the edge of high terraces with dramatic views of the Madison River below the cliff. These rock features are nearly identical in shape, contents, construction method, and settings to those described as fasting beds in the Pryor Mountains. As such, we are persuaded that these rock structures along the Madison River are fasting beds used by the Crow, Shoshone, or Blackfeet, all three of which traveled widely in this area. We can reasonably presume that many similar structures are present in Yellowstone's high elevations.

PINE NUT PROCESSING VILLAGES

In addition to spiritual guidance, Yellowstone Native Americans ventured into the mountains to hunt and gather a variety of resources, including pine nuts and game. In some of the high-elevation areas of the Absaroka and nearby Wind River Mountains, camps and villages were established by Native Americans during their collection of whitebark pine nuts in the fall. While none of these sites have actually been found in Yellowstone National Park, archaeologists from a variety of western universities—Utah State, University of Nevada, Colorado State University, and the University of Wyoming—have identified these pine nut processing villages just south and east of Yellowstone in the Absaroka and Wind River Mountains.

Among the variety of resources available in the high mountains, pine nuts were one of the most important edibles for Native Americans in the Yellowstone region. Collected in the fall each year, protein- and fat-rich pine nuts provide sustenance during the winter for many tribes throughout the region. Native Americans in California, the Great Basin, and in the Four Corners region of the southwestern United States traditionally harvested thousands of pine nuts from the pinecones of different pine tree species that grow at higher elevations (7,000 to 12,000 ft./2,100 to 3,700 m). To the north, in the Yellowstone region, Native Americans collect nuts from the whitebark pine tree (*Pinus albicaulis*). In Montana, the Blackfeet have long harvested whitebark pine nuts, as have the Shoshone in Wyoming and Idaho, including Yellowstone.

University of Montana graduate student Kodi Jae Augare-Estey wrote his master's thesis in 2011 on the practice of pine nut processing by members of the four bands of the Blackfoot tribal confederacy in northwestern Montana and southern Alberta. Their method of collecting and processing whitebark pine nuts is similar to that used by the Shoshone in the Yellowstone region. Families travel to the high elevations when the pine nuts are ripe. They knock down the pinecones with long sticks, and then burn them in small fires. The burning loosens the seeds, which can then be tapped out of the cones, shelled, and mixed with salt and water for roasting prior to eating.

Augare-Estey states that Blackfeet tribal members often followed the movements of the Clark's nutcracker in the fall, since the bird also relies heavily on pine nut collection prior to winter. The nuts provide an important source of protein for the birds, as well as for people and mammals.

In recent years, the whitebark pine has been threatened greatly by global warming; in particular, the mountain pine beetle has ravaged northwestern United States whitebark pine forests. In the ancient past, winter temperatures were cold enough to kill off the insects in the winter, but with warming global temperatures, the pine beetle survives the winter and spreads rapidly through whitebark pine forests, killing the trees.

As the Blackfeet did in northwestern Montana (and perhaps even in Yellowstone in the past), recent discoveries in the Wind River Range south of Yellowstone suggest that the various bands of the Shoshone, including the Sheep Eaters and Eastern Shoshone, have long sought the nutritional benefit of pine nuts as well. Archaeologists from the University of Nevada and Colorado State University have spearheaded much of the research of high-elevation pine nut processing villages in northwestern Wyoming near Yellowstone. To date, archaeologists have identified more than 20 villages in the high-elevation areas of the Wind River and nearby Absaroka Mountain ranges.

The most significant of these villages is called High Rise Village, which is located at an elevation between 10,500 and 10,900 ft. (3,200 and 3,322 m) within the Wind River Range (figure 6.7). The site is approximately 60 mi. (100 km) southeast of Yellowstone National Park.

FIGURE 6.7 Excavations at the High Rise Village site southeast of Yellowstone National Park (2011). *Christopher Morgan photo. University of Nevada, Reno.*

Located on a steep slope of a high mountain ridge, the site is surrounded by whitebark pine forest with alpine tundra above the site. High Rise Village measures approximately 19 acres (7.7 hectares) and contains archaeological evidence of as many as 52 lodge structures used by Native Americans. Based on their archaeological work of the 2000s and early 2010s, Colorado State University's Richard Adams and University of Nevada's Christopher Morgan suggested that the High Rise Village could possibly "be the largest, oldest, and longest occupied high-altitude village in North America."

Adams and Morgan interpret the site to be of Eastern Shoshone tribal origin, which is likely because of its location within the traditional territories of that tribe. The types of obsidian found at the site also suggest a southern Yellowstone origin for the people at the site. The Shoshone were the most predominant tribe in this portion of Yellowstone and nearby mountains in the recent past, although the Crow are known to have explored this area as well.

The living structures at High Rise Village were constructed from local rocks, and some included house floors excavated into the earth by their Native American occupants. Some of the structures still contain timbers lying on their edges that likely were once roof beams above the rock walls. Essentially, the rock and wood structures provided temporary shelter for Native American families that lived at the site for a week or more. A family probably lived in each structure, with a total population of the site of more than 200 people. Not all these people lived at the site at the same time; instead, the site likely represents the remains of multiple camps over hundreds of years, with the total population during any one gathering in the fall of between 25 and 75 people. Group size during each visit was dictated by the productivity of the pine nut harvest, with more people visiting the site in abundant years.

High Rise Village was used by the Shoshone, and perhaps other tribes, dating back to the Middle and Late Archaic periods, between 4,500 and 2,500 years ago. The most intensive eras of use were within the past 1,000 years, with use continuing at the site until 150 years ago. Most of site's radiocarbon dates are from the Late Prehistoric period, as are the majority of arrow points. As with most other Native American groups in this region during this time, the Shoshone utilized small corner- and side-notched arrow points, indicative of use of bow hunting, rather than use of the atlatl. (See figure 2.11, which shows the small size of arrow points compared to the earlier atlatl dart points.) Intermountain Ware pottery, often linked to the Shoshone, was also found at the site.

Richard Adams and Christopher Morgan's excavations at High Rise Village over the past decade indicate that Native American families hunted Rocky Mountain bighorn sheep (*Ovis canadensis canadensis*), marmot (*Marmota flaviventris*), and mountain birds such as ptarmigan (*Lagopus leucura*). They also gathered biscuit-root (*Lomatium*) and spring parsley (*Cymopterus constancei*).

Analysis of obsidian artifacts indicate that the Native Americans traveled extensively in the Yellowstone region prior to climbing the mountains to get to High Rise Village. While only one stone flake in Yellowstone came from Obsidian Cliff obsidian, two-thirds of the obsidian artifacts came from the Teton Pass and Crescent H obsidian sources near Jackson, Wyoming. A few obsidian artifacts even came from the Bear Gulch source in Idaho. All of these sources are between 60 and 150 mi. (100 and 240 km) from the site, showing extensive travel patterns, especially in areas south of Yellowstone National Park. Based on these obsidian samples, it is fairly certain that the Shoshone who lived at High Rise Village had traveled in the Snake River Valley of southern Yellowstone prior to venturing eastward into the Wind River Mountains. They likely spent much of their summer in southern Yellowstone before hiking into the mountains in the fall to harvest pine nuts and biscuitroot and to hunt for mountain sheep.

To date, no high-elevation pine nut processing villages have been identified within Yellowstone National Park. However, there has been very little archaeological survey of high-elevation settings of Yellowstone. So future archaeologists will be looking for these villages in the eastern portions of the park, within the Absaroka Mountains east of Yellowstone Lake. Whitebark pine trees are plentiful in these mountains, just as they are to the south in the Wind River Range. Surely, pine nut processing villages are present in the Yellowstone mountains, so it is only a matter of time before archaeologists find them.

BIGHORN SHEEP HUNTING SITES

The second type of high-elevation subsistence site—bighorn sheep hunting sites—are often found in association with the pine nut processing villages. Sheep hunting sites are present at higher-elevation settings throughout the Yellowstone region where bighorn sheep forage. The sites range from rock shelters used to process the animals to the actual kill sites. Kill sites are often marked by rock hunting blinds or wooden corral features used by Native Americans to trap the animals.

One of the most important archaeological sites in the Yellowstone region is called Mummy Cave. The site is located 10 mi. (16 km) east of the East Entrance to the park, on the road to Cody, Wyoming. Mummy Cave (see figure 1.11) was excavated in the late 1960s by a group of amateur and professional archaeologists, including Waldo Wedel and Wilfred Husted. The site contains more than 30 stratigraphic layers within 27 ft. (8 m) of cultural deposits. Located along the beautiful North Fork of the Shoshone River, Mummy Cave has yielded artifacts with radiocarbon dates from 9,230 years ago all the way up to the present. In the upper portions of the site's stratigraphy, a male human skeleton of likely Shoshone tribal affiliation was dated to approximately 1,300 years ago. As the namesake for the site, the man was wrapped

FIGURE 6.8 Bighorn sheep (*Ovis canadensis*) were commonly hunted by Native Americans in the mountains of Yellowstone.

in a bighorn sheep robe, with his hair tied at the back with a thong, feather, and fur ornament. Mummy Cave shows significant reliance on Rocky Mountain bighorn sheep hunting by Native Americans near Yellowstone for the past 9,000 years, from its earliest occupation to its most recent.

All throughout the rugged Rocky Mountains, bighorn sheep were important prey for Native Americans. Bighorn sheep graze in open settings, but when threatened, they flee into the rocky uplands, where they are extremely agile climbers. Native Americans hunted the sheep using drivelines and corrals, generally exploiting their instinct to seek higher ground. Figure 6.9 shows the remains of a hunting blind located on a hillside above the Yellowstone River just north of Yellowstone National Park and Gardiner, Montana. These ancient hunting features are present in many of the mountainous areas of the park and surrounding forests.

As a further testament to the importance of bighorn sheep hunting in the Yellowstone region, University of Wyoming archaeologist George Frison reported the discovery of a Native American sheep-hunting net in the Absaroka Mountains near Mummy Cave in the mid-1980s. Made from juniper bark fibers, the net dates to 8,800 years ago, indicating long-standing sheep hunting by Native Americans in

FIGURE 6.9 Native Americans used hunting blinds, such as this one north of Gardiner, Montana, to dispatch bighorn sheep.

the mountains around Yellowstone. Frison proposes that the 8,800-year-old net was likely approximately 150 ft. (45 m) in length and 5 to 6 ft. (1.5 to 2 m) high, although it was too fragile to uncoil after its discovery. He further states that two or more individuals likely held the net across a game trail while other hunters pushed the animals upslope to them. Once entwined in the net, the sheep were dispatched by the waiting Native Americans with clubs or bows and arrows.

As with pine nut collecting, late fall (before the snow flies) was the predominant season for hunting bighorn sheep. Families likely ventured to areas like Mummy Cave and High Rise Village to take advantage of both pine nuts and bighorn sheep in preparation for the winter. As a testament to the importance of bighorn sheep to Native Americans of the region, Mummy Cave also contained an 8,000-year-old bighorn sheep skull on a stone slab. In his 2004 book, *Survival by Hunting*, Frison proposes that this may be evidence for the ritual treatment of sheep, perhaps indicative of the important role the animal played in the spiritual world of the people who lived in the mountains around Yellowstone. Bighorn sheep hunting was so popular in the mountains of Yellowstone that the Shoshone, one of the most important Native American tribes in the area, are colloquially recognized as the Sheep Eaters.

ICE PATCHES AS HUNTING SITES

Ice patches, the third type of subsistence site, have been found in the high mountains of Yellowstone. Ice patches are the remnants of winter snows that remain for much of the summer in the higher-elevation portions of Yellowstone's mountains. These ice patches have existed for thousands of years and often attract game during the hot months of summer. And so Native American hunters frequented the ice patches of Yellowstone to hunt, leaving behind hunting implements that archaeologists have found.

Ice patches are not glaciers, but remnants of snow that has accumulated over many winters. Over time, the ice and snow stabilize to form almost mini-glaciers atop mountain ridges and summits. These ice and snow patches often remain without melting throughout the year at these high elevations of the Rocky Mountains near Yellowstone; this photo was taken in September. Because of global warming, though, these ice patches, as well as the margins of glaciers in the Rocky Mountains, are disappearing quickly and are exposing artifacts left behind by hunters over the past 10,000 years.

The study of melting ice patches and glaciers by archaeologists is becoming widespread all over the world at high-elevation mountain settings. In Yellowstone, the work is confined to ice patches, since no glaciers exist in the park any longer, having all melted away. In Europe and other areas of the northern hemisphere, glaciers still exist, so similar types of archaeology occur there as well. All of this research, even at glaciers, is often referred to as "ice-patch archaeology," which largely involves archaeologists venturing to high mountain peaks and slopes to examine remnant ice and snow patches, as well as glaciers where they still exist. Satellite imagery is very helpful in the identification of ice patches, and historic photos of mountain ranges can also assist in identifying ice patches and former glaciers that have now completely melted away. Once ice patches are identified in the satellite and historic images, archaeologists climb to those locations to look for artifacts. This work occurs in late summer when any new snow from the past winter has melted off the ancient ice patches.

The most important discovery in an ice patch on the edge of a melting glacier in the world is Otzi, the famous mummy of the Italian Alps. In the late 1980s, hikers found the mummified body of an ancient European hunter dating to more than 5,000 years ago. Otzi, as he was named, was apparently killed by the hands of another person as he hiked through the mountains. He was quickly enveloped in a massive ice sheet that only recently melted away. Otzi was extremely well preserved, with much of his clothing, weapons, and even stomach contents still intact.

FIGURE 6.10 In summer and fall, Native Americans visited ice patches, like this one (2013) in the southeastern corner of Yellowstone National Park, to hunt animals. *Staffan Peterson photo, National Park Service.*

From the remains, archaeologists have learned that he was likely a farmer for much of his life before venturing into the mountains. They also discovered that he had eaten ibex in his last meal before passing away on the high mountain. He carried with him a yew bow, a quiver of arrows, and a copper axe, with shoes constructed from leather and stuffed with grass for warmth. The other artifacts found with Otzi included leather leggings, a grass cape, a bearskin hat, a wooden backpack frame, and a dagger with a grass sheath. Otzi also had numerous tattoos that appear to mark locations where doctors or shamans had tried to cure multiple ailments over the course of his life. Otzi carried with him a birch bracket mushroom (*Piptoporus betulinus*) on a string that is known to have medicinal qualities to reduce pain and treat a variety of ailments. Still another type of fungus, tinder polypore (*Fomes fomentarius*), found with Otzi is known to be an excellent fire starter. From this single ice-patch discovery, archaeologists have learned a great deal about the cultures of people that lived 5,000 years ago in the Italian Alps.

The only way the ice man of the European Alps was discovered was because of the melting of an ice patch on the edge of the glacier from global warming. While archaeologists in the Yellowstone region have not found anything quite as remarkable as Otzi, they have found amazing artifacts in melting ice patches that show active Native American use of the high mountains, such as Mineral Mountain in the Absaroka Mountains, for at least 10,000 years. They were likely attracted to the ice patches because of abundant game. In the hot summers, bison, mountain sheep, deer, elk, and bear often go to the ice patches to escape the heat, roll in the snow, and eat the snow as a water source. Rolling in the snow reduces the animal's body temperature and also helps keep insects out of its fur.

Within Yellowstone and the surrounding mountain ranges, archaeologist Craig Lee (figure 6.11, left) has found a plethora of artifacts at ice patches, from stone tools to pottery and everything in between. Much of his work over the past decade was inspired by earlier high-mountain archaeologists like the University of Wyoming's George Frison and University of Colorado's James Benedict, who searched ice patches and glaciers in the Colorado Rockies from the 1960s to the 1990s, long before Craig Lee and his colleagues ventured into Yellowstone's mountains.

Retired Yellowstone National Park archaeologist Ann Johnson spearheaded the initial high-mountain ice-patch archaeology in the mid- to late 2000s in Yellowstone National Park. In her early trips with numerous colleagues, she traveled on horseback to high mountain peaks of the Gallatin and Absaroka Mountains. Later, in 2016, Craig Lee and former park archaeologist Staffan Peterson (see figure 6.11, right) embarked on a trip through the Yellowstone River thoroughfare south of Yellowstone Lake. They were transported to the southern end of the lake by motorboat, and then they hiked the thoroughfare trail that winds along the Yellowstone River south of Yellowstone Lake. Their goal was to look at ice patches within the Absaroka Mountains in the far southeastern corner of Yellowstone National Park. During their trip, they found numerous stone tool production sites in the mountains of this region, showing that Native Americans exploited chert outcrops within the bedrock of these peaks. One obsidian projectile point that they found

FIGURE 6.11 Archaeologists Craig Lee (left) and Staffan Peterson (right) explored the ice patches of Yellowstone National Park (2013), looking for Native American archaeological sites and artifacts. *Staffan Peterson photo, National Park Service.*

was geologically sourced to Bear Gulch, nearly 100 mi. (161 km) to the west in the mountains of Idaho.

In 2008, Lee and colleagues explored Parker Peak in the Absaroka Mountains in the eastern part of Yellowstone. While this survey failed to identify any material remains, it was clear that such artifacts likely were present, but might be covered by a heavy snow from the winter before the survey. Lee also examined Quadrant Mountain in the Gallatin Range in the northern portion of Yellowstone in 2008. Tracks and scat on the snow surface of one of the ice patches on Quadrant Mountain indicated that animals, including bear and elk, had recently visited the ice patch just before the archaeologists. During that trip to Quadrant Mountain, Lee and his colleagues collected a piece of spruce wood that was dated to about 600 years ago. Since spruce does not grow at these high elevations today, this ice-patch find indicates a higher tree line 600 years ago than is present at the site today. The higher tree line indicates slightly warmer temperatures in the area at that time.

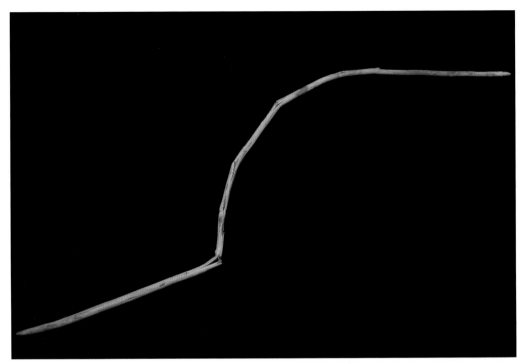

FIGURE 6.12 This atlatl dart foreshaft (with fracture) is 10,300 years old (uncalibrated 14C date of ca. 9,230 years old). Craig Lee and his colleagues found this remarkable artifact (2009) next to an ice patch near Yellowstone National Park. *Craig Lee photo. University of Colorado Institute for Arctic and Alpine Research.*

Nearby, at another archaeological site on Quadrant Mountain, Lee and his colleagues recovered six obsidian artifacts, including a 2,000-year-old Late Archaic Pelican Lake point. The artifacts were identified as being manufactured from Obsidian Cliff obsidian. With the source only 10 mi. (15 km) to the south, Native Americans likely incorporated a trip to hunt and gather in the high elevations of the Gallatin Range on their way to or from Obsidian Cliff. It is conceivable that these people (or their relatives) were also the same group that lived at the Yellowstone Bank Cache site on the banks of the Yellowstone River just north of Quadrant Mountain.

Also within the Gallatin Range, Electric Peak contains several remnant ice patches thought to contain Native American artifacts. In his expedition to Electric Peak in 2008, Lee focused on a snow patch located in the north-facing cirque of the peak. There, Lee collected six pieces of wood below the largest ice patch. He interprets these pieces of wood as having been brought there by human means,

FIGURE 6.13 This painting re-creates a scene of Native Americans hunting bighorn sheep on an ice patch. *Illustration by Eric Carlson, 2016.*

since trees have not grown at this elevation. Just as human hikers do today, Native Americans (or even early European Americans) probably used these pieces of wood as hiking sticks. Produced from pine and spruce, two of the wood samples yielded radiocarbon dates of 200 to 150 years ago.

While his studies within the park have not been as productive as he'd like, his trips to ice patches in the Absaroka Mountains east of Yellowstone have yielded remarkable artifacts. There they identified at least seven ice-patch sites that contained the remains of wooden and stone artifacts. The most remarkable of the finds is a 9,230-year-old birch atlatl foreshaft (figure 6.12) found in 2009; the shaft has a greenstick break but still holds together. The age of this foreshaft shows that it was used by Native Americans associated with the Late Paleoindian Cody Culture. These early pioneers actively used the Yellowstone region about 9,000 years ago. With the discovery of this atlatl foreshaft, it is clear that they also used the high mountains as well as the lower-elevation lakes and rivers. A similar group of Cody

Culture Native Americans likely also produced the mountain sheep-hunting net found in the same mountains by George Frison in the 1980s.

Analysis of the 9,000-year-old atlatl foreshaft determined that a Native American hunter had engraved it with two clusters of three parallel lines on opposite sides. Based on comparisons with ethnographic accounts of modern hunter-gatherer people, Lee concluded that the parallel lines were likely engraved as ownership marks to aid members of a hunting party in determining who had killed the animal. This engraving tradition was apparently quite long lasting in the region. As reported in an article in the journal *Arctic* in 2012, Lee recovered another wooden foreshaft in 2006 from an ice patch that dates to 7,000 years ago, which contains five parallel and slightly angled incisions, also interpreted to be ownership marks.

Six additional archaeological finds by Lee at ice patches in these mountains range in age from 6,700 years ago to 1,200 years ago. Native Americans produced the artifacts from a variety of wood, including birch, pine, fir, and willow. Among these artifacts are atlatl dart and foreshaft fragments, a few of which also contain ownership marks. They also found 2,000-year-old mountain sheep remains and horns that appeared to have been butchered by humans.

These amazing finds by Craig Lee and his colleagues indicate that between 9,000 and 150 years ago, Native Americans ventured into the high mountains of Yellowstone to hunt for game at ice patches, occasionally leaving behind their wooden and stone implements and butchered animal remains. Figure 6.13 re-creates one of these ice-patch hunting expeditions by a group of Native Americans.

———————

The importance of high-elevation archaeology in Yellowstone cannot be overestimated, since ice patches are continuing to reveal fragile wooden and bone artifacts. Once removed from the ice patches because of the snowmelt and exposed to the elements, these artifacts will decay quite quickly in the open air—wooden artifacts in a few years, and bone and antler artifacts within ten years. Because of continued global warming, the ice patches will continue to melt, and so it is vital for archaeologists to continue to look for and document these artifacts as they appear at ice patches.

CHAPTER SEVEN

HOT SPRINGS, THERMAL AREAS, AND GEYSERS

IN THE COLD SEASONS, the thermal features and hot springs of Yellowstone National Park provided good places for Native Americans to find game attracted to the warmth in those areas. In addition, while Native Americans sought the solace of high mountain peaks to conduct their vision quests, these hot springs and thermal features may have also been places for spiritual activities. The long-held assumption that Native Americans were fearful of these exotic geysers and thermal features is a fallacy. Thermal features, such as Midway Geyser Basin (figure 7.1), were popular attractions for Native Americans for a variety of reasons, both spiritual and subsistence.

It is no wonder that some people believed that native peoples in Yellowstone had this fear. In his 1879 park report, early park superintendent P. W. Norris stated that Native Americans greatly feared the geysers, thermal areas, and hot springs of Yellowstone National Park. In all likelihood, Superintendent Norris was simply trying to promote the notion that Native Americans did not frequent the park and that European American tourists were safe. But this misinformation likely derived from a lack of knowledge of Native American activities in the park region. Park Historian Lee Whittlesey further notes comments made in 1883 by an early park visitor, Hamilcar Hollister, regarding Native American views of Yellowstone.

FIGURE 7.1 (following) Sunset at Midway Geyser Basin. *Neal Herbert photo, National Park Service.*

Hollister quotes Native American informants as stating, "No white man should ever be told of this inferno, lest he should enter that region [Yellowstone] and form a league with the devils, and by their aid come forth and destroy all Indians."

If Native Americans followed a practice of not answering questions about Yellowstone, it was smart and effective. It might help explain why Yellowstone wasn't really explored or mapped by European Americans until the mid- to late nineteenth century. By that time, great cities had arisen across the West, but Yellowstone remained wilderness. All around them, the native peoples witnessed Euro-American expansion and a reduction of their own territories. Whittlesey indicates that Hollister's comment might provide one explanation as to why he and other early park historians could learn little about Native American use of the park. It wasn't until Peter Nabokov and Lawrence Loendorf published their books on Native American use of the park that much light was brought to the topic.

In their books, including *Restoring a Presence: American Indians and Yellowstone National Park* (2004), Nabokov and Loendorf provide ample information that the various regional Native American tribes utilized the area we now call Yellowstone National Park, including the hot springs, geysers, and thermal areas. As reported by Whittlesey, based on Nabokov and Loendorf's studies, "The Crow Indians called Yellowstone 'land of the burning ground' or 'land of vapors' while the Blackfeet called it 'many smoke.' The Flathead called it 'smoke from the ground.' The Kiowa called it 'the place of hot water.' Only the Bannock [Shoshone] had a name that did not call to mind the park's thermal regions: 'buffalo country.' Additionally, the Crow specifically called the Yellowstone geysers . . . 'sacred or powerful water.'" From these names given to Yellowstone by the various tribes of the region, it is clear that they characterized the area in terms of its hot springs and geysers.

Interviews with Crow elders by Nabokov and Loendorf indicate that they, among other tribes, believed that spirits resided in the Yellowstone geysers. In particular, the Shoshone believed that water spirits inhabited the waters of Yellowstone and vicinity. Some of the spirits were good, while some were evil. For example, Water Ghost Woman, shown here in rock art form (figure 7.2), was capable of causing or curing illnesses and often lured men into water to drown them. Water Ghost Woman was also known to steal babies and eat them. She could only be contacted by a shaman of great power.

And so for some tribes, the waters of Yellowstone, including ones associated with thermal areas, likely contained spiritual power. Whittlesey reports that explorer William Clark knew of this Native American belief, and in his 1809 travel journals interpreted this belief in water spirits to mean that the tribes feared the geysers.

FIGURE 7.2 The Shoshone people believed that Water Ghost Woman, depicted here in rock art form, could only be contacted by a Shoshone shaman of great power. Such water ghost spirits were known to inhabit thermal features, such as those in Yellowstone. *Shaman's Ridge site, Thermopolis, Wyoming. James Keyser photo, 2002.*

But we have learned that Native Americans sought the power of the geysers and thermal waters to contact the spirits that inhabited them. Instead of fearing them, they purposefully sought their help in curing illness or bringing about good (or bad) fortune.

In addition to the spiritual aspects of the thermal features, some early archaeologists who worked in the park have suggested that Native Americans likely visited hot springs in colder weather because of the game that could be found there. Game animals were drawn to the warmth at those sites as well as to the exposed forage where the hot springs melted the snow. So there appear to be two contrasting (or possibly complementary) views of the Native American use of thermal areas: first, they used them for spiritual purposes, and second, they used them for hunting purposes.

One means by which to show how Native Americans used the thermal areas, as well as to prove beyond a reasonable doubt that Native Americans did not fear the geysers and thermal waters, is through examination of the archaeological record in the various thermal areas. Many archaeological studies have been conducted in the park around the various thermal areas, hot springs, and geyser basins. Did the archaeologists find sites during the surveys? Were the sites religious in nature or related to subsistence?

Yellowstone's history is filled with multiple episodes of eruptive volcanism. This volcanism continues to this day and is most easily observed at the various thermal features, geyser basins, and hot springs of the park. Archaeologists have found numerous Native American prehistoric sites associated with these thermal features (map 7.1).

ARCHAEOLOGICAL SITES NEAR MAMMOTH HOT SPRINGS

In the northern reaches of Yellowstone National Park, Mammoth Hot Springs stands out as a vast and majestic bubbling cauldron of hot springs. The key attribute attracting Native Americans to the areas of Mammoth Hot Springs and the Boiling River was likely not only the thermal features but also the Gardner River. The Bannock Trail passes through this area, with the Gardner River a significant travel corridor during both the precontact and historic periods. By traveling along this river, Native Americans walked from the Yellowstone River into the Yellowstone Plateau to get to places like Obsidian Cliff and Yellowstone Lake. Numerous prehistoric campsites are present along the Gardner River. While the vast majority of the bigger sites are farther south near Sheepeater Cliffs, Indian Creek Campground, and Obsidian Cliff, several prehistoric Native American sites are present around both Mammoth Hot Springs and the famous tourist attraction, the Boiling River.

There are no recorded prehistoric archaeological sites within the confines of Mammoth Hot Springs proper. If the location was ever used for spiritual purposes by Native Americans, any evidence of that use is lost to the modernization and tourist activities in the area today. This area has been home to Yellowstone

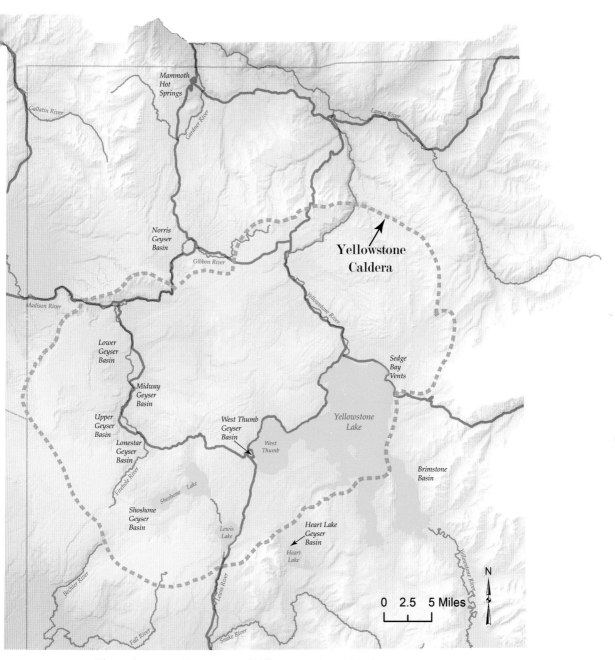

MAP 7.1 Thermal areas and hot springs of Yellowstone National Park

National Park's administrative offices for many years and, prior to that, served as a base for the cavalry assigned to protect the park in its early years.

There are, however, dozens of prehistoric Native American sites—even a few with potential religious significance—that are very close to the majestic Mammoth Hot Springs. Of note are at least 20 prehistoric stone tool production scatters located within a couple of miles northeast of Mammoth Hot Springs, along the Gardner River.

In addition, at least three sites have been identified in this area that may have had religious function for Native Americans. The sites consist of rock cairns, similar to those associated with religious activities in the mountains of the Yellowstone region.

In the 1990s, archaeologists from the Museum of the Rockies in Bozeman, Montana, identified a possible religious site approximately two miles north of the Boiling River on a 120 ft. (37 m) high bluff high above the Gardner River. Here, with a panoramic view of the Gardiner Basin below (figure 7.3), they found five rock piles that mark the top of a serpentine ridge line above the river. The first cairn is ovate-shaped and is composed of 20 large river cobbles within an area of approximately 5 to 6 ft. (1.5 to 2 m). Of the five features, this is the largest and could be the remains of a collapsed fasting bed.

Fasting beds, used by several regional native tribes to seek spiritual guidance, typically are about 5 ft. (1.5 m) long, are U-shaped (ovate), and have dramatic views of the areas below—key attributes present in this cairn. The other four rock piles contain a similar number of rocks and are of a similar size, so these features could also be the dilapidated remains of fasting beds. The cairns could be part of a hunting system (e.g., some sort of driveline system), but they did not form a line useful in driving game. Instead, the rock piles form a T-shape, perhaps best interpreted as a spiritual rock alignment akin to medicine wheel spokes.

A second site in this area is farther north, closer to the North Entrance of the park near Gardiner, Montana. This site consists of a large stone tool production site, as well as stone circles that mark the locations of former tipi lodge bases. At this site, of most importance to this discussion is the presence of 12 small rock piles. The cairns at this site are significantly smaller, comprised of five to eight partially buried rock piles about 1 ft. (31 cm) in diameter. The rock piles are oriented in a line along the edge of a southeast-northwest-oriented terrace that stands approximately 65 ft. (20 m) above the Gardner River to the east. The rock features at the beginning and end of the alignment are significantly larger. The Museum of the Rockies archaeologists who identified the site in the 1990s suggest that each cairn served as an anchor for a fence or blind for hunting game at the site. Today, bighorn sheep and pronghorn antelope are known to frequent this area.

FIGURE 7.3 This rock cairn feature sits high on a hilltop near Mammoth Hot Springs and the Boiling River, northern Yellowstone National Park.

A third rock feature is present just south of Mammoth Hot Springs that is almost certainly some sort of religious feature or effigy. This feature has a large central rock pile with two long arms of rock in two directions that end at two large clusters of rock. A similar feature is present near the confluence of the Gardner and Yellowstone Rivers, a few miles downstream. The rock features appear to take the shape of an arrow and may comprise an "arrow effigy" of unknown spiritual function.

Given that this area is traditionally linked to the Bannock Trail, some of the rock piles on hilltops could simply be trail markers. But the larger features likely served other major functions, including hunting drivelines, fasting beds, or sacred alignments. The close proximity to Mammoth Hot Springs suggests a connection between the features and the thermals. Perhaps the arrow effigy directed vision seekers to Mammoth Hot Springs, where they could seek the wisdom and power of Water Ghost Woman.

These rock features, as well as the numerous stone tool production sites, indicate active prehistoric use of the area surrounding Mammoth Hot Springs. There is little doubt that Native Americans used this area prior to the establishment of the park; they likely traveled within the Gardner River Valley and along the Bannock Trail to hunt for game, such as bighorn sheep, pronghorn antelope, and bison, all of which use the low-elevation Gardiner Basin, especially in winter. Finally, the presence of possible fasting beds and rock effigy features may indicate the spiritual significance of the thermal features of this area around Mammoth Hot Springs.

ARCHAEOLOGICAL SITES AT NORRIS AND GIBBON GEYSER BASINS

South of Mammoth Hot Springs and Obsidian Cliff is the Norris Geyser Basin, as well as the associated Gibbon Geyser Basin. Between approximately Obsidian Cliff and Gibbon River Falls is a series of large archaeological sites, several of which are situated within or directly adjacent to thermal features or hot springs. While none of the sites appears to have a religious feature, they likely support the long-term use of hot springs and thermal features for camping and for subsistence purposes by Native Americans in Yellowstone.

Just south of Obsidian Cliff, Whiterock Springs is a large hot spring and thermal feature near Solfatara Creek. This creek has numerous hot springs along its southward course toward Norris Junction and its confluence with the Gibbon River. The springs abut the southern perimeter of Obsidian Cliff, and contain numerous stone tool production sites associated with procuring the volcanic glass for that use. Based on our archaeological survey of this area, Native Americans camped at Obsidian Cliff with no fear of the nearby Whiterock Springs thermal feature.

Approximately 5 mi. (8 km) south of Whiterock Springs on the edge of the Norris Geyser Basin, the Nymph Lake site marks the location of a prehistoric Native American camp. The site is located adjacent to an active hot springs and thermal feature called the Frying Pan Hot Spring. The Native American camp itself is located atop an extinct hot spring. Frying Pan Hot Spring is on the eastern edge of Nymph Lake, with water from this lake feeding a small creek that flows southward directly into the Norris Geyser Basin and eventually into the Gibbon River. The camp was likely used by Native Americans traveling to and from the nearby Obsidian Cliff and the Gibbon River.

FIGURE 7.4 Stone tool production sites are abundant in the vicinity of the Norris Geyser Basin. Such sites are right on the edges of hot springs and thermal features, confirming that Native Americans utilized them for camping and subsistence.

Norris Geyser Basin is home to the hottest thermal features in the park—most are above 200°F (93°C). Because of the active hot springs, the water in and around Norris is acidic and not drinkable. But the Gibbon River flows nearby, providing freshwater for people who lived in the area. The two most prominent geysers at Norris Geyser Basin are Echinus Geyser and Steamboat Geyser, the tallest geyser in the world, shooting water as high as 300 to 400 ft. (100 to 125 m) into the air.

FIGURE 7.5 National Park Service and Wyoming State Archaeologist excavations at the Nymph Lake site north of the Norris Geyser Basin (2005). *National Park Service photo.*

Despite the hot, acidic, and undrinkable water, as well as the dramatic geysers, Native American prehistoric sites are abundant in this area, further testament to their lack of fear of geysers and thermal features.

The National Historic Preservation Act of 1966 mandates that federal agencies take the impacts to archaeological sites into consideration during project planning. In the early 2000s, the Federal Highways Administration planned to widen the Grand Loop Road, which would destroy the Nymph Lake archaeological site. And so the project was required to avoid any adverse effects to the site. The National Park Service, in consultation with the Wyoming State Historic Preservation Office, conducted archaeological excavations in 2005 to retrieve the important information from the Nymph Lake site before it was destroyed by road construction.

The Office of the Wyoming State Archaeologist, led by archaeologist Paul Sanders, and Yellowstone archaeologist Elaine Hale were called upon to lead the excavations at the Nymph Lake site. Park archaeologists excavated numerous shovel test pits and square excavation units at the site. They retrieved more than 90,000 stone artifacts, as well as excavated a Late Archaic hearth used by Native Americans at the site more than 2,300 years ago. Projectile points from the site included Late Archaic Pelican Lake atlatl dart points and Late Prehistoric arrow points, demonstrating 2,000 years of continuous Native American occupation. Lithic artifacts from the site also indicated that whole families were present, including children learning how to make stone tools from their elders.

Given the proximity to Obsidian Cliff, nearly all the lithic artifacts from the site were produced from obsidian. In the north block area of the site, obsidian accounts for more than 99 percent of the stone material. Source analysis of obsidian artifacts indicates Native American use of seven different sources, all oriented to the west and the south of the site. While Obsidian Cliff produced the vast majority of artifacts (76 percent), other sources represented at the site include Park Point, which is located on the eastern shore of Yellowstone Lake. Native Americans that camped at Nymph Lake had likely traveled to Yellowstone Lake prior to camping in the Norris Geyser Basin.

Four artifacts were derived from the Malad obsidian source south of Pocatello, Idaho, including two Late Archaic Pelican Lake points. Bear Gulch (about 75 mi. [120 km] west) was represented by two artifacts, including a Late Archaic point, while single artifacts of Cougar Creek obsidian, Conant Creek tuff, and Teton Pass obsidian (near Jackson, Wyoming) were also found at the site. While Obsidian Cliff is dominant, the exotic obsidians at the site suggest travel to the west and south of the site.

Few animal remains were found at the Nymph Lake site, with the few small bone fragments suggesting the hunting and processing of medium-sized mammals, such as deer, sheep, or pronghorn antelope. Protein residue analysis was conducted on stone tools from Nymph Lake. Three tested positive for the hunting or processing of sage grouse, a bird found commonly in the grassy meadows of the Gibbon River south of the site. Two bifaces and a flake tool tested positive for bison, while a retouched flake tool and a scraping tool tested positive for bighorn sheep. Single artifacts also tested positive for *Chenopodium* (goosefoot plant), pine, guinea pig (likely beaver or porcupine), rabbit, deer (elk or moose), and bear (grizzly or black). Based on these data, it appears that the Late Archaic and Late Prehistoric Native Americans at the Nymph Lake site had hunted and gathered a variety of plants and animals around the vicinity of the Norris Geyser Basin during the past 2,300 years or so.

The area around the Norris Geyser Basin (figure 7.6), especially in the vicinity of Solfatara Creek and the Gibbon River, shows very active use by Native Americans

FIGURE 7.6 Stone tools mark the locations of Native American camps above the Geyser Creek group of thermal features just south of Artists Paintpots in central Yellowstone.

in the past, including stone tool production areas. My archaeology team from the University of Montana surveyed just to the east of Norris Geyser Basin. There, on the edge of the southeasternmost hot spring of the basin, we recovered a dense concentration of obsidian flakes where a Native American hunter produced several stone tools. Such activity areas are common in this area and indicate that Native Americans had little fear of the thermal features and hot springs. Testing of the obsidian at this site showed use of not only Obsidian Cliff obsidian but also the local volcanic tuff obsidians for stone tool manufacture.

Still farther south, we recorded a prehistoric Native American site on a high bluff overlooking the Gibbon Geyser Basin, about a mile into the backcountry south of Artists Paintpots. The prehistoric site has a panoramic view of the Geyser Creek Group of thermal features, the most vigorous in the area. Here, Native Americans likely sat and watched numerous hot springs, mud pots (bubbling mud in the vicinity of a hot spring), fumaroles (a gas-filled opening in an area with active volcanism), and geysers. At this site, hundreds of obsidian flakes mark the location where a small group of hunters produced stone tools in preparation for a hunt of animals in the geyser basin below the site. Perhaps the animals were attracted to the warm thermal features on a cold autumn morning. Such a location would have been an ideal place for Native Americans to stage an attack on the animals. Rather than being afraid of the hot springs and geysers, the archaeological sites in the Norris and Gibbon Geyser Basins demonstrate that Native Americans were drawn to the areas as good places to hunt and camp.

ARCHAEOLOGICAL SITES ON THE YELLOWSTONE RIVER AND YELLOWSTONE LAKE

The Norris and Gibbon Geyser Basins are rich in prehistory, just as are the Yellowstone River and Yellowstone Lake to the west. At all of these locations, Native Americans used hot springs and thermal features to their advantage. Within the Yellowstone River Valley, the Crater Hills and Mud Volcano thermal areas were actively used. Farther south, Yellowstone Lake contains several thermal features, including the Sedge Bay Vents and Butte Springs on the north end of the lake, the Brimstone Basin on the lake's eastern shore, and the West Thumb Geyser Basin on the lake's south shore.

During an archaeological survey in the Hayden Valley of the Yellowstone River in 2015, my crew from the University of Montana surveyed in the vicinity of the Mud Volcano and the Crater Hills. Just south of the Mud Volcano sits a large prehistoric Native American archaeological site. The site is an extensive Early Archaic (8,000 to 5,000 years ago) through Late Prehistoric (<1,500 years ago) stone tool production site. Thousands of obsidian artifacts are scattered along the ground at this site near the Yellowstone River just south of Mud Volcano. Today, large herds of bison frequent this area, and this prehistoric camp likely was the location where hunters prepared their tools for a large bison hunt.

West of Mud Volcano is a collection of thermal features in an area called the Crater Hills (figure 7.7). While the Mud Volcano is easily accessible today by motor

FIGURE 7.7 Bison herds are attracted to the warm thermal features such as the Crater Hills in the Hayden Valley. Evidence reveals Native American kill sites and camps near the thermals.

vehicle, to access the Crater Hills, you must walk through grassy meadows about a mile west of the Yellowstone River. This area is also well known for its grizzly bear activity, so tourists should take this into consideration. Two people were attacked and killed by grizzly bears in this area of the Hayden Valley in 2011 between the Mary Mountain Trail and the Crater Hills.

When we ventured into this area to conduct our archaeological survey just four years after the attack, we were well aware of the danger. We made noise and talked loudly and frequently so as not to startle any bears in the area. We also carried bear spray and walked in groups of four, a minimal number considered large enough to intimidate a bear. Smaller groups of two to three individuals, and definitely not single hikers, should not venture into the Crater Hills area of the Hayden Valley. Such appropriate fear of bears is not unique to archaeologists and tourists, and surely would have been on the minds of Native Americans that lived in the Hayden Valley as well.

The Crater Hills resembles craters of the moon. Interspersed among the hills are thermal features with bubbling waters that look to be straight from the Land of Mordor in *The Lord of the Rings*. In the middle of the thermal features, my crew and I identified a large stone tool production site. In all likelihood, Native Americans sat on the edge of the thermal feature and made stone tools while they watched the bubbling hot springs below and for bears behind them. Large herds of bison are present in this area today, and also likely attracted Native American hunters to these areas, especially on cold nights and mornings.

Continuing to the south on the Grand Loop Road, three thermal areas have interesting archaeological aspects at Yellowstone Lake. On the north shore of the lake, archaeologists from the National Park Service's Midwest Archaeological Center conducted archaeological work along the East Entrance road in the mid-1990s. Led by archaeologist Kenneth Cannon, this team excavated one of the few sites with animal remains at Yellowstone Lake. The Windy Bison site (figure 7.8) is located on the edge of the lake slightly north and east of the Sedge Bay thermal vents and Steamboat Point. Animals, such as bison, deer, elk, and bear, are known to frequent these hot vents in colder weather. Here, at the Windy Bison site, 800 to 400 years ago, Native Americans stalked, killed, and butchered a bison with obsidian and chert tools. Part of an elk was also found at the site, indicating that it too was killed there. The bison was determined to be a four-year-old bull that may have been killed during a cooler season (because of a lack of insects in the remains). In all likelihood, Native Americans patiently stalked the bull bison and elk as they stayed warm next to the Sedge Bay thermal features on the north shore of Yellowstone Lake.

Another area of Yellowstone Lake that shows evidence of Native American use of thermal features is the West Thumb Geyser Basin (figure 7.9) at the southwest corner of the lake. At that spot are some of the oldest and best archaeological sites in Yellowstone, including the notable Osprey Beach site, a significant Cody Culture site that dates to 9,300 years ago. Also, on the north side of the West Thumb,

FIGURE 7.8 Native Americans killed bison and elk about 500 years ago at the Windy Bison site near the Steamboat Springs thermal features on the northern shore of Yellowstone Lake.

archaeologists have found the only prehistoric pottery in Yellowstone at the First Blood site. All around the West Thumb, as well as along the lakeshore and tributary streams around Grant Village near the geyser basin, there are prehistoric Native American archaeological sites.

ARCHAEOLOGICAL SITES AT THE SNAKE RIVER HOT SPRINGS

To the south of Yellowstone Lake and the West Thumb Geyser Basin is the Snake River Hot Springs (figure 7.10), which is near the South Entrance of Yellowstone National Park. These springs are difficult to reach since they are on the east side of the Snake River. It is nearly impossible (and certainly not recommended) to cross the Snake River in spring because of significant runoff that raises the river water level several feet. Crossing of the Snake is only recommended after June. Once across the river, the Snake River Hot Springs are located predominantly in an open

FIGURE 7.9 Numerous Native American archaeological sites are present in the vicinity of Yellowstone Lake's West Thumb Geyser Basin.

FIGURE 7.10 The author (left) and fellow University of Montana archaeologist Matt Nelson look for archaeological sites near Snake River Hot Springs (2014). This area in the southern portion of Yellowstone National Park was a popular campsite for Native Americans.

ALLUVIUM CREEK, THE BRIMSTONE BASIN AND THE WEST THUMB GEYSER BASIN

One area with thermal features that does not appear to have been extensively used by Native Americans is the Brimstone Basin on the eastern shore of Yellowstone Lake. This thermal feature is one of the most remote in the park and is only accessible by foot via the Thorofare Trail, or today by boat from Bridge Bay marina. In prehistory, the area would likely have been frequently passed by Native American hunter-gatherers walking up the eastern shore of the lake from the southern Yellowstone River to get to the northern areas of the lake. The next closest stream valley to the south is the Yellowstone River Delta and the nearby Beaverdam Creek, while Columbine Creek is the drainage just to the north. Waters from the Brimstone Basin flow westerly into Alluvium Creek, which drains into Yellowstone Lake.

In the 1870s, geologist Ferdinand Vandeveer Hayden conducted several expeditions to explore Yellowstone. In his final 1878 Yellowstone expedition report, he describes the Brimstone Basin Area this way: "This name has been given to a basin of spring deposits, which are on the northwestern slopes of the ridge that extends southwest from Mount Stevenson. It is about a mile east of the lake, and covers an area of about 3 miles in extent. It is easily seen from a distance, the white deposit on the slopes rendering it quite conspicuous, and the sulphurous odors greet the visitor some time before he reaches the place. Sulphur is abundant, and it is the source of the sulphureted hydrogen."

From 2010 to 2011, my team from the University of Montana and I conducted an archaeological survey along the eastern shore of Yellowstone Lake, including the Brimstone Basin and Alluvium Creek (figure 7.11). We identified precontact Native American archaeological sites near the mouth of the Yellowstone River, along Beaverdam Creek, and at Columbine Creek on the eastern shore of the lake. But we found little to no evidence of any precontact Native American sites along Alluvium Creek and near the Brimstone Basin.

Between 2003 and 2009, Deborah Bergfeld of the US Geological Survey led a scientific team to the Brimstone Basin to analyze the geothermal activity in the area. Her team noticed that the area is not typical of thermal areas in the park. Rather than the typical thermal vents, she noted that carbon dioxide (CO_2) gas is emitted from the ground surface, both on land and in the water, including Alluvium Creek. As she notes, "The local gas discharge is sufficiently high that it strongly affects the isotopic ratio of oxygen in waters of the local streams. Normally, surface waters all over the world fall along what is known as the meteoric water line. The abundant rising CO_2 at Brimstone Basin strips heavy oxygen (18O) from the groundwater, resulting in an unusual isotopic chemistry of the water."

Put simply, it is likely that the high levels of CO_2 discharged into Alluvium Creek made the water severely unpalatable, if not downright dangerous for consumption by prehistoric hunter-gatherers. The lack of archaeological sites along Alluvium Creek supports the hypothesis that the Brimstone Basin was, in fact, one of the few geothermal areas of the park that Native Americans might have been justifiably fearful.

FIGURE 7.11 My University of Montana team surveyed the western edge of the Brimstone Basin (in 2010), including the confluence of Alluvium Creek and Yellowstone Lake (shown here). We found little evidence that Native Americans camped in this area of the lake.

meadow across from the mouth of the Lewis River. During our surveys of this area, we identified numerous prehistoric sites along the Snake and nearby Lewis Rivers.

Among the most significant finds of my crew at the Snake River Hot Springs sites in 2014 was a red Park Point obsidian Late Paleoindian projectile point, indicating at least 9,000 years of people living in this area. Further to the east of that spot, we found several stone circles near thermal features, indicating that Native Americans placed their tipi lodges within or immediately adjacent to hot springs and thermals. The area is littered with stone tool production debris surrounding at least five stone circles. The hot springs and thermal vents literally surround the stone circles, a good indication that the people who camped there had little fear of the volcanic activity.

ARCHAEOLOGICAL SITES AT THE UPPER, MIDWAY, AND LOWER GEYSER BASINS

The most well-known geysers and springs in Yellowstone National Park are located in the Upper, Midway, and Lower Geyser Basins west of Yellowstone Lake. The Grand Loop Road runs through these three basins, following the Firehole River for much of its distance between Old Faithful on the southeast to Nez Perce Creek in the northwest. This area contains the most frequently visited thermal features in Yellowstone National Park (figure 7.12), including the Old Faithful geyser (see figure 1.3) in the Upper Geyser Basin, the Grand Prismatic Spring in the Midway Geyser Basin (see fig. 1.15), and Fountain Paint Pots in the Lower Geyser Basin. While people flock to this area today, in the past, it seems that this area was not a destination for Native Americans. Somewhat similar to the Brimstone Basin area at Yellowstone Lake, the Firehole River and associated geyser basins present a comparatively low density of archaeological sites compared to some other areas of the park.

In 2015, we conducted an archaeological survey along the Firehole River between Old Faithful and Nez Perce Creek. While we found prehistoric sites, they were surprisingly few within this 7-mi. (12-km) stretch of river. To compare, a similar stretch of river miles near Gardiner, Montana, or within the Hayden Valley of the Yellowstone River, might contain 50 to 100 prehistoric sites.

Including Old Faithful, the Upper Geyser Basin contains approximately 300 geysers in 22 areas, the largest concentration of such features anywhere in the world. In the Upper Geyser Basin, my crew made a most interesting recovery of a very large Late Archaic Pelican Lake projectile point. Old Faithful is less than 1 mi. (0.8 km) to the east of the location. As shown in this figure (figure 7.13), the projec-

FIGURE 7.12 The area around Old Faithful in the Upper Geyser Basin does not contain abundant evidence of Native American use for camping or subsistence. The area may have been important for spiritual purposes.

tile point is quite large compared to other Late Archaic Pelican Lake points from this time period (about 2,000 years ago). Produced from Obsidian Cliff obsidian, it actually resembles the large knife that we collected from near the Lake Hotel. Both of these large spear points more closely resemble Hopewell projectile points from the midwestern United States, like those of the Scioto River Hopewell culture of Ohio. It is conceivable that this projectile point was left near Old Faithful by someone who had traveled more than 2,000 mi. (3,200 km) across nearly the entire continental United States.

As with much of this area, we found little evidence of significant precontact activity. While small Native American sites are present here and there in the

2 cm

Late Archaic Pelican Lake
Oversized/Ceremonial?
Old Faithful Area
Obsidian Cliff

Late Archaic Pelican Lake
Yellowstone Lake
Obsidian Cliff

FIGURE 7.13 This large obsidian projectile point (left) was found near Old Faithful in 2015. Its large size dwarfs other typical points of the time period (right) in Yellowstone, perhaps indicating that it was made for ceremonial purposes.

Upper Geyser Basin, they are by no means as abundant as in other areas of the park. Continuing northwesterly along the Firehole River and the Grand Loop Road, the next major spring is the Grand Prismatic in the Midway Geyser Basin. We conducted a survey around its southern edges in an area that seemed conducive for prehistoric camps, but it failed to yield evidence of Native American occupation. It wasn't until we surveyed a couple of miles to the northwest that we found our first significant sites.

From approximately the location of Goose Lake along the Firehole River, the density of archaeological sites increases significantly. We found two small Native American sites at Goose Lake and then a few bigger ones near Meadows Creek in the Lower Geyser Basin and along the Firehole River near its confluence with Nez Perce Creek. One of the largest stone tool production scatters was located at a large unnamed spring and butte just southeast of Matt Spring and Flat Cone Spring (figure 7.14). Still bigger sites are present along this stretch of the Firehole River, away from the major geysers and hot springs of the Upper and Midway Geyser Basin.

It is unclear why Native Americans did not frequently utilize the Upper and Midway Geyser Basins for camps. Perhaps they were used for more spiritual purposes rather than as regular habitation areas. Maybe the waters in this area are also not palatable and amenable to human consumption. Environmental analysis of water within certain stretches of the Firehole River recorded extremely high levels of arsenic and fluoride. Nevertheless, it was determined that the water from the Firehole River near Old Faithful was safe for human consumption. Regardless, it seems that the most active hot spring locations in the Upper and Midway Geyser Basins—including Old Faithful and Grand Prismatic—experienced less active Native American activity, perhaps indicating that they preferred to camp farther

FIGURE 7.14 University of Montana archaeologists recorded a large Native American stone tool production site adjacent to a hot spring in the Lower Geyser Basin north of Goose Lake (2015).

downstream on the Firehole River to get away from perhaps unpalatable water closer to the geysers. Drinking water from some hot springs is not a great idea because of the possible sulfuric deposits, and Native Americans seemed to prefer to avoid these sulfur-rich hot spring areas for their camps.

Alternatively, the low density of Native American sites in the Upper and Midway Geyser Basins may simply reflect that the areas were not used frequently for habitation, but instead were used more for sacred and religious purposes. If so, the archaeological signatures of their sacred use may have long vanished, given more than 150 years of tourism in the area.

CHAPTER EIGHT

LINKING NATIVE AMERICAN TRIBES TO SITES IN YELLOWSTONE

WHILE IT IS CLEAR that many regional Native American tribes frequently lived in the various areas of Yellowstone National Park, tribal affiliation is difficult to prove for specific prehistoric archaeological sites. Many sites in Yellowstone—more than 99 percent of them—have no presently known means by which to accurately determine ethnic or tribal affiliation. This is because of the nature of the archaeological record and the similarities in material culture between the various tribes of the region. Early researchers Peter Nabokov and Lawrence Loendorf provide ethnographic evidence that a variety of tribes lived in Yellowstone in historic times, including the Crow and the Shoshone. The typical Yellowstone prehistoric archaeological site is comprised of stone tool production debris and fire features, as well as perhaps some animal bone or plant remains. We might also find a ground stone tool used to process meat or plants. These artifacts can tell us a great deal about the people that lived at the site, but they are unable to tell us the tribal affiliation. There is little difference between an archaeological site left by the Crow, or Shoshone, or Blackfeet, or Nez Perce (figure 8.1), or other tribes, and so disentangling which tribes used an archaeological site is nearly impossible.

There are two significant means by which archaeologists and anthropologists may suggest tribal affiliation at archaeological sites in Yellowstone: ethnographic and

FIGURE 8.1 At a Nez Perce camp, a woman is scraping a hide near a tipi (1871).
National Park Service photo.

archaeological data. First, archaeologists use knowledge about the traditional territories of the tribes. Nabokov and Loendorf interviewed Native American elders from various tribes, and they provided information regarding the areas of Yellowstone they traveled to in the past. Through these interviews, we can get an approximate sense of which tribes lived in which areas of the park in the more recent past.

Together with known traditional territories, another means to determine approximate tribal affiliation of sites is by examining stone material types. We can compare the traditional territories of modern tribes with these lithic raw material sources to estimate which tribes might have lived in the park. Examination of lithic raw material sources indicates that a variety of tribes from different regions used Yellowstone Lake in the past. Tribes from northern regions likely lived on the north end of the lake, in areas around the Lake Hotel and Fishing Bridge; it is difficult, though, to be more specific than "tribes from northern regions." Several regional Native American tribes have traditional territories in the northern half of Yellowstone, including the Nez Perce, Shoshone, Crow, Salish, and Blackfeet. This is a common predicament for examining prehistoric archaeological sites in Yellowstone and, for that matter, in much of the northwestern Great Plains and Rocky Mountains.

Another example of how we can use lithic raw materials to help understand the ethnic affiliation of an archaeological site was indicated at the High Rise Village site (figure 8.2). An analysis of the obsidian found at this site in the Wind River Mountains indicated travel in the southern reaches of Yellowstone National Park, likely along the Snake River Valley and vicinity. The most common modern tribe that used this area is known to have been the Shoshone. In all likelihood, therefore, the tribe that established High Rise Village was the Shoshone or their ancestors.

A better means to establish tribal affiliation at archaeological sites is through analysis of pottery. But this type of artifact is exceedingly rare at prehistoric Native American sites in Yellowstone National Park and elsewhere in the northwestern Great Plains and Rocky Mountains. Yellowstone was used by peoples who were highly mobile and traveled frequently throughout the region. Such people typically do not carry their goods in heavy, easily broken ceramic vessels, but rather in lightweight, flexible leather bags and basketry. Yellowstone archaeological sites generally do not contain pottery, and so they do not have the ethnic/tribal markers so often found in pottery. Pottery often has distinctive methods of manufacture and design features that can help identify the tribe that made it.

Cooking and storage vessels were occasionally produced by Native Americans out of both steatite (soft soapstone) and clay. The vessel shown in figure 8.3 was produced from soapstone, or steatite, and was found in Yellowstone, although the

FIGURE 8.2 View of the Absaroka Mountains from the High Rise Village site southeast of Yellowstone National Park. *Christopher Morgan photo, 2011. University of Nevada, Reno.*

precise location of the find is uncertain. Of all the sites in Yellowstone, only the First Blood site has yielded prehistoric Native American pottery. Excavated by Kenneth Cannon of the National Park Service in the mid-1990s, the First Blood site is located near Arnica Creek on the West Thumb of Yellowstone Lake. Prior to that work, Jacob Hoffman was the first to identify the site in the late 1950s, finding 33 pottery sherds produced from gray clay with grit (crushed stone) temper (see figure 4.9). The sherds represent the remains of a "flowerpot" shape of vessel

5 cm

FIGURE 8.3 Late Prehistoric (ca. 300 years old) steatite vessel collected in the early twentieth century in Yellowstone (uncertain location). *Smithsonian Institution collection. Paul Sanders photo. National Park Service, Office of the Wyoming State Archaeologist.*

(see figure 8.3) likely used for cooking at the site. The gray clay and crushed stone used to make the pottery at First Blood was found locally. So, in all likelihood, someone manufactured the pot at the site, used it, then left it behind when they moved on. National Park Service and Montana State University archaeologists found its broken remains 1,500 years later.

Many different tribes in the region occasionally made and used gray clay pottery with crushed rock temper. In this case, the presence of rim and base pottery sherds allowed the archaeologists to establish the overall shape of the vessel. Its flowerpot shape is diagnostic of a variety of pottery called Intermountain Ware. This type of pottery is most commonly associated with the Shoshone in the Yellowstone region.

A few sherds of Intermountain Ware pottery were also recovered from the upper levels of the Mummy Cave site on the Shoshone River east of the park. For this reason, among others, Mummy Cave is also thought to be associated with the Shoshone tribe. The pottery at First Blood and Mummy Cave dates to the past 1,500 years. In addition to pottery, soapstone vessels, such as the one shown in figure 8.3, can also be used to link sites in the Yellowstone region to the Shoshone. Several sites in the high-elevation mountains surrounding Yellowstone National Park contain soapstone vessels that indicate the presence of the Shoshone in the region.

However, sites used by Native Americans prior to 1,500 years ago are nearly impossible to identify as to their tribe of origin because of the lack of ethnic identifiers (e.g., no pottery) and the overall similar styles of projectile points and other material culture found at the sites. Therefore, for archaeological sites greater than 1,500 years old, tribal affiliation is presently nearly impossible to ascertain.

Lithic raw material links may be the only means to understand the territories of Native Americans at Yellowstone archaeological sites. By comparing the geographic range of lithic raw material sources with traditional territories of modern tribes, we can begin to understand the possible users of particular sites in Yellowstone.

The following section provides rough estimates for the seasonal mobility of tribes into and out of the Yellowstone National Park area in recent prehistory, focusing mostly on the analysis of traditional tribal territories as depicted by stone material source directionality and material culture. Following Nabokov and Loendorf's study of modern tribal use, we focus on the recent use of the park by five major tribes, including the Shoshone, Crow, Nez Perce, Blackfeet, and Salish.

THE SHOSHONE IN YELLOWSTONE

The Shoshone are thought to be linked to more sites in Yellowstone than any other tribe. As just discussed, Yellowstone Lake's First Blood site was determined to be of likely Shoshone cultural affiliation based on pottery. In addition, in chapter 6, we discussed how the High Rise Village pine nut village was likely also a Shoshone site.

Still another important Yellowstone area site, Mummy Cave is also linked to the Shoshone. The Mummy Cave site is located between Yellowstone and Cody, Wyoming. As a relatively high-elevation site (6,300 ft./1,920 m), Mummy Cave contains 27 ft. (8 m) of cultural deposits in 30 stratigraphic levels. There is long-term uniformity in the use of the site, which appears to have been a mountain sheep processing site for at least 9,300 years. Waldo Wedel and Wilfred Husted, the major archaeologists at the site, suggest that it was used for this entire period by the Shoshone. The consistency and cultural uniformity of the material culture at the site over time suggests a continuous and constant use by one tribe. Pottery at the site suggests a Shoshone tribal affiliation. Also, projectile point types, such as Rose Spring corner-notched arrow points found at the site, suggest cultural associations with Shoshone and other tribes found commonly to the south and east of Yellowstone, in areas traditionally associated with the Shoshone.

There is controversy, however, about the idea that Mummy Cave has always been a Shoshone site. The Shoshone speak a Numic, or Uto-Aztecan, language. Originating in the Great Basin region to the southwest of Yellowstone, speakers of these languages are known to have pushed northward into Montana and Wyoming within the past 1,000 years or so, in what many archaeologists refer to as the Numic Spread. If this is the case, then the Shoshone might only have been in the

Yellowstone region since this time. Nevertheless, the consistency of the archaeo-logical data at Mummy Cave—with no major observed cultural or chronological interruptions—supports the belief that the Shoshone may have been in the region for much longer than 1,000 years.

Lithic raw material trends indicate that the Shoshone actively used the south-ern tier of Yellowstone Lake. Native Americans on the south shore of the lake used a variety of cherts and obsidians for their tools, but mostly stone from southern points of origin. In support of this, pottery from the First Blood site (on the south-ern end of the lake) also confirms the Shoshone presence there within the past 1,500 to 1,000 years. Colorado State University's Richard Adams's research of the use of soapstone vessels also suggests active use of the region by the Shoshone during the past millenium.

In all likelihood, the Shoshone summered in these areas of southern Yellowstone, venturing into the Absaroka and Wind River Mountains for pine nut collection at High Rise Village among other locations, as well as for sheep hunting at ice patches and hunting blinds. Use of the High Rise Village was most intensive in the past 1,000 years, supporting an increase in the intensity of use of the Yellowstone region by the Shoshone during that period. However, High Rise Village also shows earlier occupations dating into the Late and Middle Archaic periods, as early 4,500 years ago. As with Mummy Cave, we do not know yet whether these earlier occupations of the sites show early presence of the Shoshone in these regions before 1,000 years ago, or, alternatively, whether another group of Native Americans lived there prior to the Shoshone.

The abundant wickiup structures across the Yellowstone region, such as these along Wickiup Creek (figure 8.4), have also been used by researchers to show the presence of the Shoshone in the Rocky Mountains. In a 2015 paper published in *Plains Anthropologist*, Carl Davis of the US Forest Service summarized the known wickiup structures across Montana and vicinity. He has recorded dozens of the structures, mostly comprised of temporary timber lodges used as short-term hunt-ing camps or as war lodges during the past 300 to 200 years. He recorded more than 60 conical lodge sites in the region, including 5 in Yellowstone National Park.

All of the Yellowstone lodges are located in the northern portion of the park, but there are numerous timber lodge sites in the Absaroka Mountains just to the east of the park as well. (For example, figure 1.27 shows the Alkali Creek wickiup located just east of the park.) Tribes that are known to have built and used lodges include the Shoshone, Bannock, Apache, Navaho, Paiute, and Ute, among others. In the Yellowstone region, only the Shoshone and Bannock are known to have actively

FIGURE 8.4 Wickiups along Wickiup Creek in the Gallatin Range, northern Yellowstone. *William W. Dunmire photo, National Park Service.*

used these structures, so we can reasonably presume that any such lodges in these areas are associated with these tribes. Therefore, based on their distribution and link to traditional territories, the Shoshone probably built the lodges around the eastern and northern edges of Yellowstone National Park.

The fact that all these lodges date to within the past few hundred years does not help us to determine the antiquity of the Shoshone in the region, however. Nevertheless, based on the Mummy Cave site, as well as the consistent use of lithic raw materials at sites in southern Yellowstone, it is likely that some portions of the Shoshone tribe or their ancestors have been present in the region for quite a long time, perhaps as much as 9,000 years. The continuity in the use and material culture at regional sites supports this suggestion. However, it also appears certain from a variety of data that the Shoshone increased their presence substantially in the region in the past 1,000 years. During this period, they increased their use of all areas of the park, but especially the high-elevation areas for pine nut collecting and sheep hunting, both primary subsistence activities of the Shoshone.

While we can't say for certain whether the earliest people to Yellowstone—such as the Cody Culture—are the ancestors of the Shoshone, it is plausible. One means to evaluate this in the future would be through an analysis of DNA of modern Shoshone people and ancient human remains in the region, such as those from Mummy Cave. Such studies, however, are culturally sensitive and must be accomplished with full consultation of modern tribal members, as required of the Native American Graves Protection and Repatriation Act (NAGPRA). Studies of human remains may be the only means to positively link older sites in Yellowstone with their specific tribes of origin.

THE CROW IN YELLOWSTONE

The Crow have been active in Yellowstone within the past 1,000 years. It is well established that the Crow emerged from the Hidatsa of western North Dakota sometime during this period. They migrated to their current traditional territories of southern Montana and northern Wyoming from the Dakotas within the past millennium. Many of the archaeological sites that date to this time period in Yellowstone National Park may be associated with the Crow, especially in the northern portions. If the site dates to earlier than 1,000 years ago in Yellowstone, it likely cannot be linked to the Crow, based on our current understanding of their tribal origins.

Lithic materials found at sites on the eastern shore of Yellowstone Lake clearly show an eastward directionality and likely indicate some use by the Crow, as well as perhaps the Shoshone. Again, the only real means to distinguish Shoshone from Crow sites is via pottery, and most prehistoric sites in Yellowstone lack pottery. Therefore, these sites on the eastern shore of Yellowstone Lake could reasonably be associated with either the Crow or the Shoshone. Lithic raw materials at sites in the northern portion of Yellowstone Lake, as well as sites to the north in the Gardiner Basin of northern Yellowstone National Park, show a northward orientation that may also indicate Crow (or Blackfeet, Nez Perce, or Salish) cultural affiliation.

As mentioned previously, the Crow can sometimes be identified at archaeological sites by the presence of their distinctive pottery. Crow pottery is often referred to as Crow Gray Ware or Powder River Ware. Similar to the Shoshone Intermountain Ware, Crow Gray Ware vessels (as exemplified by the one in figure 8.5), collected along Ten Sleep Creek east of Yellowstone by the Wyoming State Historic Preservation Office, have gray clay base material with grit (crushed rock) temper. Distinct from Intermountain Ware, Crow Gray Ware is typically shaped into shouldered and collared vessels, sometimes with decorations on the body.

FIGURE 8.5 Late Prehistoric (1,500 to 300 years ago) reconstructed simple stamped Crow ceramic vessel recovered from Ten Sleep Canyon, north-central Wyoming. *Michael Page photo. Office of the Wyoming State Archaeologist. Material from the University of Wyoming Archaeological Repository, Department of Anthropology, University of Wyoming.*

And so the rims and body sherds (if decorated) of the vessels are diagnostic, but are unfortunately quite rare at sites.

Crow Gray Ware is found at sites in northwestern Wyoming, although none has been found in Yellowstone National Park to date. Despite this absence, it does not mean that the Crow weren't present, just that they did not transport and leave behind pottery during their travels to Yellowstone (or that archaeologists haven't found it yet). Certainly, based on Nabokov and Loendorf's studies, including interviews with elders, the Crow have been very active in Yellowstone since their arrival during the past millennium or so. Crow sites are likely oriented in the eastern and northern areas of Yellowstone.

THE NEZ PERCE IN YELLOWSTONE

The duration of the Nez Perce presence in Yellowstone is uncertain. We know that during the Nez Perce War of 1877, Chief Joseph led 700 of his tribal members on a circuitous journey across the central reaches of the recently established Yellowstone National Park. Followed at times by as many as 2,000 US Cavalry troops, the Nez Perce nearly escaped into Canada, but were stopped by the cavalry south of the border in the Bear Paw Mountains of north-central Montana.

But we don't know how long ago the Nez Perce had made the journey to Yellowstone from their traditional homelands in Oregon, Idaho, and Washington. Nabokov and Loendorf's ethnographic study points to the presence of the Bannock Trail, an historic trail with likely ancient, prehistoric antecedents. The Bannock Trail was popular among historic-period travelers, but was well established by the Bannock, a Shoshone band from north-central Idaho. Among the tribes that actively used this trail were the Nez Perce. In 1964, park historian Aubrey Haines described the Bannock Trail as traversing the northern portion of what is today Yellowstone National Park. To its west, the trail entered the park north of West Yellowstone, Montana, near the Madison River and traversed along the edge of Mount Holmes past Indian Creek near the Gardner River across Swan Lake Flat near Mammoth to near Gardiner. Branches of the trail headed eastward from Mammoth across Crescent Hill to the Lamar River.

While it is clear that the Nez Perce used some of this trail in their harrowing 1877 traverse of the Rockies, it is unclear just how often they used it prior to European American contact. The Nez Perce's traditional homeland is northeastern Oregon, southeastern Washington, and north-central Idaho; and they traveled to the Great Plains of Montana to hunt bison. They likely would have passed through Yellowstone, and their oral traditions commonly refer to their use of thermal features and hot springs of Yellowstone during religious ceremonies. Trying to identify Nez Perce in relation to archaeological sites of Yellowstone is difficult to say the least. Sites in the northern and western portions of the park show active travel by Native Americans to the Bear Gulch obsidian source near the Idaho-Montana state line. Some sites even show use of Malad, Idaho, obsidian from near the Snake River of northern Idaho. Does the presence of these western-oriented obsidians indicate connections to the Nez Perce? Possibly, but other tribes are known to have used these western areas of the park as well, including the various bands of the Shoshone (including the Bannock and Lemhi), the Blackfeet, and the Salish.

THE BLACKFEET AND THE SALISH IN YELLOWSTONE

Nabokov and Loendorf suggest that both the Blackfeet of northern Montana and the Salish (Flathead) of northwestern Montana traveled to Yellowstone as well. DeSmet's mid-nineteenth-century maps of the region indicate that Yellowstone was part of Blackfeet territory. Archaeological sites in the northern Rocky Mountains around Glacier National Park occasionally reveal obsidian from southerly sources, including both Bear Gulch and Obsidian Cliff. This might indicate a connection between Yellowstone and the Blackfeet and/or Salish. Also, sites in Yellowstone National Park, especially those in the northern portions of the park, often show a northern orientation for lithic raw materials. One of the more common exotic lithic raw materials from sites in northern Yellowstone is the Cashman Dacite from near Ennis, Montana. This points to a directionality of travel through the Madison River Valley toward western and northwestern Montana, perhaps an indication of use by the Blackfeet and/or the Salish (Flathead). Neither of these tribes used pottery much, and so that is not a good tribal indicator for prehistoric sites in the region. The ethnographic accounts of Blackfeet and Salish use of Yellowstone are likely the best indicator that they frequently used the park in the past.

YELLOWSTONE BEFORE HISTORY

THE ARCHAEOLOGICAL DATA clearly indicate that Yellowstone has a deep Native American prehistory that extends back in time nearly 12,000 years. And we know that many Native American tribes lived in Yellowstone National Park in the past, as confirmed by the fact that today 26 tribes acknowledge a history with Yellowstone country and regularly consult with the park administrators regarding park use and policies.

There is still an enormous amount to learn about the role Native Americans played in Yellowstone's prehistory. Future researchers will not only strive to understand which tribes lived at which sites (and when), but they will also try to establish when the first people arrived in the area of the park. The earliest Yellowstone-region archaeological sites that are widely accepted by the archaeological community date to the Clovis period approximately 11,000 years ago. The well-known find, the Anzick boy from Wilsall, Montana, north of Yellowstone, dates to nearly 11,000 years ago and was linked genetically to subsequent Native Americans of North and South America, as well as to Siberian peoples of northeast Asia.

While Montana has one location that might be earlier than the Anzick site—the Lindsay mammoth site near Glendive—no pre-Clovis sites have been identified in the state. The same is true for Wyoming and Idaho, both of which have their earliest archaeological sites associated with the Clovis culture. And so, perhaps Clovis was first in the northern Rockies and Yellowstone, if not elsewhere in the region.

Clovis people did not frequent Yellowstone often though, likely because of the difficult environmental conditions after the melting of the mile-high glaciers that covered much of the park until that time. Only two Clovis points have been found in the park, one near Gardiner, Montana, and one on the southern shore of Yellowstone Lake. After Clovis, Folsom and Goshen peoples hunted now-extinct forms of bison in the northern Plains and Rockies until about 10,000 years ago. A few Goshen points have been found in the park, including one from near Lewis Falls produced from Jackson-area obsidian.

After 10,000 years ago, Yellowstone National Park witnessed an increase in use, as exemplified by the many archaeological sites left by Late Paleoindian Cody Culture Native Americans. Remains of their sites occur along the Yellowstone River at the Malin Creek site, at the Osprey Beach site on Yellowstone Lake, as well as in the form of a mountain sheep hunting net from the Absaroka Mountains just east of the park.

Since the Cody Culture, Native Americans settled into the region, establishing territories that they likely used for millennia until European American contact in the eighteenth and early nineteenth centuries. The archaeological sites of Yellowstone demonstrate the presence of Native Americans for 11,000 years, long before the park was established in 1872. Their archaeological sites are characterized by stone tools, fire pits, animal bones, plant remains, and, rarely, pottery. Occasionally, archaeologists find the remains of structures, including Shoshone wickiups and even rock wall structures such as those in the Wind River Range to the south of the park. They constructed religious structures as well, including cairns, fasting beds, and medicine wheels.

The tribes that utilized Yellowstone were highly mobile, likely entering the park in the spring, living there for much of the summer and into the fall, and then returning to their winter villages at lower elevations surrounding the park and the Yellowstone Plateau. Some intrepid hunters probably began the seasonal cycle slightly earlier in the spring to hunt hibernating bears, which were highly prized, prestigious kills because of their spiritual power. Brave hunters may have even walked across the frozen ice of Yellowstone Lake to hunt hibernating bears on the lake's islands.

These Native Americans used Obsidian Cliff's precious obsidian as well as obsidian from other sources in the park to make the tools of their survival. They traveled up the various rivers and creeks and over high mountains, and along the way, they established camps and collected a wide variety of resources, from pine nuts and wild plants to bighorn sheep, bison, and fish. Archaeological data suggest that fishing was rare by Native Americans in the park. Although some sites along the rivers (notably Malin Creek on the Yellowstone River) show evidence of fishing, to date Yellowstone Lake lacks any such sites. The timing of the arrival of the native

Yellowstone cutthroat trout to the lake is uncertain, which may be the reason for such an ephemeral signature for fishing at the lake by Native Americans.

To make the newly designated park inviting to tourists, early Yellowstone National Park advertisements in the 1870s hoped to show that Native Americans did not live in the park because they feared the geysers. The archaeological information as well as interviews with contemporary Native Americans have proven this idea to be inaccurate. There are, in fact, hundreds of precontact archaeological sites near the geysers and other thermal features, indicating that for thousands of years, Native Americans lived near them to camp, hunt, and seek spiritual guidance. In addition, Native Americans lived in every other nook and cranny in the park, including the high mountains, along rivers and lakes, and next to obsidian sources. To say that Yellowstone National Park is a pristine landscape untouched by humans discounts the 11,000 years of active use of the region by Native Americans.

All humans are descended from hunting and gathering ancestors similar to the Native Americans who lived in Yellowstone. They adapted to a harsh climate, living in all areas of the Yellowstone region and surviving sometimes difficult conditions and other times experiencing bucolic conditions. All of us had ancestors who were really good at surviving. We know this because we are here. Without our successful hunter-gatherer ancestors, I would not be writing this book and you would not be reading it. The Native American hunter-gatherers of Yellowstone mark an important chapter in the prehistory of the peoples of our planet.

REFERENCES

Please find a complete list of references online at
http://hs.umt.edu/YellowstoneArchaeology/BeforeYellowstone.

Adams, Jacob S. "Crescent Hill Chert: A Geologic and Cultural Study of a Raw Material Procurement Area in Yellowstone National Park, Wyoming." MA thesis, University of Montana, 2011.

Adams, Richard. "The Greater Yellowstone Ecosystem: Soapstone Bowls and the Mountain Shoshone." *World Archaeology* 38 (2006): 528–546.

Augare-Estey, Kodi Jae. "Whitebark Pine Restoration: Cultural Perspectives from Blackfoot Confederacy." MA thesis, University of Montana, 2011.

Barnosky, Elizabeth H. "Ecosystem Dynamics Through the Past 2,000 Years as Revealed by Fossil Mammals from Lamar Cave in Yellowstone National Park, USA." *Historical Biology* 8 (1994): 71–90.

Beal, Merrill D. *I Will Fight No More Forever: Chief Joseph and the Nez Perce War.* Seattle: University of Washington Press, 1963.

Beecher, Cathy J. "Engendering the Past: An Archaeological Examination of the Lifeways of Women in Precontact Yellowstone National Park, Wyoming." MA thesis, University of Montana, 2015.

Behnke, Robert. *Native Trout of Western North America.* Bethesda, MD: American Fisheries Society, 1992.

Bergfeld, Deborah, Jacob B. Lowenstern, Andrew G. Hunt, W. C. Pat Shanks III, and William C. Evans. *Gas and Isotope Chemistry of Thermal Features in Yellowstone National Park, Wyoming.* Reston, VA: US Geological Survey Scientific Investigations Report, 2011.

Brien, Aaron. "Bilisshissaannuua/To Go Without Water: The Importance of Fasting to the Apsaalooke." MA thesis, University of Montana, 2015.

Campbell, Matthew R., Christine C. Kozfkay, Kevin A. Meyer, Madison S. Powell, and Richard N. Williams. "Historical Influences of Volcanism and Glaciation in Shaping Mitochondrial DNA Variation and Distribution in Yellowstone Cutthroat Trout Across Its Native Range." Bethesda, VA: *Transactions of the American Fisheries Society* 140 (2011): 91–107.

Cannon, Kenneth P., and Elaine S. Hale. "From Arnica Creek to Steamboat Point: Prehistoric Use on the West and Northeast Shores of Yellowstone Lake." In *Yellowstone Archaeology: Southern Yellowstone*, edited by Douglas H. MacDonald and Elaine S. Hale, 92–115. Missoula: University of Montana Contributions to Anthropology, 2013.

Carpenter, Scott L., and Philip R. Fisher. "From Cliff to Cache: Analysis of a Middle Archaic Obsidian Cache from Southwestern Montana." In *Lithics in the West*, edited by Douglas H. MacDonald, Pei-Lin Yu, and William Andrefsky Jr., 171–191. Missoula: University of Montana Press, 2014.

Cegelski, Christine C., Matthew R. Campbell, Kevin A. Meyer, and Madison S. Powell. "Multiscale Genetic Structure of Yellowstone Cutthroat Trout in the Upper Snake River Basin." Bethesda, VA: *Transactions of the American Fisheries Society* 135 (2006): 711–726.

Ciani, Michael D. "The Bear in the Footprint: Using Ethnography to Interpret Archaeological Evidence of Bear Hunting and Bear Veneration in the Northern Rockies." MA thesis, University of Montana, 2014.

Cope, Oliver B. *Races of Cutthroat Trout in Yellowstone Lake*. Washington, DC: US Department of the Interior, Fish and Wildlife Service, 1957.

Davis, Carl M. "Not in Warfare Alone: Conical Timber Lodges in the Central Rocky Mountains and Northwestern Plains." *Plains Anthropologist* 60 (2015): 40–71.

Davis, Leslie B., Stephen Aaberg, and James Schmitt. *The Obsidian Cliff Plateau Prehistoric Lithic Source, Yellowstone National Park, Wyoming*. Mammoth, WY: Yellowstone National Park Center for Resources, 1995.

DeBoer, Warren. "Little Big Horn on the Scioto: The Rocky Mountain Connection to Ohio Hopewell." *American Antiquity* 69 (2004): 85–107.

Dillehay, Thomas D., et al. "Monte Verde: Seaweed, Food, Medicine, and the Peopling of South America." *Science* 784 (2008): 784–786.

Erlandson, Jon M., T. J. Braje, K. M. Gill, and M. H. Graham. "Ecology of the Kelp Highway: Did Marine Resources Facilitate Human Dispersal from Northeast Asia to the Americas?" *Journal of Island and Coastal Archaeology* 10 (2015): 392–411.

Firestone, Richard B., et al. "Evidence for an Extraterrestrial Impact 12,900 Years Ago That Contributed to the Megafaunal Extinctions and the Younger Dryas Cooling." *Proceedings of the National Academy of Sciences* 104 (2007): 16016–16021.

Frison, George C. *Survival by Hunting: Prehistoric Human Predators and Animal Prey*. Berkeley: University of California, 2004.

Grayson, Donald K., and David J. Meltzer. "Revisiting Paleoindian Exploitation of Extinct North American Mammals." *Journal of Archaeological Science* 56 (2015): 177–193.

Gresswell, Robert E., William J. Liss, and Gary L. Larson. "Life-History Organization of Yellowstone Cutthroat Trout in Yellowstone Lake." *Canadian Journal of Fisheries and Aquatic Sciences* 51 (1994): 298–309.

Griffin, James B., A. A. Gordus, and G. A. Wright. "Identification of the Sources of Hopewellian Obsidian in the Middle West." *American Antiquity* 34 (1969): 1–14.

Hoffman, J. Jacob. "Intermountain Pottery on Yellowstone Lake." *Archaeology in Montana* 2 (1961): 3–7.

Holmes, William H. "Notes on an Extensive Deposit of Obsidian in Yellowstone National Park." *The American Naturalist* 13 (1879): 247–250.

Hughes, Richard E. "The Sources of Hopewell Obsidian: 40 Years after Griffin." In *Recreating Hopewell*, edited by Douglas K. Charles and Jane Buikstra, 361–375. Gainesville: University Press of Florida, 2006.

Husted, Wilfred M., and Robert Edgar. *The Archaeology of Mummy Cave: An Introduction to Shoshonean Prehistory*. Washington, DC: National Park Service, 2002.

Jenkins, Dennis L., et al. "Clovis Age Western Stemmed Projectile Points and Human Coprolites at the Paisley Caves." *Science* 337 (2012): 223–228.

Johnson, Ann M., and Brian O. K. Reeves. "Summer on Yellowstone Lake 9,300 Years Ago: The Osprey Beach Site." *Plains Anthropologist*, 2013.

Kornfeld, Marcel, George C. Frison, and Mary L. Larson. *Prehistoric Hunter-Gatherers of the High Plains and Rockies*. London: Altamira Press, 2009.

Lee, Craig M., Robert L. Kelly, Rachel Reckin, Ira L. Matt, and Pei-Lin Yu. "Ice Patch Archaeology in Western North America." *SAA Archaeological Record* 14 (2014): 15–19.

MacDonald, Douglas H., et al. "The Best of Both Worlds: Completing Cultural Resource Management Obligations While Conducting Archaeological Research at Yellowstone." Paper presented at the Yellowstone Science Conference, Mammoth Hot Springs, Wyoming, 2012.

MacDonald, Douglas H., and Elaine S. Hale (editors). *Yellowstone Archaeology: Northern Yellowstone*. Missoula: University of Montana Contributions to Anthropology, 2011.

MacDonald, Douglas H., and Elaine S. Hale (editors). *Yellowstone Archaeology: Southern Yellowstone*. Missoula: University of Montana Contributions to Anthropology, 2013.

MacDonald, Douglas H., Jordan C. McIntyre, and Michael C. Livers. "Understanding the Role of Yellowstone Lake in the Prehistory of Interior Northwestern North America." *North American Archaeologist* 33 (2012): 251–289.

MacDonald, Douglas H., William Andrefsky, and Pei-Lin Yu (editors). *Lithics in the West: Using Lithic Analysis to Solve Archaeological Problems in Western North America*. Missoula: University of Montana Press, 2014. Morgan, Christopher, Ashley Losey, and Richard Adams. "High-Altitude Hunter-Gatherer Residential Occupations in Wyoming's Wind River Range." *North American Archaeologist* 33 (2012): 35–79.

Nabokov, Peter, and Lawrence Loendorf. *American Indians and Yellowstone National Park*. Mammoth, WY: Yellowstone National Park Center for Resources, 2002.

Nabokov, Peter, and Lawrence Loendorf. *Restoring a Presence: American Indians and Yellowstone National Park*. Norman: University of Oklahoma Press, 2004.

Nagorsen, David W., and Grant Keddie. "Late Pleistocene Mountain Goats (*Oreamnos americanus)* from Vancouver Island: Biogeographic Implications." *Journal of Mammology* 81 (2000): 666–675.

Norris, Philetus W. *Annual Report of the Superintendent of the Yellowstone National Park*. Washington, DC: US Government Printing Office, 1879.

———. *Annual Report of the Superintendent of the Yellowstone National Park to the Secretery of the Interior, for the Year of 1880*. Washington, DC: US Government Printing Office, 1881.

Novak, Mark A., Jeffrey L. Kershner, and Karen E. Mock. *Molecular Genetic Investigation of Yellowstone Cutthroat Trout and Finespotted Snake River Cutthroat Trout*. Laramie: Wyoming Game and Fish Commission, 2005.

Pierce, Kenneth L., Kenneth P. Cannon, Grant A. Meyer, Matthew J. Trebesch, and Raymond D. Watts. "Postglacial Inflation Cycles, Tilting, and Faulting in the Yellowstone Caldera Based on Yellowstone Lake Shorelines." In *Integrated Geoscience Studies in the Greater Yellowstone Area*, edited by Lisa A. Morgan, 127–168. Denver, CO: US Geological Survey, 2007.

Potter, Ben A., Joel D. Irish, Joshua D. Reuthera, and Holly J. McKinney. "New Insights into Eastern Beringian Mortuary Behavior: A Terminal Pleistocene Double Infant." *Proceedings of the National Academy of Science* 111 (2014): 17060–17065.

Rasmussen, Morten, Sarah L. Anzick, Michael R. Waters, et al. "The Genome of a Late Pleistocene Human from a Clovis Burial in Western Montana." *Nature*, February 13, 2014.

Reckin, Rachel. "Ice Patch Archaeology in Global Perspective: Archaeological Discoveries from Alpine Ice Patches Worldwide and Their Relationship with Paleoclimates." *Journal of World Prehistory* 26 (2013): 323–385.

Sanders, Paul H., Carmen J. Clayton, and Elaine S. Hale. *Archaeological Data Recovery, Phases 1 and 2 at the Nymph Lake Site (48YE114): A 2,200-Year-Old Obsidian Workshop Near Obsidian Cliff in Yellowstone National Park, Wyoming*. Mammoth, WY: Yellowstone National Park Center for Resources, 2011.

Scheiber, Laura L., and Judson B. Finlay. "Obsidian Source Use in the Greater Yellowstone Area, Wyoming Basin, and Central Rocky Mountains." *American Antiquity* 76 (2011): 372–394.

Steward, Julian H. *Basin Plateau Aboriginal Sociopolitical Groups*. Washington, DC: Bureau of American Ethnology Bulletin 120, 1941.

Surovell, Todd A., et al. "An Independent Evaluation of the Younger Dryas Extraterrestrial Impact Hypothesis." *Proceedings of the National Academy of Sciences* 106 (2009): 18155–18158.

Surovell, Todd A., S. R. Pelton, R. Anderson-Sprecher, and A. D. Myers. "Test of Martin's Overkill Hypothesis Using Radiocarbon Dates on Extinct Megafauna." *Proceedings of the National Academy of Sciences* 113 (2016): 886–891.

Taylor, D. C., K. Wood, and J. Jacob Hoffman. *Preliminary Archeological Investigation in the Yellowstone National Park*. Missoula: Montana State University, 1964.

Vivian, Brian C., Brian O. K. Reeves, and Ann M. Johnson. *Historical Resources Mitigative Excavations at Site 24YE353: Malin Creek Site Report*. Mammoth, WY: Yellowstone National Park Center for Resources, 2009.

Waters, Michael R., et al. "Pre-Clovis Mastodon Hunting 13,800 Years Ago at the Manis Site, Washington." *Science* 334 (2011): 351–353.

Waters, Michael R., Thomas W. Stafford Jr., Brian Kooyman, and L. V. Hills. "Late Pleistocene Horse and Camel Hunting at the Southern Margin of the Ice-Free Corridor: Reassessing the Age of Wally's Beach, Canada." *Proceedings of the National Academy of Science* 112 (2015): 4263–4267.

Whitlock, Cathy R. "Postglacial Vegetation and Climate of Grant Teton and Southern Yellowstone." *Ecological Monograph* 63 (1993): 173–198.

Whittlesey, Lee H. "Native Americans, the Earliest Interpreters: What Is Known About Their Legends and Stories of Yellowstone National Park and the Complexities of Interpreting Them." *George Wright Forum* 2002: 260–279.

Wildschut, William. *Crow Indian Medicine Bundles*. New York: Contributions from the Museum of the American Indian Heye Foundation, 1975.

INDEX

Page references in italics refer to illustrations